Kathryn Magnolia Johnson

Armand A. Gonzalzles

Kathryn Magnolia Johnson

ISBN-13: 978-1-9855780-0-5

www.529Books.com

Editor: Lisa Cerasoli
Interior Design: Lauren Michelle
Cover: Claire Moore

This book is dedicated to my father, Kuroki Bertram Gonzalzles, who found peace in his family history.

———————————————

Contents

Figures

Kathryn Magnolia Johnson

Foreword

In this remarkable book, Armand Gonzalzles introduces us to Kathryn Magnolia Johnson, someone we all will benefit from knowing. I remember being an eighth grader in Sandusky, Ohio. We were required to study the history of the state and, specifically, its heroes and heroines. This phenomenal Ohioan, who was born in Darke County and lived a portion of her life in Greenville—a town that was reportedly the namesake of her great, great grandfather, General Nathanael Greene—never appeared in our history books.

When Dr. Gonzalzles first told me about his great grand aunt, Kathryn, I could hardly wait to gain access to her full story. As a result of his careful and thorough approach to Kathryn's life works—told in her own voice—we all finally have an opportunity to learn about the courage, perseverance, and phenomenal contributions this freedom fighter made in the battle for social justice domestically and internationally.

Renowned Sociologist W.E.B. Du Bois—Kathryn's National Association for the Advancement of Colored People (NAACP) colleague—famously declared in his classic work the *Souls of Black Folk* (1903): *"The problem of the twentieth century is the problem of the color line."* Early in her life, Kathryn discovered this color line to be one of the most divisive issues she would ever encounter. It manifested itself in the internal dynamics among "colored people" as exemplified by the interactions between the lighter and darker members of her own family, and even more dramatically in the dealings between "coloreds" and whites. These interracial experiences were thrust upon her as the only child of color in the otherwise all-white Cedar Springs elementary school, and were greatly accentuated throughout the remainder of her life.

"The more things change, the more they stay the same." That was a common phrase uttered by my elders growing up. Frankly, I had no idea what that meant. This book brings that phrase into clear light for me now. This story, beginning in 1878, is a historical depiction of the social and political environment during the early-to-mid-1900s. However, the theme bleeds throughout the nineteenth century and into the twenty-first. All the critical issues in race relations that were prevalent during that era of Jim Crow laws and customs, as well as the period immediately thereafter, is expanded upon in Kathryn's journey—and much of the same race dynamics persist today. In 1906, as the Dean of Women at Shorter College, she witnessed the Argenta Race Riot in Little Rock, Arkansas; in 2017, we witnessed the racist attacks in Charlottesville, Virginia. During Kathryn's stint as a high school teacher in Kansas City, Kansas, she witnessed and exposed a principal's inappropriate sexual behavior toward female students; headlines in 2017 media platforms feature an avalanche of reports of such behaviors. "The more things change, the more they stay the same."

Readers will be in awe and inspired by Kathryn's travels throughout this country, defying the physical dangers presented by racist reactions to her speeches and teachings. Her volunteer efforts to educate the "colored" troops fighting in France during the First World War, along with her efforts to provide resources to poor people in Africa and Spain, are equally as compelling.

In this book, Dr. Gonzalzles informs us that "In 1940, Kathryn runs on the Republican ticket for representative in the first Congressional District of Illinois." She doesn't win but the contest makes her a vanguard for women in politics. In 2000, Barak Obama ran unsuccessfully for Congress in the very same district prior to his relatively rapid ascendance through the Illinois and U.S. Senate to the presidency. Of course, Kathryn had no way to fathom an Obama presidency, a two-term one, at that. But her work as a political activist certainly can be credited as a building block toward his eight-year stint in the White House.

Kathryn died on November 13, 1954, seven months after the May 17, 1954 U.S. Supreme Court ruling in Brown vs. Board of Education of Topeka, Kansas case ending de jure segregation in the United States. Although she was unnamed in the credits, we can be assured that as the first field agent for the NAACP, the very organization that secured this landmark ruling, Kathryn Magnolia Johnson was a key contributor to this victory.

It is important to note that, although the original accounts of her life are supplied through her diaries, various letters, and news and magazine articles, it was Dr. Gonzalzles who skillfully organized and synthesized the astonishing accomplishments of his great grand aunt, into such an exhilarating story. For that we, the readers, salute him.

—Michael Bennett, PhD, tenured professor and former chairman of the Department of Sociology at Depaul University

Chapter One

The Color Line

"For what, forsooth, shall a Negro want with pride, amid the studied humiliation of fifty million fellows."

—W.E.B. Du Bois

MY FATHER DIED WHEN I was four years old. He left a family of eight children. I was the youngest. My older sisters, Juliannah and Nancy, bore much of the emotional burden, having had Father for much of their lives, their hurt and anger appeared deeper and more lingering. Unfortunately, I never had an opportunity to form that special connection, but I really believe the loss, and subsequent lack of fatherly support, helped me develop a powerful sense of survival and immense determination.

Ten years after our father's death, my mother, Jane Lucinda McKown-Johnson, moved us from, Longtown, Ohio, to New Paris. Mother married again. This time she married a man with a complexion darker than that of her own or my late father's, and because of his dark skin, all my brothers and sisters left home—only my youngest brother, Jesse, remained. It was 1889. I was eleven years old and didn't quite understand what the confusion was all about. But soon (meaning a few years past the "age of reason"), I became aware of the "color line."

The color line, passed down from generation to generation, is a color-based prejudice manifesting itself through verbal and nonverbal communication, and negatively impacting the lives of colored people. From New York to Los Angeles, this color line exists as an unconscious bias against those of darker color, permeating our culture even today. In Washington D.C., the daughter of a friend of mine was denied a teaching

job because of her dark complexion, even though she was highly qualified. She taught seven years in Raleigh, North Carolina before she could teach in her own hometown.

The state of Ohio had a color line: a law specifying that if a person looked white they could vote. My father, Walter Johnson, was such a person. His complexion was very fair, and many people in the county didn't realize he was a colored man, and for this reason he could vote.

Figure 1. Walter Johnson, Kathryn's father.

My birthplace, Longtown, originated in 1818 when James Clemens, a slave owned by aging plantation owner Adam Sellers, was freed. Adam Sellers, wanting a better life for his slaves, approved and supported James Clemens's marriage to his mulatto daughter, Sophia Sellers.

Many of the ex-slaves that settled freedmen communities like Longtown were mulatto, their fair complexions allowing many to pass for white. They were the children of their masters, a result of extramarital affairs, or other miscegenistic activity between wanton slave owner and unwilling female slave.

Most of the thirteen colonies passed anti-miscegenation laws as early as the 1600s—laws meant to prevent interracial relationships and thus prevent mixed race children. Most people paid little attention to the anti-miscegenation laws, which was evidenced by the complexions of many

Longtown residents, as well as other freedmen settlements throughout Ohio.

In the words of W.E.B. Du Bois: *"When all the best of the Negroes were domestic servants in the best of the white families, there were bonds of intimacy, affection, and sometimes blood relationship, between the races. They lived in the same home, shared in the family life, and often attended the same church, and talked and conversed with each other."*

Working indoors, living in plantation houses, as opposed to dirt-floor, one-room shacks where most slaves lived, the fair-skinned slaves wore clothing bought by their masters and were educated by their owners, white settlers, even officers of the law, those same officers that were supposed to uphold southern laws against education of coloreds, laws only upheld for darker-skinned Negroes. A "paper bag test," per say, determining legal adherence, showing a double standard perpetuating the erroneous concept that lightness of complexion was a measure of worth and intelligence.

Colored settlements also had a color line. In the Longtown Darke County settlement, the fairer a child, the better his or her chance of marrying well. Some parents threatened a child with disinheritance for marrying a Negro of darker complexion.

We had two colored churches in Longtown. One Sunday, a visiting minister was invited to speak at one of them. Looking at the congregation, he thought his audience was white and proceeded to "deliver his soul" against the culture of color prejudice that pervaded white society. To his embarrassment, he learned his entire audience was designated "colored," (the darker-skinned people went to the other colored church).

Even though there was a form of social stigma based on color in Longtown, its success was lack of Jim-Crowism. Eventually, liberalism helped Longtown become a stop on the underground railroad, a launching pad for ex-slaves—a place where Quaker abolitionists, liberal whites, and freed men of color provided room, board, and education to men, women, and children that were escaping to Canada where slavery was prohibited.

I was born in Longtown on December 15, 1878. Colloquially called "Long," many of its citizens were descendants of slaves or farmers, and were farmers themselves. Longtown, in the middle of Darke County, on the Ohio side of the Indiana-Ohio border, was surrounded by flat farmland. No longer a stop on the underground railroad, Longtown had evolved into a uniquely special community, especially considering the times. A bastion for liberal ideology, relative integration, and miscegenation, it had the distinction of being the most racially tolerant, unorthodox community in America.

Figure 2. Lucinda Jean McKown (mother), Frederick Douglass Johnson (brother), and Walter Johnson (father).

After Father's death, when mother moved the family to New Paris, I started going to Cedar Springs public school. There were three colored families in the town, and I was the only child of color assigned to that school.

Cedar Springs public school was a country school, a one-room structure and one person teaching all eight grades. The school was on top of a hill just above town, had no running water, and no well; water had to be taken from springs that bubbled through the small resort town, and carried to the school in buckets. Those same springs provided water for tourists staying at the resort, and those businesses and households in the surrounding community. I was one of the students who went down the well-used pathway to the base of the hill, returning with a bucket of cool spring water to quench the thirst of twenty-five or thirty waiting students.

In the classroom, I learned as rapidly as any. I remember one student quite well; his name was Fred Halderman. Fred and I used to work on our arithmetic problems together. A brilliant scholar, he considered me his intellectual equal, always asking the teacher's permission to study with me.

I was never tardy nor was I a disciplinary problem, yet slowly, I became conscious of an unspoken gap, a perceived difference between myself and the other students, growing wider and wider by the day. I began to feel different and realized that I was generally alone.

Then one day on my way home from school this gap became unbridgeable. A childhood controversy developed, reaching a climax, a girl named Jessie Mills venomously called me a nigger. I resented it bitterly; a fight ensued, ending with me throwing Miss Mills to the ground and pummeling her with all my might.

Later that year an even more hurtful insult came from a textbook we were given to study, a book we were expected to accept as infallibly true. The book was the largest, the heaviest of all the ones we had to carry. It was called *Eclectic Geography*, written by Adolf von Steinwehr and D.G. Brinton. The book contained many large geographic maps; it was so large that it took up most of the space on our desk. One section included pictures and discussions about the different races of man: the white race, the red race, the brown race, and the yellow race. All were represented accordingly except the black race. Underneath a black man's picture, it stated: *"This is an Ethiopian, he belongs to the most inferior race on the face of the globe."* I was both amazed and stunned. My schoolmates turned to me saying, "That's your folks!" I was crushed, not understanding how a just God would make five different races of man and make one inferior to the others.

I knew of books by William Wells Brown, William Nell, Frederick Douglass, and other noted Negroes that had written narratives on Negro accomplishments, but those books were never allowed in public schools. I began thinking long and hard about the material available to us, paying more attention to other textbooks, trying to find one that gave the African or the colored man credit for any accomplishment, but I couldn't. Some reported nothing and others mentioned only that Negroes had been taken from Africa and brought to the coast of Virginia as slaves in 1619, as if a footnote.

It was only after I passed the Boxwell Examination, admitting me to New Paris High School, that once again I came face to face with the racial impact of the color line. After completing eighth grade, students had to pass the Boxwell Examination to attend the nearest high school. No colored person had ever graduated from New Paris High School. Jessie Mills, the girl I pummeled, her father, Mr. Wilson P. Mills, started an open protest to my entering New Paris High. "No colored girl," he argued, "should ever be allowed to graduate from New Paris High School."

His reasoning was that there were no jobs requiring a high school diploma in the town of New Paris for colored girls; therefore, I wouldn't be able to benefit from a high school education. No jobs for colored girls in New Paris—that was true. But was that my fault? I was shocked, having no idea that our nearest white neighbor was so vehemently opposed to my pursuing an education. In Mr. Mills' opinion—and that of many other white people—the education of the Negro was neither important nor necessary. My color defined my station in life and outweighed the need for a high school diploma or further education.

Figure 3. Kathryn Magnolia Johnson age 14 years, graduation picture, New Paris High School.

Some years later, I learned that a white woman, Mrs. Mary Reid, who had always been friendly, sat in opposition to Mr. Mills, arguing that there was no reason why a colored person should not enter the New Paris High

School and graduate. "It is my opinion," Mrs. Reid argued, "that New Paris did not control all the positions in the United States in which a high school education could be used."

I entered the high school, studied hard, and made sure to stay on good terms with everyone. However, at recess time when we went to the playground, I was never invited to join the other children in any of the games. I would watch them play as I stood alone.

Figure 4. Graduating class at New Paris High School, circa 1896, from left—Roxie Conzims, Merrill Mitchell, Willie Mikesell, Reed Pearl, Kathryn M. Johnson.

Because I studied very hard and always knew my lessons, I made what I thought were the highest grades in my class. Each year, Miami University of Oxford, Ohio, offered a scholarship to the graduate who had achieved the highest grades. The scholarship of 1895 was awarded to Pearl Paul— the girl who sat immediately in front of me, the girl who I had tutored on numerous occasions. Unfortunately, she died before the summer was over and never used the scholarship; it was awarded to another white student. Then, some forty years later, in 1935, Fanny Reid Murray, the daughter of Mrs. Mary Reid, the lady who supported my entrance into New Paris High school, asked me, "Did you know you had the highest grades in your graduation class at New Paris High in 1895?" The truth was, I had never known my high school class standing. "No," I answered. Once again, another example of color negating the need for an education.

Chapter Two

Parentage

"Consider, my reader: If you were today a man of some education and knowledge, but born a Japanese, an East Indian, or a Negro what would you do and think?"
—W.E.B. Du Bois

MY FATHER, WALTER JOHNSON, WAS born in Kentucky near Lexington on December 11,1827. Walter's father, Joseph Johnson, was born in Charlotte County, Virginia on June 11, 1801. Joseph's Mother, Sarah Johnson, was a white woman, the daughter of the plantation owner or possibly the overseer of the plantation. Dating back to the mid-1600s, the state of Virginia and other southern colonies passed laws stating that children of slave women take the status of their mother, regardless of the father's identity. My grandfather was the son of a white woman by a colored man, and taking the identity of his white mother, was born free.

Benjamin Brawley says in his book, *Social History of the Negro*: "The son of a white woman by a colored man was born free in Old Virginia. However, the son of a colored woman by a white man was born a slave."

He was correct. When my grandfather was about twenty-one years old, he left his mother's home and went to Kentucky to petition the court for "free" papers so that he would not be taken and enslaved.

The original copies of Joseph's free papers were stolen; however, I have a copy that states:

State of Kentucky
October 8, 1836

Be it remembered that at a county court therein and held for the County of Jessamine, in the state aforesaid, on Monday, the nineteenth of September one thousand eight hundred and thirty-six, the following order was made.

Joseph Johnson, a man of color, this day appears in court and on his motion and the Court being satisfied from proof adduced that he was born free, his mother being a white woman, in order that a certificate of freedom be given to him, he being thirty-five years old, five feet, ten inches high, a bright mulatto.

I, Daniel B. Price, clerk of the county court for the court aforesaid, do certify that the foregoing is truly transcribed from the records of the said Court, and that in conformity thereto, I do certify that the said Joseph Johnson is entitled to all the privileges of a free man.

In testimony, whereof I hereunto set my hand and affix the seal of said Court, this 8th day of October, 1836.

Test. Dan B. Price, C.J.C.C.
Seal
Jessamine County Court

In Kentucky, Joseph Johnson, my grandfather, married Clarrissa Lewis, an American Indian woman. They moved to Darke County where other members of the Lewis family were living. I never saw my grandmother Clarrissa, but my mother Jane Lucinda McKown said that the Lewis's, "had a great deal of Indian blood in them." My father's sister used to say that the Lewis's were called, "Eastern Cherokees." They had come from the eastern section of North Carolina and were descendants of the Cherokees that were forced from their land by the federal government during the infamous 1830s Trail of Tears.

While I never saw my paternal grandmother, I did have the fortune of visiting one of her sisters. Her married name was Fry, and her first name was Nancy. When I met her, she was living in Springfield, Illinois. Nancy lived in a nice frame cottage on the road leading to Oak Ridge Cemetery where Abraham Lincoln is buried. She was very fair in complexion with coarse, straight, black hair that she parted down the middle. While we visited, I could hear the clipity-clop of hoof-beats as horses pulled hearses, carrying the embalmed to their resting places in the cemetery.

There was another sister living in Detroit, Michigan who married a Clark. Great-Aunt Martha Clark and her husband had taken part in the California Gold Rush of 1849, and after making a small fortune, returned to Detroit, where they spent the rest of their lives. Martha and her husband had one son, Walter Clark, who moved to Washington, D.C. and worked for one of the Government agencies. I once crossed the tracks of Walter's life while working for the NAACP, one of those very peculiar experiences where one thinks, *This is a small world.*

I was in Cleveland for the 1916 Midwestern Conference of the NAACP. While there, I met an attorney from Detroit. He asked if I would be willing to speak at the Detroit branch of the NAACP; I accepted his invitation. The attorney, a Mr. Warren, agreed to meet me at the train station, but upon arrival, I saw no one on the platform or in the station that resembled Mr. Warren. I went to a pay phone and called him. He explained that because he lived quite some distance away, he had decided to have a Mr. Buzzard meet me at the station. He described Mr. Buzzard as an elderly brown-skinned man, and seeing only one elderly brown-skinned man in the station, I hung up and walked toward him.

His home was a casual stroll from the station, and as we approached I saw a large sign over the door that read: *Clark House.* Looking at the name, I suddenly thought of Great-Aunt Martha, and when Mr. Buzzard introduced his wife, I found myself telling her about Martha and her son, Walter.

"Well, I'm Walter Clark's widow," Mrs. Buzzard said. "Walter has been deceased for some time."

She showed me a group picture of my father, my mother, and my oldest brother, Frederick. She also had a picture of my youngest brother, Jesse. After seeing those pictures and conversing, I decided to stay in Detroit longer than I had expected.

Mrs. Buzzard and I talked about the family. My mother was born Lucinda Jane McKown on July 2, 1819 in Virginia. Her parents, Archibald Sr. and Mary McKown, were free people of color. Archibald Sr.'s father was Daniel McKown, who had come to this country from Edinburg, Scotland in the 1750s. Daniel's wife was Hindu, and they were married prior to settling in Virginia. They had one son, Archibald Sr., my great grandfather—a sailor who had gone to sea sometime around the end of the eighteenth century. Returning to this country through the port of New Orleans then traveling to Virginia, he gathered his large family and moved to Rush County, Indiana.

William Trail Jr., recorded all this information in a pamphlet written for the 1915 family reunion. William's Mother, Sarah McKown was born in Virginia in 1800. His father, William Trail Sr., was born into slavery in Montgomery County, Maryland in 1784. His owners were Basil and Barbara Trail. When William Trail Sr. was about twelve years old, his master moved to Spartanburg, South Carolina. He was sold several times, but believing no man had a right to own him, he chose to work during his off-hours, made enough money to buy a horse, and rode to freedom across the Ohio river to Cincinnati. Once across the river, he continued to Indiana, where he settled in Connersville. His master got wind of his location, contacted the sheriff, and William was caught, arrested as a fugitive slave, shackled, and headed back south with the sheriff. But young William Sr. freed himself, fighting fist and knife he got away, then hid where he could and made his way back to Indiana. He was caught again, this time lodged in jail. While there, he signed a contract to pay three

12

hundred dollars for his freedom. He found out that human beings could not be sold in the free state of Indiana, so while in jail waiting for his release, William's neighbors hauled logs to the front, made a fire, and watched over him all night, hoping to prevent him from being harmed or returned to slavery. Successful, young Trail was freed at last.

He found work clearing forest land, eventually making enough money to buy twenty-five acres in Rush County. He built a cabin and lived there for about eight years. When Archibald Sr. moved to Rush County with his large family, young William Trail Sr. courted and married Archibald's daughter, Sarah McKown.

In Rush County, Archibald McKown Sr. owned eight hundred acres of land. Some years passed and he decided to lease part of that land to the budding town of Shirley, Indiana for a term of ninety-nine years. The 1950s came and the lease expired on grandfather Archibald's land. The town of Shirley was still there, but after multiple communications with their mayor and legal department, it became apparent there was no intention of returning this land, which we didn't expect. Exhausting our attempts to stake claim to that land, we retained an attorney. The attorney went to Shirley to speak with the town "Fathers." The attorney left Shirley. Afraid of the KKK, he discouraged us from further pursuit.

Tarleton McKown, my mother's father, married Julia Greene, the granddaughter of General Nathanael Greene. Tarleton and Julia moved from Indiana to Darke County, Ohio, settled and bought land in Longtown, where they farmed and raised a family. The following receipt shows the details of the property purchase:

Receivers Office at Fort Wayne
No. 13681
Received from Tarleton McKown
Of Rush County, Indiana

The sum of 100 dollars, being in full for the N.E. ¼ of the southeast quarter of section No. 2 of township No.20 and of range No. 6, East, containing eight acres, at the rate of one dollar and twenty-five cents per acre, sold this day. $100.

For John Spencer
C.H. Hubbard—Receiver

Tarleton McKown probably moved his family to Darke County for the same reasons that motivated my father's family—the Union Literary Institute: a place where colored children were given a chance for an education. It was sometimes called the "Darke County Seminary." They felt welcomed there, as they did at the churches in Longtown.

When my mother moved our family to New Paris, there were no churches for colored people to attend without being insulted. I once heard a female Quaker preach in a town nearby; I was a teenager who felt converted by her teachings. I knew, too, that the Quakers were instrumental in the operation of the underground railroad, and that one section of that escape passage ran through Richmond. Slaves escaping across the Ohio River to Cincinnati, like "Eliza" in *Uncle Tom's Cabin*, were hidden during the day, then taken by night to the next underground station. The Quakers hid them from one stop to the other under loads of hay, straw, or fodder, until the slaves could make their way to freedom in Canada or Europe.

There was a Quaker meeting house in Richmond that my mother and I frequented. At their large yearly meetings, they would build pulpits on the spacious lawns in front of their meeting houses, allowing the preachers—both men and women—to speak to the gathering. People came from near and far, lunch baskets full of food and refreshments. I wanted very much to join the Quaker church, but as inclusive as they seemed, none were interested in having colored people. I had a certain fear about trying to integrate myself into their membership; I never tried to join. The teachings of the Quakers lingered, but I decided to join the Richmond African Methodist Church—ten miles away.

The Quakers didn't believe in baptism by water, a belief supported by several passages in the Bible. Acts 1:5 says:

"For John truly baptized with water, but ye shall be baptized with the Holy Ghost, not many days hence."

I had qualms about baptism by water and thought it unnecessary. But, I remembered a story my mother told me about my grandmother, Julia Greene-McKown. My grandmother was concerned about going to her death without being baptized by water. She was not satisfied with the spiritual life she had led. She was too weak to go to the baptismal pool, so her family brought a horse trough to her bedside where she was baptized. This story convinced me to be baptized by water, thinking that maybe one day I might feel the same. I also wanted to have a church that would welcome me, so one morning I was baptized in the Jersey Creek, which runs through Kansas City.

When I look back at my parentage, I find a mixture of cultures and races: Hindu, Eastern Cherokee, African, and Caucasian. I was considered colored without regard for my ancestry. Unlike those without African blood, I realized that my family's African roots inhibited our personal freedoms, security, advancement for self and family, as well as an inability to find a decent church to call home.

What was the American Negro? What was I? Was I black or white? Indian, African, or Hindu? Was my parentage so unworthy? While still a child, I set out on a journey to discover answers to these questions, questions that became the center of my universe. Even though I have traveled to almost every state, the answers to these questions have still alluded me—answers that might explain the harsh and biased treatment of the American Negro.

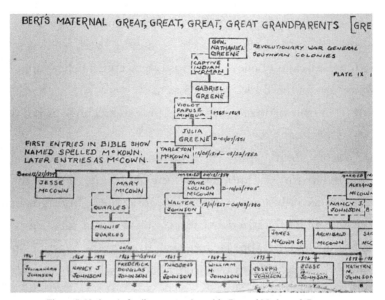

Figure 5. Kathryn's family tree, starting with General Nathanael Greene.

Chapter Three

Wilberforce University

"I did not know anything about Latin and Greek, but I did know of Wilberforce. The breath of that great name had swept the water and dropped into Southern Ohio, where southerners had taken their cure at Tawawa Springs and where white Methodists had planted a school of the African Methodists."

—W.E.B. Du Bois

MY STEPFATHER, HARPER ORCHARD, WAS a slave in North Carolina. He could neither read nor write, but he was certain that every child in his household would have an education.

It was my stepfather who told me about the rich history of Wilberforce University. He was a member of the African Methodist Episcopal Church, a denomination that was founded in Philadelphia by Richard Allen in 1816. The Right Reverend Allen and other black Methodist congregants wanted freedom to practice their religion. This was not the case in the all-white St. George's Methodist Episcopal Church of Philadelphia, where Richard Allen and other Negro communicants were forced to get up from their knees and wait on their feet until the white congregants had received communion. Unwilling to accept such humiliation, the Right Reverend Allen and all the black Methodists rose from their knees, walked out of the church, and went to a nearby blacksmith shop where they held worship services. This was the beginning of the first and oldest colored Protestant denomination in existence. The

Right Reverend became the first bishop of the A.M.E. Church. Today that A.M.E. Church has more than a million members throughout the world, with churches in Africa, South America, West Indies, and America.

It was through the A.M.E. Church of Ohio, in collaboration with the all-white Methodist Episcopal Church, that in 1856 the A.M.E. Bishop, Daniel Alexander Payne, founded Wilberforce University, the oldest private black university in America. The school was named after William Wilberforce—one of England's great abolitionists, and an ardent crusader against slavery.

Bishop Payne was instrumental in acquiring the grounds. As a man, he was driven to his knees on many an occasion; he knew that prayer was the only place to go, setting the example at Wilberforce. He was also a man who worked hard. During his youth, he read about John Brown of Haddington, a great Scottish divine and author. John Brown learned Latin, Greek, and Hebrew without formal instruction. His story was an inspiration, a calling to Bishop Payne, who now believed that with arduous work and study, he, too, could accomplish anything. In 1829, while in Charleston, Bishop Payne used that inspiration to open a school for colored children. He enrolled his own three children as the first students—an example for the colored community. Then to support the school, he charged fifty cents a month for the children of other families. He taught for six years, making great academic progress among his students, but in the process, he attracted the attention of white people. The town took measures to close the school, stopping him from educating his community. In April of 1835, the State of Carolina, through its legislators, passed house bill No. 2639:

"Be it enacted by the Honorable, the Senate and House of Representatives, now met, and sitting in General Assembly, and by the authority of the same, if any person shall hereafter teach any Negro to read, or write, or cause or procure any Negro to read

or write, such person, if a free person of Negro descent, shall be whipped, not exceeding fifty lashes."

Young Payne soon left that section of the country, entered the Lutheran Theological Seminary at Gettysburg, Pennsylvania, and for several years taught there. He became Bishop of the A.M.E. Church and moved to Cincinnati. A day came, when on his knees in prayer, uplifting his hands to the heavens, he made a covenant with God to purchase Tawawa Springs and reopen Wilberforce University. It had been closed in 1862 because of the Civil War. Then, in 1863, the A.M.E. Church paid ten thousand for the land and the buildings, making the reopening of Wilberforce University a reality. Bishop Payne became its first President, its first leader, and its first covenant: "Arduous work and study."

My stepfather suggested I go there for higher education. Never in all my young life had I imagined that there was such a paradise on earth as Wilberforce University.

The campus was beautiful. All the buildings were set against a backdrop of natural woods. The larger main building was back against the far tree line, and the smaller buildings were on either side of a massive lush lawn, the buildings collectively forming a U-shape. The waters of the Tawawa Springs rippled through a ravine in the surrounding woods. It was not the beauty of the campus, but rather the people, that made Wilberforce such a paradise. I'd finally entered a new world where my existence was "okay" and acknowledged.

Figure 6. Kathryn's on entry to Wilberforce.

My cultural experience at Wilberforce was exceptional. Instead of being one of few, I was one of many. With only three white professors, all other students and faculty were colored. I remember two of the three white teachers very well: Mme. Knowlton, who directed the music department, and Mrs. C. Bierce–Scarborough, Director of the Normal Department, wife of Professor William S. Scarborough—a man of color. Professor W.S. Scarborough was a graduate of Oberlin College, and an author of several textbooks, including one on Greek history. His mother, who was from Macon, Georgia, was a selfless woman who lived with them and took in laundry to help her son through school. I don't recall the name of the third white faculty, however, I do recall his position, head of the shoe-making section of the Department of Industries; Wilberforce University had preceded Tuskegee in development of a Department of Industries.

Figure 7. Class at Wilberforce, circa 1893.

The three white teachers projected no color prejudice. In fact, in the early days of Negro education, whites were closely involved with the development of many colored educational institutions. The Methodist

Episcopal Church as an example, purchased the land for Wilberforce in 1856 and, through its Freedman's Aid Society, continued to support the school, mimicking the Union Literary Institute of Darke County started by southerners that wished to educate their illegitimate colored descendants. In the early years, mulatto descendants were the majority in most colored colleges and universities.

On April 12, 1861, the Civil War started. A year later, it resulted in the closing of Wilberforce, because those southerners that wished freedom and education for their slaves had to start supporting the Confederacy. All their funds were needed to help sustain the Army of the South—the army that was fighting to preserve the institution of slavery. Then in 1863, two years before the end of the Civil War, the school was purchased by the African Methodist Episcopal Church and reopened as the first private colored university. The new founders were Bishop Daniel A. Payne, Bishop James A. Shorter, and Professor John G. Mitchell. Professor Mitchell was the head of the Darke County College, the first school of higher learning ever established for people of color in America.

The lack of color prejudice gave me a feeling of calm, satisfaction, and security—a feeling I had never experienced. More importantly, Wilberforce opened a new world, one which allowed me to meet and interact with many inspiring people, many of whom would become the founders of the Civil Rights Movement.

One of my inspirations was Hallie Quinn Brown, the daughter of freed slaves and one of Wilberforce's earlier graduates. She matriculated in 1873, with a Bachelor of Science. Hallie was well-traveled, having crossed the ocean eight times, lecturing before Queen Victoria of Great Britain, the World Missionary Conventions in Scotland, and the World Conventions of the Women's Christian Temperance Union, held in London. Miss Brown's lectures were well-received, and exemplified her reputation as an intelligent and forceful woman.

During one of her European visits, Miss Brown was asked to compose a letter to a philanthropist in London. The philanthropist, a Mrs. Emory, was well known, and Hallie was to request a meeting to discuss "a goodly some of money" for the construction of a much-needed girls' dormitory for Wilberforce. At the time of the request, Miss Brown was in Edinburg, Scotland, and knew neither Mrs. Emory's first name nor her address. She decided to send the letter to: *Mrs. Emory, Philanthropist, London, England.* Hallie soon received a reply, setting a date for travel to London and a meeting.

At the meeting, Hallie pleaded her cause but was unable to reach Mrs. Emory's philanthropic heart. Then, just before she was to sail home, an envelope arrived containing two tickets to attend a labor meeting, a meeting scheduled at one of London's great auditoriums; Hallie was invited to sit on stage with Mrs. Emory.

The meeting commenced, speeches were made, prayers were offered, and then later that evening the featured speaker, a man from Boston, Massachusetts, ended his speech and got down on his knees to pray. Everyone in the audience and everyone on stage knelt with him. Hallie Brown prayed so earnestly, her fingernails made imprints in the palms of her hands. She prayed that the Lord would touch the speaker, inspiring him to say something that might reach the philanthropic heart of Mrs. Emory.

The speaker prayed:

"Lord, reach the heart of the man or the woman with the 'strong box,' who has money hidden away when it should be brought out and used for the benefit of the people in need."

At that point, Mrs. Emory leaned over, put her arm around Miss Brown, and whispered, "I'm going to give Wilberforce University sixteen thousand dollars for that new girls' dormitory."

Miss Brown replied, "Thank you!" talking to both the Lord and Mrs. Emory.

The prayer ended, Mrs. Emory reached to the nearby table, picked up a blank envelope and wrote: *I, Mrs. Emory of London, England, promise to give Wilberforce University sixteen thousand dollars with which to build a girls' dormitory.*

Hallie came home a hero and Emory Hall stands today as a memorial to both Mrs. Emory's generosity and Miss Brown's long-standing support of Wilberforce University.

Through the sponsorship of the Methodist Episcopal Church, a sizable number of native Africans were also enrolled at Wilberforce. At one time, I had twenty-two native African schoolmates, some from West Africa, but most from South Africa. When interacting with them, I found myself thinking of that textbook—the one that was so big it took up almost my entire desk, the one that said Africans were the most inferior of all races. I found myself looking for any indication that maybe there was some truth in *Eclectic Geography.* I couldn't, because those assumptions were not only wrong, but racist in origin, and misguiding about Africans and all people of color.

I still remember some of my African schoolmates. One friend, Charles, accidentally got off the train at Springfield, Ohio one day, about twenty miles from the university. He ran all the way to Wilberforce, demonstrating not just that Africans were great runners, but that they understood the opportunity, the gift, the importance of education—the importance of Wilberforce.

Then there was one African student, Charlotte Manye, who will forever stand out. She had the most beautiful singing voice, one that could not be ignored—smooth and melodic, rich with pathos, a voice that was transfixing as she run up the stairs to Union Hall daily, singing, *"He knows, He knows, He knows."*

23

Brought to this country by an Englishmen, Charlotte, was on tour with fifteen other African singers. Bishop Derrick, from the A.M.E. Church, heard Charlotte's beautiful voice and asked the manager if she could stay and attend Wilberforce under the protection of the Board of Missions. The manager declined, because he had promised the parents that the performers would return. Nevertheless, Charlotte figured out how to stay and spent eight years at Wilberforce, graduating with a Bachelor of Science.

Back home in South Africa, Charlotte's mother had become ill and died. When Charlotte returned home in 1908, she built a school in honor of her, fifty feet from her mother's gravesite. She named the school Wilberforce Institute. Today, it's one of the leading schools in South Africa, and continues to have strong ties to the A.M.E. Church.

I remember another African graduate—he made a mark, not only on African history, but on the world. His name was Hastings Banda.

During Hastings' childhood, a Presbyterian minister established a mission close to his home. Hastings had never learned to read nor write (and had never left his village). Many of the villagers thought the world ended at the horizon. Hastings' father allowed him to attend the mission school, not for educational reasons, but because the mission gave them salt, a spice that was scarce in that part of the country. When Hastings was about fourteen, he heard of a mission school somewhere in Rhodesia where he might further his education. He asked his father's permission to go, but his father declined because the school was eleven hundred miles away and the journey would take him through dangerous bush and jungle.

Determined, young Hastings ran away.

He walked and ran the eleven hundred miles in thirty days, through perilous bush, sometimes so thick he could not see the sun. When he reached Rhodesia, he found the black bishop, and upon seeing him, felt overwhelmed with joy and kissed the bishop's hand. Hastings found work and entered the mission school. He studied hard until a way opened for him to travel to America and attend Wilberforce University (1925). After Wilberforce, Hastings gained entry to Indiana University and then University of Chicago, where he became an assistant professor of anthropology. He continued on to medical school, and then transferred to Meharry Medical College, where he received his MD.

Lastly, there was Charles Young, a handsome black man, a Lieutenant, an instructor in military science, a professor of higher mathematics, a music director, and a composer. His achievements put an end to any argument that people of color were inferior to anyone. Yet, with all his accomplishments, he was as humble as a child, and would come to the religious meetings and play the old-fashioned organ for the services.

I don't remember when I first saw him; I do remember the pride I felt as I watched him parade his cadets around the grounds for drill practice. He was a graduate of West Point, only the third colored man to graduate from that prestigious military college. He, like the other graduates, was baptized with the fire of color prejudice at West Point, yet he was steadfast despite those racial assaults.

Even though Charles's conduct was without reproach and his scholarship excellent, the white cadets would not even serve themselves from the same dish that he had used. Through merit, he rose to the rank of Colonel. After his graduation, he was assigned to the Buffalo Soldiers and fought in the Spanish-American War with Colonel Roosevelt. When World War I started, Colonel Roosevelt wanted to organize a regiment with Colonel Young as one of its officers, but President Woodrow Wilson would not allow it.

Colonel Young was fifth in line for promotion to the rank of Brigadier General. However, to prevent a colored man from attaining that rank, the War Department retired him, stating he was incapacitated due to high blood pressure. When Colonel Young got word of his forced retirement, he mounted his horse and road from Wilberforce University in Ohio to

Washington, D.C., demonstrating to everyone that he was in perfect health.

When he arrived in D.C., he met with the Secretary of War, and after some investigation, Young was reinstated and promoted to the rank of full colonel. The War Department then stationed him in Liberia as Military Attaché. Colonel Young died in Liberia from jungle fever, and after a year, his body was brought back to the United States.

I was in Washington when Colonel Young's body arrived for burial. The morning of the funeral, I spoke about the life of Colonel Charles Young in an address to a student body from one of the colored high schools. That afternoon, all the colored schools in the city were dismissed, school children lined the streets, watching teary-eyed as the flag-covered casket moved slowly past them on its way to Arlington Cemetery. Four war horses were brought from Fort Meyers to pull the gun carriage, behind which many able-bodied people followed. They buried Colonel Young, sounded taps, and fired a salute. To this day, he remains in Arlington Cemetery near the Tomb of the Unknown Soldier.

After Colonel Young's death, *The Nation*, a highly respected and widely circulated black journal, published an editorial: "Life and Times of Colonel Charles Young." It stated plainly how Colonel Young had persevered to become the highest-ranking black man in the armed services until his death in 1922. On the same occasion, W.E. Burghardt Du Bois wrote in the February 22, 1922 issue of the *Crisis*, that Charles Young's life was a "triumph of tragedy," and added that he seldom manifested pain, mental or physical, always turning the other cheek.

While at Wilberforce University, I began to understand how impactful color prejudice was, and would continue to be, for so many. This understanding was to lay the foundation for what was to be a great part of my life's work.

Throughout my life, I have seen this color prejudice manifested both silently and violently. It had become apparent to me that the authors and publishers of academic textbooks were involved in a well-designed conspiracy, a conspiracy intended to create a sense of inferiority among all people that have the blood of Africa running through their veins.

The workings of this conspiracy took two forms: The first was active (violent); it sought to degrade the Negro race in its entirety through the demeaning act of segregation. The second form was silent; it sought to diminish the accomplishments of individual men and women of color by excluding them from academic textbooks.

Textbooks should contain the facts; history books should speak the truth. The accomplishments of great men and women of color, scientists, inventors, scholars, and military personal should be made public, especially to people of color. How can a race live in pride? How can an individual breathe the air of self-esteem if his or her race, his or her people, have all been "nobodies?"

I began looking for any books, academic or not, that shone a friendly light on the many accomplishments of the Negro race. I found one book in the old library at Wilberforce's Shorter Hall. The book was called, *Men of Mark*, and there were positive representations of colored men and women, narratives describing the impact their accomplishments had on their communities. But one book was not enough, considering the degradation and silence inside the pages of so many others. My questions and concerns continued. Through prayer, I had hoped to find the answers. Fortunately, one of the finest and most memorable recollections I have about Wilberforce University was their attitude toward prayer. You see, prayer was required. It was both refreshing and spiritually satisfying to me; yet, not all students felt as I did. We had assigned seats in chapel. They were numbered. If a number was showing, the missing student received a black mark. Enough of those could result in expulsion. I'm thankful for a steady regimen of prayer while attending the university. Practice, after all, makes perfect.

Today's schools aren't as strict, though I believe if these institutions were to return to that level of discipline, the students would fare better. Sadly, people of this nation have moved away from prayer, from spiritual habits. I know the Bible, having listened to my mother's readings— readings done at bedtime as she knelt and prayed before the family altar— and I continued reading my Bible as I knelt at my family altar every night.

When General Douglas MacArthur victoriously returned from war, the country was filled with great jubilation, like the jubilation witnessed at the triumphal entry of Jesus Christ into Jerusalem. On that day, General MacArthur said one thing that will forever stand out above all else: *"Wars are futile; they never settle anything. It must be of the spirit if we are to save the flesh."* Things of the spirit are the only things that are lasting. Bishop Payne realized that, having learned it when he and others founded Wilberforce University. He had come from the Deep South, where laws were passed that would subject him to beatings if he taught colored people how to read and write.

Any person who had a message of value, who had accomplished something of worth, who was honest and God-loving, was welcomed at Wilberforce University. Paul Laurence Dunbar, the poet laureate of his day, wrote his most popular poems in Negro dialect, but read them at Wilberforce using pure English:

> *An angel robed in spotless white*
> *Stooped down and kissed the sleeping night;*
> *Night woke to blush; the sprite was gone;*
> *Men saw the blush and called it dawn.*

Or, when he spoke in the untutored colored man's dialect:

Lay me down beneaf the willers in de grass,
Whah de branch'll go a-singin' as it pass;
An w'en I's a -layin' low
I kin hyeah it as it go
Singin', 'sleep my honey, tak yo' res' at las.

If I could choose a place to live during the twilight of my years, it would be Wilberforce University. Living amid the quiet of the campus, the beauty, the culture, the spirituality, the rhythm, and among the inspiration of the teachers who toiled, never ceasing to give zest and courage to students they knew must go out and do better work than others, so that they might overcome the unjust disadvantage within their daily lives. I was made an example of this notion when one of my teachers from New Paris told me about state tuition certificates available to qualified colored students wanting to attend Wilberforce. I applied and qualified for the state to pay my tuition. After teaching for three years, I was financially able to return to Wilberforce to complete my Bachelor's degree, but then I faced an employment problem. New Paris was void of jobs for educated woman of color; everywhere I inquired, the doors were closed.

Figure 8. Kathryn's graduation picture, Wilberforce, circa 1905.

I turned my thoughts to Darke County, the settlement where my mother was raised and where I was born. There were three or four schools in the county that employed colored teachers. One of the schools was in Greenville—my older brothers had taught there—so I went to Greenville, Ohio, took the public-school examination, and upon passing, I was able to secure a position as a teacher in one of the Darke County public schools.

Chapter Four

Race Riot at Shorter College

"There, heaven-tall, earth-wide, hung the stranger on the crimson cross, riven and blood stained, with thorn-crowned head and pierced hands."

—W.E.B. Du Bois

I TAUGHT AT THE WILBERFORCE public school for only one year, staying home the following year to care for my mother who had become quite ill. Concerned, I urged Mother to go to a doctor, worried that her ailment was far worse than anyone had expected, but she always found a reason not to go—perhaps knowing in her soul that this affliction had doomed her.

In March of 1905, she went to Springfield, Illinois to visit her sister, Nancy. When she returned a month later, her arm in great pain and slinged, she was ready to see the doctor.

The doctor's office was in Richmond, Indiana. He examined her carefully, and with a look of concern, he told us she had a cancer known as sarcoma. I didn't understand what he meant, and not wanting to alarm Mother, I left her with a friend and went outside to telephone him.

"Sarcoma," he'd told me, "is a form of invasive cancer."

A friend (at the time a journeyman hairdresser) told me that she'd seen several clients with that diagnosis. In desperation, I spent much of my time talking with anyone that knew anything about sarcoma. I read books, magazines, advertisements, anything and everything that offered information and, more importantly, offered hope. Finally, we met a man near Eaton, Ohio who had a scar on his face from the healed cancer. He said he'd been cured by a man upstate. I decided to take my mother upstate.

When we met with him, he told us, "That man's cancer had been cured using an ointment, but in your mother's case, the roots of the disease have grown too deep for an ointment to reach. Your mother's sarcoma requires surgical removal."

We saw no other alternative. The operation was performed and afterwards she seemed to improve, regaining the ability to lift her arm to do things like comb her hair. This gave us hope.

In the meantime, I was offered a teaching job at the State Normal School in Elizabeth City, North Carolina. I was a bit hesitant since I'd never been in the South before, but my mother encouraged me to go and, with her support, I overcame my hesitancy. I traveled by way of the Norfolk and Western Railroad, going through the mountains of West Virginia, then changing trains to the Norfolk and Southern, and its "colored only coach"—something else I'd never experienced before. I didn't move from the seat I'd been in, which was probably a "white section only" seat, since crossing south of the Mason-Dixon Line. No one seemed to recognize me as colored. As the train traveled deeper into the South, I looked out the window and saw something else I'd never seen— a cotton field. The raw, white cotton peeping from the bolls, the fields where slaves lived and died, their wives mistreated, their children sold off, their families destroyed. I couldn't stop the developing sense of dread. It was almost cotton-picking time.

The streets of Elizabeth City were paved with oyster shells, fisheries only a short distance away on the Atlantic Coast. Ox carts were still being used for transporting goods and materials. The postmaster lived just across the street from where I was staying, and each day a colored lady came and left his house. The lady was his family's housekeeper. One day

I stopped her and asked, "How much are you being paid for the housework?"

She said, "One dollar per week."

I was astonished. I knew things were bad, but not as bad as that.

I needed a dress made for work, so after a few inquiries, one of the teachers referred me to a white woman who was a dressmaker. When she needed me for a fitting, she would watch for me, calling out as I walked by. She never called me "Miss," going to almost insulting lengths to keep from doing so. She would shout, "Say, you! Yes, you're the one I want. Come in for a fitting." Afterwards, when I needed another dress made, I found a colored dressmaker who was not afraid to call me "Miss."

I taught English at State Normal and after the first week, I realized very few students were proficient in spelling or pronunciation. They had come from country schools where their education was limited. Spelling out loud in the assembly room, while standing in a row, was the best way to teach both pronunciation and spelling. During an oral spelling lesson, a boy by the name of Appollas Dey was given the word *coffee*. He began repeating the first letter. Finally, he blurted out, "C-o-u-g-h-e-y." The classroom roared with laughter. I corrected Appollas and gave the class an early dismissal. Today, this style of teaching is no longer used, but I still believe it's the best method.

After the oral exercises, we would write the words using diacritical marking to accent the syllables. The students were taught to use the dictionary and pronounce unfamiliar words based on their syllable sounds. The students seldom used personal pronouns, and the letter *r* was rarely sounded. For example, the word *court*, as in *courthouse*, was pronounced "coat."

The school year passed quickly and soon it was time for me to return to Ohio. My brother was living in Washington, D.C., so I decided to go that route, so I could visit with him and his family. At the time, they had a young baby. When I arrived at their home, much to my surprise, they were prepared to accompany me to New Paris. I thought this was a bit unusual since I hadn't contacted them, and traveling with a young infant wasn't easy, but I said nothing.

On our way to New Paris, we stopped at Wilberforce to visit an old college friend, Bishop Lee. He told me that my mother's cancer had recurred. Noting my distress, Bishop Lee took out his Bible, opened it, and placed his finger on Psalm 91, which says, "He that dwelleth in the secret place of the Most High shall abide under the shadow of the Almighty. I will say of the Lord, He is my refuge and my fortress; my God; in Him will I trust. Surely, He shall deliver thee from the snare of the fowler, and from the noisome pestilence. He shall cover thee with his feathers, and under His wings shalt thou trust."

This comforted me immensely, but I immediately went to the nearest phone to call my mother, thinking that if she could walk to the phone, there was hope. She answered, and upon hearing her voice, I felt an urgent need to go to her; I did without delay.

My mother told me she had spoken with my brother, but he hadn't shared that with me. Perhaps he knew the hopelessness of her illness, an illness she could not overcome, and knowing that I was on my way to New Paris, he decided to ready his family for the trip.

That entire summer I watched my mother fight a desperate battle against Mr. Death, and like a robber waiting for all to sleep, waiting for that last light to go off, he stood outside my door. My youngest brother, Jesse, was at home, and I often gave him reports on my mother's wellbeing. He would look at me and say, "She'll never get well." This would exasperate me terribly, realizing that he had no hope. Mr. Death entered, and my mother passed away. After the funeral, I found out why Jesse would always say that. Night after night he would dream that he was standing by her grave, while she was being lowered in for a that last long sleep.

My mother was orphaned in her early teens and even though her father, Tarleton McKown, had owned a farm in Darke County, orphaned children did not always fare well. Then, as an adult, she'd been left a widow with eight children. She did her best, working so hard her knuckles were enlarged and her fingers crooked almost at right angles, but she worked to raise her large family. I would like to quote this poem as a tribute to her memory:

"No dainty, spineless things, your hands, bejeweled,
Of alabaster hue, and subtle scent,
But large and worn, with twisted fingers schooled
In myriad tasks, and knuckles prominent-
How many dishes washed and dried—who knows?
Or beds prepared? You sewed and scrubbed each day,
And sunshine warmed your line of snowy clothes.
And lingered o'er the harvest tucked away
Upon your shelves. You fashioned cakes and pies
Fresh loaves of fragrant, crunchy bread. The sands
Of time ran fast. You did not compromise with pain;
There flowed from your ugly hands
New courage for a man, and peace that filled
The heart of every stricken child. Did I say
Ugly hands? The night I saw them stilled
Forever, 'neath the lamplight soft, no cry
No tears, no futile words came to extol,
Because their beauty flooded all my soul."

—Unknown

Mother died two weeks after the State Normal School in Elizabeth City reopened. I'd sent a letter of resignation expecting a prolonged stay at home, but after my mother's death, I notified the school and soon received a wire asking that I return. After her passing, I felt a deep loss, an emotional void, an emptiness that was too great for me to attempt work—I remained at home all winter and spring.

In June, I went to Wilberforce for the commencement exercises. On campus, I met Bishop Lee, he asked if I would go to Little Rock, Arkansas to take the position of Dean of Women at Shorter College. I accepted, and this changed the entire course of my life.

It was the fall of 1906, I was almost twenty-eight years old. I'd been in Little Rock for about three weeks when the Argenta Race Riot started, a race riot that engulfed the entire colored business section of North Little Rock.

At two o'clock on a Sunday morning, I was awakened by the sound of gunfire coming from the street just outside my dormitory building. I later learned that in Little Rock, the firing of guns meant there was a fire raging somewhere in the city. This gunfire was due to both—the riot, and multiple fires set by the rioters.

I got out of bed, went to the window, and saw men walking around the one-story cottage across the street from the school. They were tearing off the shutters, piling them on the front porch, and setting them on fire. Their faces, exposed by the glow, were those of white men.

As the gunfire increased, more and more women in the dormitory woke up, running to their windows to see what was happening. The cottage across the street soon became a roaring furnace, our faces easily seen by the blaze. The white mob looked up and spewed a series of racial slurs. They started firing their guns at our second and third floor windows, telling us to get our "black heads" inside. The girls ran back to their rooms and hid under beds and inside closets.

A week before this happened, I had a daytime vision, like a warning from a psychic that we were to be amid a disastrous affair, but even before that premonition and even before leaving my home in Ohio, I decided that maybe I should take a gun with me. My brother, Jesse, had a .22 revolver and he gave it to me for safe passage. I pulled out that .22, afraid that the mob might come in and find it. I kept looking for a safe place to hide it. Realizing I was spending more time moving from one place to another, I stopped and went back to the window to see what the mob was doing.

The section of the city that contained most of the colored businesses was an inferno, flames reaching toward the heavens. The fire department was putting out the fires as best they could. The mob came onto our campus, and men began pouring coal oil on the steps of the boys' dormitory. I watched in terror as they lit the oil, the liquid exploding into a roaring fire, the blaze crawling up to envelop the building. I realized that if the boys ran out, they stood a good chance of being shot. If they stayed in the building, they would be burned alive. I lay down across a bed, closed my eyes and prayed, "Lord, save the building, but I don't see how it can be done."

A half hour later, I mustered enough courage to get up and go back to the window. I looked out, astonished; the fire was out. It was not yet daylight, and I was afraid to venture across campus to see how much of the blaze had been extinguished, but as the sun rose, I gathered a dozen girls, went downstairs, and stepped out into the sooty morning air. As we started moving toward the smoking dormitory, we saw Granville Lewis, one of our teachers, run out of the building, his shirt matted with blood. He told us that he had seen the fire, started running over to put it out, and was shot in the chest.

All day Sunday, the rioters marched up and down the street on parade, guns on their shoulders, shouting racial slurs, their faces twisted in hate as if they hungered for more carnage. The women of our dormitory dressed and went across the street to the college chapel, where we held Sunday school classes. We were so on edge that if a pin had dropped, it would've sounded like a gunshot. We decided to return to the dormitories where we stayed the rest of the day.

As night came, gunfire continued. As if we were in a war zone, our anxiety was at an all-time high; none of us went to bed. One of the male professors joined us, thinking that his presence would ease our concerns. It didn't. I kept sensing tragedy, as if some other horrific occurrence was either happening, or going to happen—that feeling you get when someone's life is about to end, someone you might know. At daylight, my feelings from the night before became reality. There was a whispered report, a colored man lynched from a telegraph pole, body shot full of holes, no doubt his only crime, being colored. I wanted to go to the crime scene. It was only a few blocks from the girls' dormitory, but I didn't, as fear fostered common sense.

All day Monday, messages kept coming to us that the mob was planning to dynamite the girls' dormitory. No classes were held that day, fear underlying our every thought, education taking a second seat to survival, prayer our only respite. At seven o'clock, we gathered in the chapel for a student prayer meeting. It was my turn to lead, and I walked in singing, *"My faith looks up to thee, Thou lamb of Calvary."* I looked out over our student body and realized that there were more people than ever before. Large numbers of colored community had come in from the surrounding neighborhoods, afraid to stay in their homes.

Everyone prayed that evening, no one was ashamed to get on their knees. They were concerned about the mob, afraid, uncertain of their immediate future. Knowing this fear was justified, we prayed, "Lord, have mercy, save us now, not from our sins, but from the white people that mean us harm."

We still had no idea what triggered the riot.

Student prayer meetings usually lasted about an hour, but circumstances as they were, this meeting could have lasted all night. It was abruptly interrupted when the Little Rock chief of police and a dozen of his officers entered the dormitory, promising to protect us. While on patrol, they must've heard the agony in our voices as we prayed for the Lord's salvation. I kept thinking, *Prayer changes things*—the vulnerable, the hopeless, those young students thinking they had no place to go and suddenly realizing the uncertainty, the frailty of life, the gravity of the situation. It forced them to their knees, imploring them to pray, to cry out in desperation, "Lord, save us!"

The chief of police comforted us, telling us it was okay to go to bed, telling us that we would have a police guard until all the danger was over. We went upstairs, tired, weary, still anxious, but satisfied with what the chief had said. Feeling that the police had come in response to our prayers to protect us, we fell asleep.

One of the teachers didn't believe the chief had come to protect us. Instead, she thought it was a Trojan horse—that the police were in league with the rioters. This teacher had never led a prayer meeting until that night—the night that poor, innocent man was lynched. She came into the prayer hall, her trunk packed and sitting on the floor beside her, fell on her knees, and prayed loudly until she could be heard from one end of the hall to the other, her desperation naked for all to see. An occasional stifled laugh could be heard, as some found humor in her despair, even during this ongoing tragedy.

With the promise of protection, the school session continued, and we finally found out what initiated the riot. Several weeks earlier, two colored men had been killed, setting the stage for racial trouble. The first killing occurred when a former white policeman entered a bar and started a fight with a colored man, killing him. The fight was over a colored woman, presumably one this white ex-policeman was having an affair with. The body of the man was transported to the Colum Brothers' undertaking parlor, the only colored funeral establishment in town. The coroner suspecting murder, wanted an inquest into the man's death, but when the coroner went to Colum's to perform the inquiry, several white hoodlums got wind of it, forced their way into the establishment, and tried to prevent the inquest. These hoodlums threatened to burn the parlor to the ground, because this colored man, though dead, had defended a colored woman against a white man.

The funeral home run by Garrett Colum—along with his two brothers, Charles and Robert—was approached by a small group of people wanting to pay their respects to the victim. A white Argenta policeman blocked the entry to Colum's, and was attacked by Garrett. Gunfire ensued, and Robert Colum lay dead. This defiance, this opposition against white authority, infuriated the crowd and started the riot. The remaining two Colum brothers escaped, fled the city, and some thirty-five years went by before anyone in Little Rock heard of them again. Some thought they had drowned in the Arkansas River, some thought they had gone to the Philippines, but no one knew for certain what had become of them. After the race riot, there were no criminal charges against anyone for the deaths of three black men, no one was found responsible for the burning of colored homes and businesses, and it appeared no one cared about the destruction of lives.

Years later, while working for the NAACP, I was in Detroit on business when I stumbled upon some news about the Colum brothers. I was dining with a small group at a friend's home and noticed a woman, one I didn't know, sitting to my right. This woman had very little to say. Every now and then she would turn and look at me. Finally, she asked, "Are you the Ms. Johnson that used to teach at Shorter College in Little Rock, Arkansas?"

I said, "Yes."

"Well, I'm the niece of the Colum brothers."

I was astonished and asked, "What ever became of them?"

"One of my uncles fled to Canada, changed his name, returned to the United States, and is living in Springfield, Missouri. I'm not sure what happened to my other uncle, but my mother believes he actually did escape to the Philippines."

I started thinking about the Negro man, the one who was lynched. Homer G. Blackman was guilty of no crime. The day of the riot, he was serving as a court witness in a neighboring town. He returned that evening, not knowing there was a riot in Little Rock, and when crossing the Arkansas River bridge, he was spotted by one of the rioters. The rioter cried out, "There he goes! There he goes!" Mr. Blackman was overtaken, captured, shackled, and jailed. That evening, a mob broke into the jail, took him, strung a rope over a light pole, lynched him, shot him multiple times, and left him hanging dead for all to see. He was known to be a good citizen and was building a home in preparation for marriage. Mr. Blackman lost his life, but many others were injured for the rest of their lives.

When I looked out my window the night of the riot, I saw a white man pass by, moving with intention, as if he were going somewhere. The rioters called to him, saying, "Hey there, if you are a white man, come this way, but if you are a nigger, you'd better trot." The man, not wanting to get mixed up in the rioting, started running. The rioters started shooting. The man was hit in the hip and fell to the ground, screaming. When I saw him next, it was at the college. He was limping, using a crutch, and I realized the gunshot he sustained had crippled him for life.

Aside from my .22 caliber, there was not a single firearm at the school, and none were accessible. Before the police chief had arrived, we tried to get a message to the state troopers to no avail. Some students tried to run away. They boarded trains, begging conductors to allow them free rides home, saying their fathers would pay the fare when they arrived. These students were innocent, but persecuted mercilessly, witnessing violence, sensing fear, experiencing all the extremes of emotion; emotions that would linger for a very long time.

Soon after the race riot, prayer week began. We decided to host a revival much like the one held at Wheaton College, a revival that awakened the hearts and souls of both students and community. It began earlier than planned, spontaneous in the aftermath of the riot.

The whole experience made me ponder the fate of the colored man in America—his history, and his future. First slavery, then emancipation, reconstruction, followed by Jim Crowism and race riots—riots responsible for the killing of more colored people at one time than even the institution of slavery. These riots were born out of the cruelty of slavery, out of mob violence, out of inhumane, war-like aggression; the helplessness of colored people during these race riots was heartbreaking.

The week of prayer was ushered in with great enthusiasm. Expectations high, we were anticipating students from other schools, people from surrounding communities and, of course, the coming of the Lord. We sang, "Whosoever Will, Let Him Come," and with that song as our rallying cry, they all came.

The music awakened us at four o'clock in the morning. We dressed and enthusiastically crossed the campus to the boys' dormitory where sunrise prayer meetings were underway in one of the classrooms. Chapel services began each morning and lasted all day. No attempt was made to resume classes. Everyone was feeling the spirit; it was a religious, a psychic phenomenon. There were tears of laughter, tears of sadness, screams of joy, and screams sorrow. Many were held in the grip of the Holy Spirit, some stiffened and collapsed, shouting to the heavens, "Hallelujah, 'tis done!" Every classroom, every dormitory, was filled with an electrifying presence that could not be defined.

On the last morning of the revival, a young man was trying to shield himself from the force possessing the campus, its buildings and people. This young man was unable to understand the spiritual power and magnetism. The double doors entering the chapel swung open, and four men entered, half-carrying, half-dragging a giant man, probably six feet four inches tall, unable to talk, helplessly held in the grip of the Holy Spirit. They gently set him on the front seat. The four men told us his name was Goodloe, and upon hearing his name, the young man, trapped in a trance-like state, could only say, "Lord, have mercy!"

The riot, burning of the boys' dormitory, racial slurs, shooting of Professor Lewis, lynching of Homer Blackman, followed by the revival, and the conversion of Mr. Goodloe, gave me greater insight into the experiences of the enslaved. Slaves sang spirituals—a.k.a. "corn ditties"—with great power and wonderful rhythm spawned from the injustice, hopelessness, and fear felt every day of their enslaved lives. The riot gave us a window of understanding into the past, opening our minds and souls to feelings that made us wish, just as the slaves must have, for a band of angels to come and carry us home, as in the old Negro spiritual melody, "Swing Low Sweet Chariot."

> *"I looked over yonder and what did I see,*
> *Comin' for to carry me home,*
> *A band of angels comin' after me,*
> *Comin' for to carry me home."*

Those enslaved wearied of mob violence, persecutions, abominations, atrocities, and other horrors described in the Theodore Dwight Weld book, *American Slavery as It Is: Testimony of a Thousand Witnesses.* Slaves with prayer as their only respite, not allowed to sing and dance in praise of the Lord, would go deep into the woods for secret "camp meetings," where they shared their songs, their joys, and their miseries. They would take big iron pots, turn them on their sides so the well would catch the sounds of their songs, prayers, and expressions of their wounded hearts. God could hear them, but the master couldn't. They sang:

"Way down yonder by myself
Couldn't hear nobody pray."

Few of them could read, but they learned about John the Baptist and wanted to be ready when that band of angels came:

"I want to be ready,
I want to be ready,
I want to be ready,
To walk in Jerusalem, just like John."

Those songs brought heaven down to earth, as did the songs of the student body.

The week of prayer at Shorter College was an experience that would prepare me for my time at the high school in Kansas City, Kansas—and for my work with the National Association for the Advancement of Colored People.

Living in a world of discrimination, segregation, and injustice, I have never had a full breath of freedom while in my native land. If churches would practice what they preach and schools would adopt a more inclusive curriculum, young people with dark faces wouldn't grow up in a world that, for them, is stifled, cramped, and distorted. There are things of the spirit that laws cannot control; these Godly things are greater and more powerful than all man-made laws, more powerful than the atom or hydrogen bomb—these spiritual things could change the world if allowed do so. But we must continue to make laws, with the hope that someday they will be enforced.

In 1951, the Topeka branch of the NAACP sued the Topeka Board of Education. The suit stated that segregation in the schools created a sense of inferiority in colored children, and a feeling of superiority in the white children. The white child becomes "puffed up," domineering, conceited, and egotistical, while the colored child becomes "deflated," subservient, subordinate, and self-hateful.

It's a bad trait, consciously cultivated in the white child through segregated schools. The white schools with their beautiful buildings, new equipment, and current but misleading textbooks, and the colored schools, housed in rundown buildings, broken equipment, and outdated, misleading textbooks.

The colored child wonders why he is put aside in worn-out buildings formerly occupied by whites. He wonders why the desks are marked and scarred with derogatory words about his race and color, while white children have new desks. He wonders why he has such poor and limited equipment for the science room, while white children have all the equipment they need. He wonders why certain subjects are not taught in his school, while white children have an unlimited curriculum.

When he picks up his textbooks, he wonders why there are no pictures of colored people inside. The only pictures he sees with dark faces are those of poorly dressed people with gunny sacks hanging around their necks. These people are picking cotton, labeled as "slaves."

These uncertainties cause the child to wonder about himself, who he is, what is his value. When he asks someone about it, he is told something that makes him swallow hard; he learns that his fore parents were slaves.

People who have migrated from the South want segregated schools, because they want their children to have the opportunity to learn; they don't possess the courage to fight for places in the mixed schools. They have been persecuted all their lives and see no hope for change. They take the path of least resistance. But where there are segregated schools, colored schools are in the poorest buildings, with worn-out furnishings taken from the white schools. If there are only a few pupils for a certain class in German, or French, or science, the subject is dropped from the curriculum. This sets the colored students back a year or so, and when they enter normal school or college, they are academically disadvantaged.

The reason white and colored people don't relate to each other is because they don't know one another. They grow up in different worlds. They are segregated in school and church, in both the North and the South. Church and school: these are our country's greatest institutions. The Christian church is built on the foundation of "brotherhood of man," but segregation reaches its peak at high noon on Sunday—what hypocrisy.

I once heard a story about the Savior of mankind trying to get into a church on Fifth Avenue in New York City. An unsophisticated colored man came along and said to the Savior, "I've been trying to get into that church down there, too." The Savior replied: "Well, I've been trying for some time myself to get in there, and I can't, and I know you can't!"

Mrs. Faith Rich served as the Education Committee Chairman of the Westside Chicago Branch of the National Association for the Advancement of Colored People (NAACP), though she was involved in many other aspects of the organization. The Education Committee focused on the desegregation of the Chicago Public Schools, and sought a revision of textbooks to remove bias against African Americans, Catholics, and Jews. Mrs. Rich conducted a study of bias in public school textbooks.

The following is quoted from the first page of her report, issued in 1946:

"Father, I thought you told me the Ku Klux Klan was bad," Henry said.

"Son, I did tell you that. It was bad," Mr. McGee replied.

"Our history book doesn't say so. It says the Klan was good to punish bad Negroes."

"Where did you find that?" Mr. McGee asked.

Mr. McGee picked up the book and read:

"The Klan accomplished three things for the South. It frightened the Negroes into better behavior; it made the carpetbaggers more careful; and it showed the nation that southern people would not quietly endure outrages." (Coleman, Charles Hubert, and Edgar B. Wesley. 1939. *America's Road to Now.* Pages 389–390.)

Mr. McGee's son, Henry, goes to Sherwood School at 57th and Princeton. This conversation took place last fall when Henry's class was studying *America's Road to Now*, a textbook on the approved list of the Chicago Board of Education. Henry's book was no exception, as the following pages from his sister's history book will show:

"The new state government also ratified the Fifteenth Amendment, which put the Negroes right to vote in the Constitution. So, the United States gave the vote to the men who had recently been slaves, most of whom could not read or write and knew nothing of managing the affairs of government, before it gave the vote to white women, many of whom are highly educated and knew much about public affairs." (*Exploring American History.* "Fifteenth Amendment Gives Negroes the Vote." Pages 502–503.)

Unfortunately, neither Sherwood School nor textbooks on American History are exceptions. Gunnar Myrdal, distinguished Swedish Social Scientist, chosen for his impartiality, writes: "A pro-southern bias is, however, not restricted to southern writers. Ever since the great National Compromise of the 1870s, when reconstruction was liquidated, the need for rationalization of the anomalous position and treatment of the Negro has been national in scope. Contrary to the belief commonly held in the South, the present writer has reached the conviction that not only the public in the North, but also northern social scientists are rather pro-southern in their biases." (Myrdal, Gunnar. 1944. *An American Dilemma: The Negro Problem and Modern Democracy*, Volume 2. Pages 1037-1038.)

The form in which race prejudice occurs in these school books, makes it hard to realize how inaccurate, unscientific, and dangerous they are. The careless or indifferent reader doesn't notice he is absorbing distortions, implications, and irrelevant comparisons. Many readers, regardless of age, might feel that the authors are only presenting the facts. But, if they reread whole chapters a few times, their attention directed to certain points, they will realize that much of the text is not fact, but rather propaganda of southern landlords, which has filtered down through many minds and been linked to many modern issues.

Thus, the church, the school, and the textbook point the finger of scorn at the dark brothers.

One Summer I went to Grand Forks, North Dakota to visit a cousin—a great farming area, that reminded me of Darke County. The University of North Dakota was within walking distance, so I registered for a course in English. Most of the students were of Scandinavian decent, and when we sang at chapel services, most of the songs were in their native language.

I was asked to tell them about the race riot I experienced at Shorter College, and was even interviewed by *The Grand Forks Daily Herald*. (This was published in the July 30, 1909 edition.) After the interview, I stopped at one of the farms and talked with a farmer. We had a great discussion involving political, religious, and social issues, finding many points of mutual agreement. I sensed no overt color prejudice; however, the churches were segregated.

On Sundays, I attended a small colored church, founded by my cousin, Mrs. Sarah L. Smith. It was the first colored church founded in that state. There were only about a dozen colored families in the city, but they were never invited into the other churches. They found religious comfort in a Methodist church, and each Sunday the church sent a man out to preach. He was not much of a speaker, but he seemed to be earnest, as with great emotion, he told about his conversion. He had been a drunkard and in the gutter, but eventually lost his appetite for liquor and had gone into the ministry. Each time he told the story, tears would course down his cheeks.

The color-based separation of churches has laid the foundation for segregation throughout all other institutions in this country. Today we have an incredulous reputation among the dark people of the world. It's difficult to make other races believe in the doctrine of the "brotherhood of man," when we don't practice it.

Chapter Five

Field Worker for *The Crisis,* and the NAACP

"It all came, this age of miracles because a few persons in 1909 determined to celebrate Lincoln's birthday properly by calling for the final emancipation of the American Negro. I came at their call. My salary even for a year, was not assured, but it was the "voice without reply." The result has been the national association for the advancement of colored people and the crisis."

—W.E.B. Du Bois

AFTER THE RACE RIOT AT Shorter College in October of 1906, I remained at the school for the remainder of the school term, then went to Kansas City, Kansas, where I taught for three years at Sumner High School. The school had begun complying with Kansas House Bill No. 890, allowing for segregation in Kansas high schools.

The Shorter College race riot left a deep, long-lasting impression on me. This was the first time I had experienced, face to face, the evil of racism. This fostered a determination to free those colored victims from that terrible feeling of impotence—the helplessness one feels when violently attacked unprovoked with no protection or redress from the law. I felt that I had to do something to prevent lynchings, burnings, and other cruelties plaguing the colored communities.

That kind of protection required an organization, a very large organization with money and legal talent. An organization of people who were unselfish, highly capable, and courageous enough to go out into the field and awaken colored people to their own needs, their own rights, their own possibilities, and potentials. I knew of no such organization, but I made up my mind that if such an organization ever formed, I would join and offer my service.

While at Sumner High School, we changed principals, and I found myself in the middle of a heated fight. The new principal was a graduate of Dartmouth, an immoral man who demonstrated no sense of professionalism. The female students came in groups, telling me about his advances on them when in his office or when visiting their homes uninvited when their parents were away.

Then, one day, when speaking to a group of girls, I felt a sudden burst of resentment. I said, "Well, this matter should be reported to the school board!"

A few days later, the principal sent for me, asking if I had made that statement. I told him, "Yes."

He then said, "We'll have to fight this thing out before the school board."

And we did, with great vigor. Three of the girls swore in affidavits about the principal's advancements toward them; I took those affidavits to the committee. During the reading of the testimony, the principal was present, talking with such confusion that a member of the committee told him to "hush," adding that he was guilty.

However, no action was taken. I went to Mr. Pearson, the superintendent, to discuss the matter. He said, "Well, all colored men are immoral anyway. If we turn him out, we'll only get another man just like him, so we may as well keep him."

That, I could not agree with.

Because of this controversy, I was dropped from the high school faculty, but it wasn't the last time I would hear of this matter.

There was a great need for a colored YWCA (Young Women's Christian Association) in Kansas City, and I helped organized one. As I've mentioned before, I don't believe there should be segregation in Christian institutions, but if you are colored, it is often a matter of having a separate institution or no institution at all. A few years ago, because of my role as founder of the Kansas City YWCA, I was asked to speak at the mortgage payoff celebration. Speaking with members and those who benefited from YWCA services, I felt assured that the organization would continue to do splendid work in Kansas.

In November of 1910, I was still laying the foundation for the Kansas City YWCA, when the first issue of *The Crisis* appeared. It was a small magazine, heralding the beginning of a new movement called the "National Association for the Advancement of Colored People."

There were only one thousand copies of the first edition, and I received one of those. I immediately wrote and asked for the privilege of introducing the magazine to my section of the country. I soon received a positive response with a supply of *The Crisis*, which I put in every barbershop, restaurant, and any and every colored business in town. I spoke about the magazine and its purpose in every church, and to every audience that allowed me to. I sold the magazine! Soon, Miss Mary White Ovington, the mother and current secretary of the NAACP, wrote me and said that I was one of the four most active agents for the magazine in the United States.

What was this magazine, this new organization? This movement that fired me up and made me enthusiastic about getting others fired up, as well. In an early issue of *The Crisis*, William English Walling, the first chairman of the NAACP's Executive Board, wrote an article entitled, "The Founding of the NAACP," in which he said that he and his wife were in Chicago at the time of the race riot in Springfield, Illinois in 1908, and took the first train to Springfield to get firsthand information. Mr. Walling wrote the story of that race riot for the *New York Independent*, a paper capable of free thought, an attribute not found in any other American journal to date. Mr. Walling and his wife had just returned from a trip to Russia and were lecturing in New York City. Mr. Walling, a white man, told his audience that the race situation in this country was, in some respect, worse than anything he had seen under the Czar during his visit to Russia.

Mary White Ovington read Mr. Walling's article in the *New York Independent*, and sometime after his New York lecture, she contacted him, telling him that an organization should and could be formed to work for and protect the legal rights of colored people, and the prevention of lynchings. Mr. Walling agreed, and the two of them felt they could start such an organization since they both knew many spirited and influential people interested in doing the same.

At the time, Miss Ovington was working on her first book, *Half a Man*. For six years, Miss Ovington investigated the status of Negroes in New York City. During this investigation, she met a young colored man who had just returned from Germany where he was doing graduate study work. He told her he had come from one of the Gulf states, and she asked him if he intended to go back to the South to teach. He explained that his father, although financially successful in the South, had advised him to live in the North where his manhood would be respected. He said that his father could hardly endure the South, so in the summers he always came North where he could be a man. Then the son quickly corrected himself and said, "No, half a man. A Negro is wholly a man only in Europe."

Half a man, Miss Ovington thought—a good title. The book traces the status of the black man from the first slave ship that entered New York harbor in 1626, to the 1711 public slave market on Wall Street, to the New York slave rebellion of 1712, through to 1911 when *Half a Man* was published. Miss Ovington even sent me a signed copy. In the book, she writes: "The slaves were pursued when they attempted flight, captured and executed; some hanged, some burned at the stake, some left suspended in chains to starve to death." These atrocities were supported by a 1706 New York law that also included Indians:

"New York declares blacks, Indians, and slaves who kill white people to be subject to the death penalty."

Dr. Franz Boaz, past head of the Department of Anthropology at Columbia University, wrote the foreword for *Half a Man*. In it, he states:

"Miss Ovington's description of the status of the Negro in New York City is based on the most painstaking inquiry into his social and economic condition, and brings out in the most forceful way the difficulties under which the race is laboring, even in the large cosmopolitan population of New York. It is a refutation of the claims that the Negro has equal opportunity with the whites, and that his failure to advance more rapidly than he has is due to innate inability."

He went on to say:

"Many students of Anthropology recognize that no proof can be given of any inferiority of the Negro race; that without doubt the bulk of the individuals composing the race are equal in mental aptitude to the bulk of our own people; that although their heredity aptitudes may lie in slightly different directions, it is very improbable that most individuals composing the white race should possess greater ability than the Negro race."

Miss Ovington was ready to propose the founding of an organization such as the NAACP to William English Walling. She knew several prominent colored people whom she felt she could approach. Among them was Bishop Alexander Walters of the African Methodist Episcopal Zion Church, a church founded by James Varick. He later became Bishop Varick, who left the John Street Methodist Episcopal Church with thirty other members in 1796, because among other things, he had been denied the right to preach there.

Reverend William H. Brooks, pastor of St. Mark Episcopal Church, which was located on 53rd Street, was also invited to the first meeting. Mr. Walling invited the prominent journalist and muckraker, Charles Edward

Russell, a Jewish social worker and activist, Henry Moskowitz, the American nurse and sociologist, Lillian Wald, and the social reformer, Florence Molthrop Kelley.

At the first annual conference, arrangements were made to recruit a colored leader with nationwide prominence. They chose Dr. W.E. Burghart Du Bois, who accepted the position as the first editor of *The Crisis*. In Mr. Walling's article, he reported that before the conference, most of the attention had been given to securing the interest of colored people, and the advanced emancipated elements among the white community. But he always dated the launching of the organization from the day Dr. Du Bois joined the group. He added that the organization had a second birth when the services of the noted lawyer, novelist, and poet, James Weldon Johnson, were secured as executive secretary.

It was Mr. Walling's suggestion that the main organ of the association be named *The Crisis*, because he felt that they were amid a racial crisis.

The small group, headed by the late Mary Ovington, selected Oswald Garrison Villard to send out a call for people throughout the United States to join this new emancipation movement. That call was issued on February 12, 1909—the anniversary of Lincoln's birth, about a year after the Springfield race riot.

The Crisis was largely responsible for the growth of the NAACP, especially the branches throughout the country. For example, when I first went to Texas, a branch couldn't be organized, but many, many people still bought *The Crisis*. Often, after speaking to people in those colored Texas communities, there would be a stampede for copies of the magazine. It laid the groundwork for awakening the people, and now many of the Texas branches are doing tremendous and effective work.

I still have a copy of that first *The Crisis* issue, dated November 1910. On its front cover is a picture of a little dark boy playing with a hoop. At the top of the cover are the words: *THE CRISIS*, A record of the Darker races, Vol. I, November 1910, No. I

Noted Editors of *The Crisis*

Underneath the heading is a list of editors: W.E. Burghart Du Bois, Oswald Garrison Villard, J. Max Barber, Charles Edward Russell, Kelley Miller, W.S. Braithwaithe, and M.D. Maclean.

Dr. W. E. Burghart Du Bois, the chief editor, was the founder of the Niagara Movement that had its first meeting at Niagara Falls in 1905. The next meeting was at Storer College in Harper's Ferry, West Virginia. Storer College sits high on a mountain, overlooking the Shenandoah River. It's not far from the arsenal that was captured by John Brown in his effort to free at both Niagara Falls and Storer College. Men and women came from all over the United States to join Dr. Du Bois in fighting the ongoing and ever-growing problem of racial discrimination. This movement was not a part of the NAACP, but it brought its founder, Dr. Du Bois, such prominence that when an editor for *The Crisis* was needed, the name of Dr. Du Bois headed the list of men qualified to fill the position.

Dr. Du Bois, a graduate of Fisk University, Harvard and the University of Berlin, was author of many books, his first being, *The Souls of Black Folk*. This book made him internationally famous because of the beauty and pathos of its life language.

Oswald Garrison Villard, was a grandson of William Lloyd Garrison, the great and ardent abolitionist. Mr. Villard was president of the *New York Evening Post*. J. Max Barber, a colored man from Atlanta, worked menial tasks in a hotel to earn his way through dental school. Charles Edward Russell, also listed on the cover, a white newspaper man that had strong convictions about the negative racial impact of the color line. Kelley Miller—a colored man who was head of the Department of Mathematics at Howard University. William Stanley Braithwaite—a colored poet on staff of the *Boston Transcript*, and Mary D. McClean, a white newspaperwoman who worked with Dr. Du Bois.

Printed on page 10 of *The Crisis* was the following statement, setting forth the purposes and policies of the magazine:

"The object of this publication is to set forth those facts and arguments which show the danger of race prejudice, particularly as manifested today towards colored people. It takes its name from the fact that the editors believe that this is a critical time in the history of the advancement of men. Catholicity and tolerance, reason and forbearance, can today make the world's old dream of human brotherhood approach realization, while bigotry and prejudice, emphasized race consciousness and force, can repeat the awful history of the contact of nations and groups in the past. We strive for this higher and broader vision of peace and goodwill.

"The policy of *The Crisis*, will be simple and well-defined. It will first and foremost be a newspaper. It will record important happenings and movements in the world which bear on the great problem of interracial relations, especially those that affect the Negro American.

"Secondly, it will be a review of opinion and literature, recording briefly, books, articles, and important expressions of opinion in the white and colored press on the race problem.

"Thirdly, it will publish a few short articles.

"Finally, its editorial page will stand for the rights of men, irrespective of color or race, for the highest ideals of American democracy, and for reasonable but persistent attempt to gain these rights and realize these ideals. The magazine will be the organ of no clique nor party, and will avoid personal rancor of all sorts. In the absence of proof to the contrary, it will assume of purpose on the part of all men, North and South, white and black."

Page 12 of the issue described the organization of the NAACP, which *The Crisis* was to be spokesman: "On the one hundredth anniversary of

Lincoln's birth, a call was issued in New York, signed by prominent people from all over the country, for a conference on the status of the colored people. The first conference was held in New York, May 31 and June 1, 1909. The second conference was held in New York, May 13-14, 1910. The second conference organized a permanent body to be known as the National Association for the Advancement of Colored People."

Plans for the organization included, among other things, the publication of *The Crisis*. I enthusiastically sold copies, and soon was asked to do fieldwork. My charge? To increase magazine sales and subscriptions while spreading the message of the NAACP. I accepted the offer, making my own itinerary, and started working in Hannibal, Missouri—the home of Mark Twain.

The organization didn't have money at the time, so from magazine sales, I paid myself a small salary to cover my expenses. The New York office supplied circulars, my picture, and advertising for *The Crisis*.

The work of the organization was badly needed in a state like Missouri, an ideologically southern state, yet located north of the Mason-Dixon Line. Cotton was grown in its southeastern section, the crop that made slavery profitable. Missouri was known as "slave breeding country," because slavery was ubiquitous throughout the state—slaveholders had no qualms about selling their own mulatto children across state lines and into the deep South, where cotton production was more profitable.

Some years after visiting St. Louis, I was on a speaking tour through the southeastern section of Missouri and saw the old St. Louis courthouse with its slave block still standing—a block where slaves had their teeth examined and muscles felt to judge their health and strength before being auctioned off to the highest bidder.

The Missouri trains were not segregated, people of color could ride in any train car and sit in any seat, but they could not eat in the restaurants, acquire a room in the hotels, or go to college. George Washington Carver was born in Missouri. As a young man he crossed into the state of Kansas, hoping to attend a newly established Presbyterian college near his place of birth. When he arrived, he was told that they didn't take "niggers." He then left Kansas and went to Iowa where he was allowed an education. He entered Iowa State University, eventually earning his Master's Degree in Agriculture.

On Easter Sunday 1906, three colored men were lynched in Springfield, Missouri. Two of the men, who were wrongly accused of assault and rape, were freed after their boss assured the authorities of their whereabouts and obvious innocence. The wrongly accused men were jailed a second time to protect them from a developing lynch mob. Then the mob broke into the jail, and took the two men, along with a third man that had nothing to do with the alleged crime. The mob went to the public square, threw ropes over the light post, and lynched all three. Cursing and swearing, the mob broke into a general store, took empty goods boxes, and set a great bonfire.

I arrived in Hannibal with several copies of *The Crisis*, along with five hundred circulars advertising speaking engagements. I had never tried this form of advertising, but my past experiences with the NAACP encouraged me.

I was in Hannibal only on Sunday, but in that time, I managed to speak to quite a few congregations, explaining in short narratives the history and purpose of the NAACP. I found it best to speak just before the benediction, and after the collection, relieving any uneasiness the minister might have about church expenses, especially his own salary. Often the minister would follow my talk with one of his own, encouraging the congregation to buy copies of *The Crisis*, take out a year's subscription, or both.

The ushers stood at the door, handling the copies, passing them to members of the congregation and collecting the dimes, while I vacillated between standing and sitting at a table just below the pulpit. The congregants were very responsive, many came up and shook my hand and some, wanting a year's subscription, gave me their names and addresses, telling me when to come by and get their dollar.

In southeastern Missouri, my first stop was Cape Girardeau, and after I was told that it would be dangerous to spend the night anywhere else in that section of Missouri, I decided to stay. I was provided with a car and driver, traveling hundreds of miles to speak at night, then I returned to the safety of Cape Girardeau, away from danger. I was both speaking for, and campaigning for, the NAACP.

My first speaking engagement was in Jackson, Missouri. The pastor of the A.M.E. church took the initiative to hold the event in his church, ignoring threats from city authorities warning colored people about potential harm if they "went to hear that woman speak." Sadly, the congregation heeded that warning, and only a handful of people were present.

I was told that many colored men were shot in Jackson for not voting as they were told. Wondering how anyone would know who voted for what in secret balloting, I inquired. Here's what I was told: "Well, the ballots have numbers and the colored voters are watched, their numbers transferred from the ballot and placed on another slip of paper beside the voter's name. This made it possible to check on voter's allegiance. Those that didn't vote as instructed would face serious harm or death."

I then went to Carrutherville, Missouri—a town where few colored speakers dared to visit. The last time a colored speaker had visited Carrutherville, he completed the lecture, went home, put on his bedclothes, went to bed, and was shot—the bullet entered from the foot of the bed, severely wounding his lower legs. The hall he spoke in was subsequently burned to the ground.

As we made our way into the more rural areas, we found ourselves within three miles of the Arkansas state line. I saw a group of colored men and women picking cotton in a field just a short distance from the road, and asked the driver to pull over. When my driver stopped the car, a man from the group looked our way, stopped picking, and came toward us. We told him we were looking for a colored church that was nearby, and would like an opportunity to speak to the congregation. Shaking his head, he turned and went back to his picking group. The group gathered around him as if in a huddle, then leaving that group, he started going toward a man that was standing far to the side; they spoke. The other man turned and started walking toward us. Speaking as he approached, he told us that he owned this land and was the pastor of the colored church, but that it was much too dangerous for us to speak to the congregation. Pointing across the road, he said, "See that house there? A white man lives there, whose son was killed a year ago. I had met the white man when I arrived in the area to take my pastoral duties. The man cried as he told me about his son, killed as he took a truckload of colored people to voter registration."

We continued our journey and drove to the colored schoolhouses, where we had secured pre-arranged meetings. These schoolhouses were one-room log shacks, no desks, no equipment, benches made of boards nailed to blocks of wood. A woman I spoke with in Cape Girardeau told me she had to walk through muddy roads in big rubber boots to get to the one-room shacks called schools; she was the teacher. In contrast, white children had centralized schools, new desks, new equipment, new chairs, and school buses to transport both students and teachers.

In Booneville, Missouri, I stopped at their all-white public high school and met with the principal. I was hoping to speak to him about subscribing to *The Crisis*, but while in his office, the principal's teenage daughter walked in and, noting I was colored, said, "Did you know that Frederick Douglass was white?"

I asked, "Why do you think he was white?"

She responded, "Because Daddy is the high school principal and he knows."

I got up and left without talking to the principal.

We had our ups and downs, but overall, I found the community response to the sale of *The Crisis* gratifying. In Columbia, Missouri, I visited the University of Missouri and, with nervous courageousness, went to the head of the Department of Journalism to ask if he would agree to a school subscription of *The Crisis*; encouragingly, he did so.

The experience at University of Missouri motivated me to try the same at Stephens College, also located in the city of Columbia. Originally called "Columbia Female College," Stephens College was for white girls; no colored students were welcome in either school. I was not successful with that subscription.

There was a woman of color in town, named Annie Fisher. Mrs. Fisher made a modest fortune selling "Beaten Biscuits." Her biscuits were made using a special machine that whipped them into a light, fluffy dough on the inside, but were crusty on the outside. Mrs. Fisher had a lovely home, rental units, a restaurant, a catering business—all patronized by the white Stephens College students, as well as the white population in the town and the country. Mrs. Fisher's product was par excellence, and, because of its quality, she had orders coming in from all over the country. The biscuits were so famous that they were on President William Taft's table when he visited the Missouri State Fair on Mule Day in 1911.

When it was all said and done, I spoke to audiences in Hannibal, Louisiana, Mexico, Sedalia, Columbia, Booneville, Monroe, Moberly, Lexington, Joplin, Springfield, Fayette, Fulton, Jefferson City, St. Louis, and Kansas City.

I made a second journey across Missouri, visiting Joplin, Springfield, Fayette, and Jefferson City. I sold nearly two thousand copies of *The Crisis* in less than two months during my first visit—many were yearly subscriptions. I began the second trip on July 5, 1912, and on September 28, 1912, I received the following letter from W.E.B. Du Bois:

My Dear Miss Johnson:

We cannot think of giving you up as agent for The Crisis *after all the excellent work you have done for us. If you cannot take whole charge of the Kansas City agency, you might use the young man to help you, but we still want to keep you as agent. I regret to say that the notice was too short to have your circulars printed and sent to Sedalia. I hope that the failure to get them did not hinder you too much. I am sure you must think at times we do not appreciate all you and other friends do, but you must remember that all of us in this office are overworked, and that it is impossible to give our agents always that amount and degree of cooperation, which we would like to.*

When The Crisis *gets on more satisfactory basis financially, and we can have a larger number of workers, we shall hope to do better. At present, let us hope to have your continued cooperation as our representative in the West.*

Very sincerely yours,
W.E.B. Du Bois

When I left Lexington, I went to Kansas, the state that I called home at the time. As a child in Ohio, I had a desire to see Kansas because it was the state that many people referred to when they said, "Go west and grow up with the country." Kansas had a history that captivated the minds of colored people and abolitionists like John Brown.

John Brown

Although born in Torrington, Connecticut on May 9, 1800, John Brown spent much of his young life in Ohio, where he absorbed the abolitionist ideology. His abolitionism was further enhanced when traveling through the state of Michigan, where he witnessed the vicious beating of a young slave boy. As a young adult, he went to Plainfield, Massachusetts, where he enrolled in prep school, and then transferred to a congregationalist school in Litchfield, hoping to become a minister.

Money prevented him from finishing school, so young John Brown returned to Ohio and worked for his father's tannery business. He again left Ohio, and tried but failed at several businesses in Pennsylvania, Massachusetts, and New York. Despite all his failings, he continued his strong anti-slavery stance, focusing specifically on the state of Kansas.

Kansas was to be admitted to the Union as either a free or slave state, dependent on the way the inhabitants voted in the upcoming election. Squatters for both the abolitionists and pro-slavery sides moved into Kansas to attain voting privileges, hoping that their vote could secure the decision for a free or slave state.

John Brown sent two of his sons down the Ohio River, up the Mississippi, and over to the Missouri River so they would be in Kansas for this important voting event. The boat in St. Louis was filled with pro-slavery, tobacco-spitting, profane, southern white men bound for Kansas.

During the river journey, an illness invaded the boat, killing John Brown's four-year-old grandson. At the first port stop, the Brown family went ashore to bury him, but the burial was interrupted when they returned to get a shovel and found the boat had left; the pro-slavery passengers had realized the Browns were abolitionists. The Brown family had to acquire a steam-powered vehicle to take them to Kansas City.

John Brown followed his sons, brought guns and ammunition, stopped by to get his grandson's little body, then settled in Osawatomie.

The 1856 voting day came, and thousands of illegal voters swarmed into the state of Missouri. The Browns found themselves in the thick of a fight that ended with the killing of five pro-slavery men in what became known as the Battle of Osawatomie.

A price was put on John Brown's head, but he escaped to Iowa, and Kansas gained the moniker, "Bleeding Kansas." This famous event was memorialized in a poem, written by Eugene Ware, a native Kansonian.

"States are not great
Except as men may make them great;
Men are not great except they do or dare

And there is one
Whose faith, whose fight, whose failing,
Fame shall placard upon the walls of time
He dared begin-
Despite the unavailing
He dared begin when failure was a crime

When over Africa
Some future cycle
Shall sweep the lake gemmed uplands
With its surge;
When as with trumpet
Of Archangel Michael,
Culture shall bid a colored race emerge;

There future orators to cultured freedmen
Shall tell of valor, and resound with praise
Stories of Kansas.

From boulevards
O'er looking both Nyanzas,
The statured bronze shall glitter in the sun
With rugged lettering:

JOHN BROWN OF KANSAS;

HE DARED BEGIN

❖

Before I began doing fieldwork for *The Crisis*, I had introduced the magazine throughout Kansas City and helped to organize the Kansas branch of the NAACP. Because of my familiarity there, I decided to make my first stop Lawrence, the seat of the State University, a school that allowed attendance by colored people. I remember one colored man who migrated from Mississippi to study medicine. He was in love with a Mississippi girl and, thinking he might lose her if he left her behind, he married her and brought her along. However, integration of Kansas schools was not ubiquitous.

In the state of Kansas, the grade schools were segregated, but the high schools were integrated. However, in Kansas City, the high schools were also segregated, this race separation occurring for a brief time before I went there to teach. This happened following an altercation on a playground that ended with the death of a white student at the hands of a black non-student.

School segregation only accentuated an already widening racial divide. I thought the schools should be mixed from the beginning, allowing children to know each other's cultures and similarities in the primary grades, and throughout their early learning years. I believe then, there would be less trouble in the high schools. Mixing both students and teachers is the only democratic way. It should begin in the nursery, and continue throughout college.

It is difficult to change segregation if our churches are racially divided. As I've said before, it's well known that segregation reaches its peak at high noon on Sunday, when white people go to their churches and colored people go to theirs. The hypocrisy of the doctrine, "the brotherhood of man," is apparent in our churches, and exemplifies "preached but not practiced."

Legislation can't impact racial attitude, nor can it change its negative psychological effects. Legislation can't combat the prejudice in the hearts of parents. On the playground, the white child mimics the ideology of the parent, casting daggers out of the corner of his or her eyes, which says to the colored child, "I don't want you around, you are inferior to me." He may call the colored child an ugly name, or turn his back in silence as the child approaches. This negative verbal communication, this body language of hate, is psychologically hurtful and misguided, and aimed exclusively at black children, which pushes both children in the wrong direction. Even worse, it sometimes causes the colored child to drop out of school, giving up the unrealized gift of education.

I spoke in Lawrence, then went to Topeka, where I organized their first local branch of the NAACP since starting my tenure as a field worker. St. Louis and Kansas City, Missouri had branches, but fear of harm in the more rural parts of the state made branch organization impossible.

Kansas City, a place where slaves, freedmen, and abolitionists intermingled, sharing experiences and ideas—where the first colored volunteer regiment for the Union Army was founded—where the largest colored settlement, Nicodemus, was established—where John Brown made his mark on history, a history that motivated people to organize. In Topeka, they met and formed a branch, but asked to leave the office of president open, saying they would take care of that later.

After leaving Topeka, I visited several other cities: Atchison, Emporia, Parsons, Wichita, Fort Scott, and Coffeyville. In Parsons, many in the colored community were enthusiastic about the prospect of having a branch of the NAACP. I recall a dentist who was quite energetic and willing to do anything needed to organize a local branch. He and others had in mind a possible leader, a white woman who had been a member of the Parsons Board of Education. An appointment was made for me to speak with her.

I arrived early for that appointment, and explained the purpose of this new abolition movement.

She listened patiently, and when I finished, she said, "Well what do you think of that Jack Johnson affair?"

This was about the time when Jack Johnson had married his second white wife. I think this one was from Minneapolis.

I said, "Well, Jack Johnson couldn't have married her if she hadn't married him."

Then she exploded with: "I think it's an outrage. A woman rears a pure, sweet girl like that, then a big black brute like Jack Johnson comes along and hypnotizes and marries her! The other night, my daughter went to Topeka, and sleeping in the berth just above her was a big, black nigger!"

She continued with this rhetoric, until it became quite clear that the colored people of Parsons were mistaken about her. They thought she was their friend, but after hearing her position, I realized that nothing could be done to organize a branch of the NAACP in Parsons.

Another letter arrived from Miss Mary Childs Nerney, secretary of the NAACP. The letter was dated May 22, and it voiced concern about the caliber of people applying for leadership positions in the branches, specifically the Muskogee branch. She wanted me to report on a list of people she included in her letter that were to make up the leadership, and whether they would work for the organization that was now becoming quite a power force in the movement for Negro rights. This was to be a confidential report.

I moved on to Muskogee, Oklahoma, where I was asked to let Miss Nerney know my thoughts concerning the Muskogee people in charge of organizing this new branch. I felt I had a better chance of organizing a branch in Muskogee, certainly better than Parsons. Muskogee seemed to be the most progressive city in the state, and several well-to-do businessmen were present at our first meeting. One was the owner of a large department store called Elliotts, where several colored folks were employed. Throughout Oklahoma, there were many Indians mixed with colored. This was especially obvious in Muskogee, and many were wealthy because of the oil lands they owned.

Reaching out to people in Muskogee was made easier through their church network, and the ease of communication made me feel very hopeful for the potential success of this branch. We had a meeting at the Colored Methodist Episcopal Church and organized what I believe was the first NAACP branch south of the Mason-Dixon Line. I am quoting Miss Nerney's letter of congratulations, dated April 29, 1913:

Dear Miss Johnson:

Thank you for your letter of April 25 enclosing six dollars to cover Association memberships. We are delighted at your success and congratulate you. I suppose we have your good efforts to thank for the constitutions which just reached us from Muskogee. Even before I got your letter, I inferred that you were our good angel.

Is it not nice that Dr. Du Bois is making his western trip?

I know he is going to be successful.

All the memberships that you send will be acknowledged directly. Do you think you could use some of our annual reports for free distribution? I am sending you a sample under a separate cover.

Very Sincerely,
Mary Childs Nerney

I replied to Miss Nerney's letter on May 28, 1913, telling her in detail about the membership of the Muskogee branch, and included a partial list of the forty-two members, their standing in the community, and their assets.

I then went to Oklahoma City and received the following letter from Miss Nerney:

May 27, 1913

My Dear Miss Johnson:

We have just received an application from Oklahoma City to be admitted as a branch of the National Association. I enclose a list of the proposed members.
Please let me know if they are all right. Are any of them white?
With best wishes.

Very Sincerely,
Mary Childs Nerney

All the twenty-six proposed members were colored, and I understand the Oklahoma City branch is still prospering. In fact, in 1952, that branch invited the National Organization to hold its annual meeting in their city.

While in Oklahoma, I visited Okmulgee, Guthrie, and Langston. Langston University, founded in 1890 as a state university for colored people, was the only black college in Oklahoma. Boley, Oklahoma was a predominantly colored pioneer town founded in 1903 on land owned by the Creek Nation, and subsequent Native American ancestry among its citizens. Taft, Oklahoma was another all colored town, also founded on Creek Freedman land, not very far from Muskogee and McAllister, and for reasons unknown to me, named in honor of President William Howard Taft.

Boley was an interesting place. The railroad station had a Jim Crow section for whites. State law dictated that the races must be in separate waiting rooms. An unaccommodating room was set aside for the whites, much like the railroads had for blacks elsewhere in the South. Very few white people ever visited the town—only a few musicians came through, and the small waiting room was apparently big enough for them.

Boley had a bank and several other businesses, all colored. There was a department store that employed twenty-two clerks, cashiers, and others. Boley also had a school building constructed with fine brick. One night, the town elders drove me to a very nice rural school building about ten miles out. It was set back among many trees, where I spoke to the people by coal oil lamps.

In McAllister, I stopped to speak with a veterinarian, the first colored person I had ever met in that profession. The veterinarian's wife and I went out to tour the new state penitentiary, a makeshift facility with fewer than one hundred prisoners, mostly male. We told the officer at the door what we wanted, he seated us, and after waiting a long time and seeing others come in after us and taken through the prison, we protested.

The officer said with a smirk, "Well, we can't find anyone who wants to take you niggers through."

Furious, I went home and called the Warden. I told him I was a well-known public figure and I was going to speak about him all over the state. He told me to come back the next day and someone would be at the door, waiting to take me through. I went and was treated with respect and with every courtesy.

Chapter Six

With the A.E.F. in France

St. Nazaire, France, 1919

AMERICA DECLARED WAR ON GERMANY in April 1917, but our armed forces numbers (126,000) were insufficient. In response, the government instituted the draft act in May 1917, requiring all males between 21- 31 years of age to register for the draft. African Americans quickly volunteered, seeking to prove their value and gain equality in an unjust America. "Colored folks should be patriotic," was heard throughout the colored communities.

Staring at the War map hanging on the wall of our small New York YWCA office, I also felt the need to serve. It was the Spring of 1918 when the call came asking for volunteers to serve as welfare workers with the YMCA. I readied myself, completed the necessary requirements, said goodbye to friends and family and boarded the transport ship in June of 1918.

When we arrived in Paris we met several other workers, including the first colored female YMCA secretary, she had been ordered home, unacceptable to the Army, a result of southern officers bringing their racism to France. Colored YMCA secretaries waiting in the U.S., were then delayed, leaving only three colored women to manage the spirits of 150,000 colored troops. We suffered from this shortage through the middle of 1919. Winter approached, and nothing had changed.

It was Christmastime for the thousands of colored soldiers stationed in St. Nazaire—the Army doing its best to provide them a nice holiday, realizing it would take months to bring them all home. Mrs. Hunton and I did all we could to entertain and teach the troops during this time. We organized religious and educational services, field trips, art and culinary experiences—cultural experiences these troops would never experience in their own country due to racism.

Many of the colored draftees came from the country, rural areas where there were no schools and they could neither read nor write. When it came time to sign for their pay checks, they couldn't sign their names. Addie Hunton and I decided to start teaching these men how to do both. Recognizing the success of their educational work, the Army got involved mandating their school.

Most of the troops were illiterate and, after the 1919 signing of the Armistice that ended WWI, colored soldiers were directed to come to my school. I worked with them all winter, hoping they would have some knowledge of the three "R's," before leaving Army camps and YMCA huts. My work soon began to show results, as documented by the following letter from the Army Educational Commission:

Dear Miss Johnson:

With best wishes for the success of your work and kindest regards, I thank you very much for the samples of the letters written by your earnest students. These, I assure you, are very interesting and inspiring. I shall be glad to receive any more material of the same nature that you can send.

You will be interested to know that I have tried to write something about the work you are doing at St. Nazaire, and have turned the articles over to the YMCA Publicity Department for dissemination in America.

Sincerely yours,
C.R. Miller
Army Educational Commission
12 Rue D'Aguesseau, Paris

The American Library Association sent boxes of books that would assure enjoyable reading material for the colored soldiers. The following letter demonstrates how they cooperated with us:

Dear Miss Johnson:

Your recent letter had been received, and we take pleasure in sending you by grande vitesse, six cases of fiction, containing about seventy volumes each.

As you were stationed at St. Nazaire, you are, of course, familiar with our assistant, but in case you have not a circular with you, I am enclosing one.

We shall be glad to hear from you from time to time in regard to circulation, or anything we can do to assist you.

Religion is synonymous with spiritual support for oppressed people, but when I arrived in St. Nazaire, colored troops didn't have a chaplain, even though they were required to attend religious services every Sunday morning. A sign hanging in the YMCA hut read: *Religious Services, Sunday, 11:00 AM.*

That next Sunday morning, I went to the chapel hut. When I walked in, I didn't find troops, but I did find the YMCA secretary looking perplexed, as if he didn't expect anyone. The secretary was a visiting Episcopalian minister from Boston, a fellow student I knew from Wilberforce. He couldn't understand the soldiers' absence from religious services.

Most of the soldiers came from Christian homes, making their absence even more difficult to understand. I made some inquiries, and after a few Sundays I was asked to lead the morning services. I had a fair crowd and I found the soldiers confused and conflicted, not understanding why the Army supplied them with guns for killing, along with a ministry for teaching the gospel of the "Prince of Peace."

That morning I used a passage from Joshua 5:6. "And the children of Israel wandered forty years in the wilderness; and all the men of war who came out of Egypt were consumed because they obeyed not the voice of the Lord."

I wondered if this would apply today.

My work at St. Nazaire attracted unexpected praise. The following is a letter from the YMCA's Regional Director of Women's Work:

St. Nazaire
March 31, 1919

Miss Kathryn Johnson has been in the hut for colored men since July 19. Her work has been along educational lines. She has conducted classes in elementary education for the illiterate. On account of her splendid work, many of the men are now able to sign the payroll. Also, besides holding the Bible classes, she has conducted a forum, instructing men in the cause of the war, and giving the reasons why they were in the service. Many of them did not know why they came here.

Miss Johnson's library is quiet and orderly. She, herself, is an earnest, energetic worker, and should be commended for the things she has accomplished and the work she has done."

Susannah Ridgeway
Regional Director, Women's Work
Aries in France

Another chaplain visited, but he had no religious or cultural connection with the troops. He was followed by a colored chaplain named

Jefferson. The troops' expectations were high, but he stayed only a few weeks.

The signing of the Armistice increased expectations for going home, but chaplains were still needed for Sunday services and funerals. Even though the war was over, soldiers still died and thousands more were buried in American cemeteries on French soil. Through all the excitement, Addie Hunton and I continued to work for the benefit of the colored troops.

Challes Eaux

In February of 1919, my colleague, Mrs. Hunton left her hut and went to the leave area at Challes les Eaux, "The Place of Waters," located in the Alps, just three miles from Chambery. There were many places of interest near the two towns, so we arranged excursions for the new soldiers coming into St. Nazaire.

In the heart of Chambery stands a statue of four elephants, their trunks and tusks elevated. Projecting up from the center of the four elephants, Hannibal, standing at the top of the fifty-foot obelisk. This monument is in memory of Hannibal's crossing of the Alps in 218 BC. Nearby is "Hannibal's Pass," where he came through the Alps with thirty-eight African elephants and 35,000 men, on their way to Italy. This immense herd of elephants worked with their trunks to loosen huge boulders, ones that rolled down the mountainside toward the Romans.

YMCA, MEN AND WOMEN AND SOLDIERS TAKEN IN FRONT OF THE STATUE OF ELEPHANTS, CHAUMBERG FRANCE, MAY 1919

Figure 9. Chambery, France, very near Challes Les Eaux, the "Fontaine des Éléphants" and the WWI colored soldiers, 1919.

Hannibal's Pass was one of the diversions arranged for the soldiers, but very few could make the full trip, many falling out winded, unable to make it even halfway up the mountain.

I would say to them, "Come on, young man. It's wonderful up there. You can make it."

"No, Miss Johnson, I can't."

The dozen or so soldiers that made it to the top enjoyed the wide verandas of the beautiful Hotel L'Astragale. We enjoyed the majesty of the Pyrenees Mountains rising to the heavens and the Rhone River running like a silver thread through the valley below.

On our descent, we'd gather the soldiers that were unable to make the climb. They rested at the foot of the mountain, enjoying the shores of Lac du Bourget, the deepest and largest lake in France, its randomly shifting thermal winds making it one of the most dangerous lakes in the world.

Just above Lake Lac du Bourget is Aix Les Bain, "Place of Baths." Hot, mineral-rich waters bubble up from the floor of the grottoes, inviting people to bathe in the healing liquid. Draining down to the bottom of

Lake Lac du Bourget, these waters also bubble up from the lake bottom, forming whirlpools, dangerous for swimmers and small craft.

We took a small steamer to Hautecombe Abbey, a towering structure on the cliffs above Lake Lac du Bourget. It was originally a Catholic monastery founded in the twelfth century for Cistercian monks. For a brief time, it belonged to the king and queen of Italy, and was known as the "House of Savoy," home to one of the oldest royal families in the world, but eventually, it returned to a home for twenty-one monks. The monks were forbidden to look at the face of a woman, so only one came out to receive us. The others stayed in cloister to greet the soldiers.

Figure 10. Soldiers at Hautecombe Abby with female French photographer in middle.

I often wondered what these monks did, cut off from the world, no highway or railroad, their only contact with the outside world through a treacherous route across a whirlpool-filled lake. I thought maybe some were students…until the day I explored the grounds. I noticed a barn-like structure about fifty feet from the monastery, and when I looked inside, I saw large wine vats; the monks were also vintners.

In the Abbey's chapel, the ceilings were adorned with beautiful frescoes, the walls interspersed with niches entombing saints. A casket made of glass, extending into a small chapel, contained the embalmed body of a sixteen-year-old boy, martyred for his faith. In the choir loft, there were music books on easels with notes larger than I had ever seen.

Within walking distance of the Abbey, there were waterfalls crashing down from the top of the Alps. These were known as the "Cascades of the End of the World"—its name derived from a mystical tale about the ancients that looked down on these waterfalls and said, "Well, here is perhaps the end of the world."

Figure 11. "Cascades of the End of the World," near Hautecombe Abby.

We visited Mont Revard, its summit over 5,000 feet. We were transported up the mountain on a cogwheel train, a rack-and-pinion transport system commonly used to carry passengers and materials up steep elevations. The cogwheel gripped a toothed middle rail, preventing slippage backwards. Sometimes the gradient seemed perpendicular, causing concern, many of us wondering what would happen if that mechanism failed, but we arrived without incident.

There was an observatory on the summit that allowed us views of three different countries, France, Italy, and Switzerland. There were snow-covered Alps, and scattered about on plateaus were rental kiosks with sleds and skis for the enjoyment of visitors. Near the YMCA headquarters was a tiny chapel on top of Mont Saint Michel d'Aiguilhe. This could only be reached by climbing 268 steps—not an easy task. One day, a group left ahead of me. I hurriedly followed, hoping to get there before they left the chapel. I decided to take a short cut and in doing so, came upon two little shepherd girls. Tired, I sat down to talk with them. The little girls, speaking with the innocence of children, told me that the white soldiers came before the colored soldiers, spread hateful propaganda, saying, "Soldat noir villain." Or in English, "Black soldiers are villains."

Race-based propaganda, spread by white soldiers in small towns and villages, was an attempt to poison France with America's unjust "Jim Crowism," but most French people did not accept this social construct. One evening, we were at dinner in the hotel Chateaubriand, and the hostess commented that the white soldiers had visited the night before, but the colored soldiers were more courteous and well-behaved. As we finished our meal, the mayor and city officials came to say goodbye, graciously inviting us back, telling the soldiers to come and live in their town, suggesting they might consider marrying their daughters.

Black Madonna

A truly magnetic attraction was on the foothills of Mont Granier, in an area between Modane and Chambery. Three miles from our compound stood Our Lady of Mayans church, with its "Black Virgin" historically worshiped by Saint Francis de Sales.

A powerful earthquake hit this area in 1248, causing the four-thousand-foot Mont Granier to partially collapse, sending boulders the size of houses down the mountainside. Entire villages were destroyed, but the church of Myans was spared, a huge boulder coming to rest at its door, as if stopped by an unseen hand.

The story of this miracle was told throughout the world. School children from surrounding towns and villages arrived on Tramways every Monday. People from all over the world would come to worship before the *Black Madonna*, and our colored troops were in awe, wanting to visit the Myans' church every Sunday.

L. Bisey Neuchales
400. Notre-Dame de MYANS (Savoie) — La Vierge Miraculeuse

Figure 12. Black Madonna.

In the basement of the church, just behind the pulpit, stood the Madonna, surrounded by cases and crutches, the words "Thank You" written or carved into their finishes. The statue evoked a sense of amazement for the colored soldiers, and many took an intense interest in her blackness. "The Savior is white, and the devil is black." That was the teaching, but this statue questioned that belief, a statue made by people who saw the Savior's mother as black. This Madonna was one of over four hundred in Europe, nearly half of them in France.

After one of our Sunday visits, we noticed that a dark-skinned soldier was missing. We went back to the chapel and there he was, still standing behind the pulpit, gazing at the Madonna. Watching him, I tried to imagine what thoughts were racing through his mind. All his life, suffering because of his blackness, segregated and spit upon, denied employment, and in his own country, unable to attend a church without fear of insult. But suppose the Savior was black…. What then?

The French didn't seem race conscious. They certainly understood the difference between white and black Americans, but made no presumptions. We met a French woman from town, one who often followed us, taking pictures. We offered to buy the photos, wanting to have reminders of our experiences, especially the more humorous ones. She socialized with us, ate with us, commiserated with us, and never once seemed to project any sense of difference.

Figure 13. French Photographer Madame Reulet with colored troops and YMCA Secretaries in St. Nazaire, France. Kathryn seated.

Mont Blanc Chamonix

June approached and leave areas began closing, the secretaries decided to take this fleeting opportunity to visit the Chamonix. So, we took a day or two off and went by train to Mont Blanc Chamonix. Along the way, we were visually entertained by the Bridal Veil Falls. These long, narrow streams of water cascading down the mountainside, glistening, foaming, spraying and roaring like little Niagaras.

As we arrived at Chamonix, we marveled at its beauty— a quaint village set on the foothills of Mont Blanc. The River Arve was flowing gracefully between small houses, their balconies adorned with colorful flowers. St. Michael's church was set against a backdrop of greenery, a statue of de Saussure in the village square. We had never experienced such tranquility.

It was 1,500 feet to the valley glacier "Mere De Glace" (Sea of Ice). Sunset was a few hours away, so we had time to make the climb. Our guide provided us with wooden alpine sticks, their handles with leather loops that secured to our wrist. When we neared the top, the snow was so deep that we had to use the sticks to assure safe footing. Despite much care, I stepped into deep snow that was over the tops of my boots, but we finally made it.

Across the three miles of snow and creviced ice, we saw a hotel. The guide wanted to lead us there, but I didn't like the risk involved, so I declined. When we returned home, someone told us a bishop of the A.M.E. church and six graduates of the University of Edinburg went to see the "Sea of Ice." The group tied themselves together, but one man slipped, went down between the crevices, and pulled three others with him. The jagged ice cut their rope, and all were lost.

The "Sea of Ice" looked as though it had been there since the beginning of time. The snow was packed down between the mountain peaks, blanketing a valley eighteen miles long and three miles wide. It was the latter part of May, the ice was beginning to melt, and icy water was roaring furiously down the mountain, but the snow never completely melted.

We spent the night in Chamonix and woke in time to see the sun rise over Mont Blanc, setting the Glacier du Boisson afire with heavenly beauty.

As we descended from the "Sea of Ice," just below the snowline, the warmth of spring allowed the flowers to lift their heads. We gathered a handful of primroses and as we did, a mountain goat, with its feet perched on the side of a gigantic rock, turned its head and looked at us, as if asking, "What are you doing?" That goat stood there with such great balance, a miracle from God.

On our journey back to Challes Eaux, we reached a point where two nations met. We went through Annemasse on the Swiss border. The Swiss troops stood at attention, forbidding us to cross into Switzerland, but a well-placed franc into the hands of an officer allowed us to place our feet on Swiss soil.

We stopped at the beautiful Hotel Splendide, built in 1904. Across the lake, one could see Tramways traversing the streets of Lucerne, and small boats moving up and down the lake.

The Hotel Splendide was expensive—twenty-four dollars a night for myself and the French girl who accompanied me as our interpreter. She couldn't afford the room cost, and refused to let us to pay, so she left.

It was well known that some French businesses overcharged Americans. The next morning, we overheard AEF officers loudly condemning the hotel for this practice.

We walked down to the beach, hoping to enjoy a pleasant afternoon, but sadly we came upon the body of a woman with golden hair. The tides had gone out and left her body. It reminded me of Charles Kingsley's poem in *McGuffey's Fifth Eclectic Reader*, which I studied at my grammar school in New Paris, Ohio. (28)

> *"Oh, Mary, go and call the cattle home,*
> *And call the cattle home,*
> *And call the cattle home*
> *Across the sands of Dee!*
> *The western wind was wild and dank with foam,*
> *And all alone went she.*

> *The creeping tide came up along the sand*
> *And o'er and o'er the sand*
> *And round and round the sand,*
> *As far as eye could see,*
> *The blinding mist came down and hid the land*
> *And never home came she.*

Oh! Is it weed or fish, or floating hair
A tress o' golden hair,
O' drowned maiden's hair,
Above the nets at sea;
Was never salmon yet that shone so fair
Among the stakes on Dee.

They rowed her in across the rolling foam,
The cruel, crawling foam,
The cruel, hungry foam,
To her grave beside the sea;
But still the boatmen hear her call the cattle home,
Across the sands of Dee."

We never found out what happened to that poor young lady, how she lived or how she died. We never found out her name, or whether she had family. We only knew that she went "to her grave beside the sea."

The band from St. Nazaire was visiting. I remember hearing them when I first arrived; it was somewhat dysfunctional. Their timing was off, their notes discordant, their wind instruments out of synch, but now the band could really play, and we were happy to have them.

One morning, we were waiting for the train to take us on a sightseeing trip. One of the band members, a tall young man in a playful mood, climbed up one of the trees that shadowed the station. He didn't notice the electric wires treading through the branches and accidently put his hand on one. His body jerked, then he went limp and tumbled down, hitting the ground hard. He was dead, the band heartbroken, our trip now a tragedy.

The band members buried him in the French cemetery in Chambery. They needed mourning bands, but because of gambling, they had no money. Feeling compelled to help, I bought black crepe and made the mourning bands.

Gambling was common in the Army, and as with all else, some were better at it than others. One young man always had more money than the others, and repeatedly requested that I send his winnings home. I sent about $1,200 home for him. More educated than most, this young man usually won all the money—the others won nothing.

The leave areas were for the support of troop morale. Every four months, troops were allowed a week off to do whatever they wanted. The French troops could go home to their families. The British, when the channel traffic would allow, could go home to Britain, but the Americans couldn't go back to America, due to time restraints. The YMCA, along with French authorities, planned excursions to hotels and resorts in the Savoy area to entertain the American troops.

When a new set of colored troops came to the leave areas, they were amazed to see colored women working with the YMCA. Once, while sitting on a couch in one of the large recreation rooms, a young man came striding in. Ready to greet him with some words of cheer, I got up and started toward him, but he turned around and left the room. He later returned, explaining that he was overcome with emotion and didn't want me to see his tears.

Noted celebrities visited the St. Nazaire camps and leave areas. Major Robert Russa Morton, the President of Tuskegee Institute, was sent by President Woodrow Wilson to investigate the psycho-social condition of colored American soldiers. Upon finding gross discrimination, he encouraged the troops to fight discrimination when they returned to the U.S.

Ralph Tyler of Columbus, Ohio, a noted journalist—the only accredited black foreign press correspondent in Europe—reported on colored American troop activity in France.

Julius Rosenwald, a white American businessman, philanthropist, part owner of Sears Roebuck, and a member of the Board of Directors for Tuskegee Institute, established the Rosenwald Foundation, which opened schools for colored children throughout rural Alabama. While in St. Nazaire, he left $200 for the colored soldiers, money used to establish a school for automotive mechanics.

From New York, Broadway theater crews performed for the soldiers. One performance used a small dog found in a German dugout. The dog, saved after being exposed to poison gas, played the part of a "cootie." Cooties, or lice, were a big problem for the troops. The bites and burrows resulting from these infestations caused intense itching and subsequent sores, often requiring treatment at delousing stations.

The YMCA hut at St. Nazaire adopted a dog named Bull; he was a rather large dog. The soldiers fed Bull and let him sleep in a chair by the old American stove used to warm the hut. The dog developed mange due to mites—like those that infested the troops, but peculiar to animals. We took him to a veterinarian, and after a while, he was cured. One of the colored officers wanted to keep him, but I told him he belonged to all the soldiers and took to him back to camp.

I learned that Bull was an American dog and had arrived aboard the *Leviathan*, the German cruise ship that was captured and used by the U.S. as a troop transport. Many of these transports were out of Hoboken, New Jersey—the main port of debarkation for the American Expeditionary Forces.

When the soldiers found out that Bull was from Hoboken, they treated him as a soldier, dressed him up, collared him, and sewed stripes on a blanket, giving him the rank of Captain. Bull seemed proud, as if he knew he was being honored.

❖

In the Spring of 1919, I traveled north to the town of Verdun. On this journey, I saw rusting tanks on deserted battlefields, un-used shells piled up like cords of wood, and poppies were everywhere. These red flowers waved in the breeze, creating a dazzling mirage. One could easily see where the Canadian military doctor and artillery commander, Major John McCrae, found inspiration for his famous poem, "In Flanders Field."

> *"In Flanders fields, the poppies blow*
> *Between the crosses, row on row,*
> *That mark our place; and in the sky*
> *The larks, still bravely singing, fly*
> *Scarce heard amid the guns below.*
>
> *We are the Dead. Short days ago*
> *We lived, felt dawn, saw sunset glow,*
> *Loved and were loved, and now we lie*
> *In Flanders fields.*
>
> *Take up our quarrel with the foe:*
> *To you from failing hands we throw*
> *The torch; be yours to hold it high.*
> *If ye break faith with us who die*
> *We shall not sleep, though poppies grow*
> *In Flanders fields."*

Another poet, Author Newberry Choyce, was also inspired to write a book of poems, *Memory Poems of Love and War*. He wrote one poem about the dead who lay on Arras Road, entitled, "Memory."

"I know a lone spot on the Arras road
Where I shall hardly bear to walk again

For fear of waking those great souls I loved
Who struggled to a death of piteous pain.

Ah! I should hear their laughter on the way,
And round my heart their boyish sighs would creep;

Till I must long to leave the rushing world
And steal away to join them in their sleep.

For only they who tread the tortured path
Of those torn roads where swaying poplars sigh,

Can dream how God could give no greater bliss
Than this hushed peace beneath the sad French sky."

I received an unexpected telegram from my brother, Joseph L. Johnson, MD, of Columbus, Ohio: *When are you coming to Paris?*

I was surprised to learn that he was so close by. My brother, who was recently appointed United States Minister to Liberia, had come through Paris to attend the Peace Conference at Versailles. Excited to see him, I left for Paris the next day. We made an unavoidable but brief fuel stop in Lyons, then drove by the great Cathedral of Lyons. When we arrived in Paris, I immediately went to the American Legation building to inquire about my brother. He received his mail there, but no one knew where he was or where he might be staying.

The next day, I was in the YMCA foyer. I looked up toward the balcony and there was my brother, pointing at me. He wasn't staying at the legation building, but at a hotel only two blocks away from the Paris YMCA headquarters.

That evening we had dinner, reminisced about Longtown, and the people we'd known and loved. The following day, we went to the Meuse-Argonne American Cemetery, where soldiers were re-burying our fallen patriots.

Meuse-Argonne American Cemetery

Many of those bodies came from "No Man's Land," that desolate area I had driven through on my way to and from Verdun. The dead were buried in temporary graves, each with a cross at its head. On the cross was a dog tag, like the one around the dead soldier's neck. Often, there were only parts of bodies, with no means of identification, placed in temporary shallow graves, leaving a hand or foot protruding from the earth. I can't describe the acrid odor that inundated us during that thirty-mile drive.

At the permanent cemetery in Meuse-Argonne, the bodies were re-buried. The colored soldiers were given this terrible task. It was a task too sacred to be assigned to the German prisoners, and too horrible for the white soldiers, but it was "just right" for the colored soldiers.

At night, the electric lights shone brightly over the cemetery, and as they performed their grim tasks, the colored soldiers sang, "Ain't Gonna Study War No More," a spiritual song recalled from their forefathers during slavery. Twenty-three thousand soldiers were re-buried.

The white soldiers—made up of officers, enlisted men, and clerks—didn't offer to lend a hand. Instead, they stayed in their well-stocked recreation huts, run by the Knights of Columbus. Over their huts were signs that read: *No Negroes Allowed.* When the colored soldiers saw these signs, they became furious about this blatant discrimination. They tore down the signs and destroyed the recreation huts.

❖

On our way, back to Paris, we stopped at Belleau Wood, the place of the "Battle of Belleau," June 1918. As in Romagne, the fallen bodies were being re-buried. Tired, we stopped and had dinner there with the YMCA secretaries.

Figure 14. American cemetery at Belleau Woods, France.

The next afternoon, we drove fifty miles to Fere-En-Tardenois. As we approached the area, we saw an open hillside, void of shrubbery or trees, and pockmarked with open graves, laden with wooden boxes. The "Battle of Tardenois" had taken place on these hilly fields, just above a valley traced by the River Ardre. Thousands of soldiers died and were buried in these shallow graves. It was a Sunday, and we were in the kitchen having dinner, listening as the soldiers engaged in solemn conversation. They were discussing the re-burials scheduled for the next day.

Later that evening, we decided to go to the Rheims. When we arrived at the Chateau Thierry depot, we were told that the train to Rheims was cancelled. There was a train to Epernay waiting to pull out of the station, the conductor was standing on the platform adjacent to one of the cars, and hearing our conversation with the ticket agent, told us to get on his train, that a train to Rheims would be waiting in Epernay. We boarded his train. But, when we arrived at Epernay station, there was no train, no place to sit, no place to lie down, soldiers lying around on the floor, taking up every available space, using their bags as pillows.

We hired a Frenchman to carry our bags as we searched for a hotel, but none could be found. We came back and sat down on a curb. I was so exhausted I could hardly sit upright. We asked a man driving a "voiture"—a vehicle with a buggy top and a high front seat—if we could spend the night in it. He said no. He had to take his horse home to feed. A woman came out of the station dressed in a black bombazine; she had overheard our conversation with the buggy driver and beckoned us to follow her. After a two-block walk, we arrived at her house. She took us upstairs and put us in an out-sized bed with high feather tick. The bed was so high that we had to get on a stool to climb in.

The next morning, we made our way to the station, where the train to Paris was scheduled to leave at 3:15 AM. When we arrived in Paris, we went to Rheims and visited the Hindenburg Line. This was the defeated German western defensive, or "Siegfried Position," built during the winter of 1916–1917. We looked for souvenirs and found helmets and hand grenades.

My brother had to prepare for his conference, so we hugged, spoke of the future, and he was on his way. As he was leaving, we noticed a man sprawled on a street bench with a large bottle of wine in his hand. The man was using a phony French dialect, asking us a series of questions to test our loyalty. He then laughed and told us he was from Baltimore and worked for the government. Why he asked questions, we never understood.

I visited the historic Church of Joan of Arc in Rouen. This ancient cathedral was in ruins, its historic significance was not because of its matchless beauty, but because of Joan of Arc, France's great heroine, who was burned at the stake. I asked if they would rebuild it. A Frenchmen said, "Qui, Qui!"

I asked, "How long will the re-building take?"

He said, "Trente Anis." Thirty years.

We arrived at the ancient coastal city of Brest, where I ran into Miss Richen, my coworker. She was concerned about our trying to find living quarters in Pontenezen, and said it would be best to get rooms in Brest. Against that good advice, I persuaded her to try and secure accommodations at the women's dormitory tent in camp Pontenezen, our new assignment. Camp Pontenezen, a "rest camp," was thirty miles from Brest, and we soon found out that all the rooms were taken.

Fortunately, we ran into B. F. Lee Jr., one of the YMCA undersecretaries, and son of the past president of Wilberforce, Bishop B. F. Lee. He was gracious enough to give us his room. The hut secretary was a white man, who remained for a few nights, then left and gave us full charge, but before he left, someone tried to frighten us.

One night, shortly before we were to retire, a large hand appeared at one of our flexoglass windows. The fingers made dents in the cloth. The next day we reported this incident, but nothing more was ever said, our report was never responded to.

There were forty thousand colored soldiers at Camp Pontenezen and only one colored YMCA secretary. Soldiers were constantly coming in to spend limited time in the camp, awaiting transportation from Brest back to America. Realizing how underserved our troops were, Miss Richen and I requested permission from Major Roberts to work at the camp; he agreed.

We wanted to put together a hut that would be a place of relaxation and peace for the colored soldiers, but we had very few resources. The soldiers agreed to donate three hundred francs to buy draperies, chairs, and other extras for the rest hut. We named it the "Frederick Douglass

Hut." We tore down partitions, put up shelves, and organized a library. We served refreshments every day. The inspection major made his rounds, praising our labors.

Figure 15. YMCA hut at Camp Pontenezen.

Camp Pontenezen was located on the site of the old Napoleon Barracks, a mud hole. Six boardwalks were made to try and keep us clear of the never-ending mud. These boards were placed about two inches apart, somewhat like the webbed feet of a duck, thus the walks were called "duck boards." They were nailed together, providing an almost mud-free walkway and were made wide enough for the large Army trucks that frequently came in and out of the camp.

The "Frederick Douglass Hut" was where Miss Althea Rochon and I served until the camp was closed. Every morning we awoke to beautiful strains of military music, and at night we fell asleep to the sound of taps. Our hut had a large auditorium with a projection screen and we showed motion pictures every evening. Sleeping quarters were in the rear. A small locomotive brought supplies twice a day, and my window was between the noisy locomotive and the "duck board" highway, those sounds of marching feet echoed as companies, battalions, and divisions exited the camp to board ships heading home to America.

We organized a library in a room that was previously used as a barbershop. Reconfiguring the room, we added shelving for five hundred books. Wherever we were assigned, the American Library Association, at our request, would send boxes of books. We made flower boxes for the windows, and found a French gardener who gave us flowers that were delicate in color, fragrant, and quite beautiful.

We arranged field trips. Eight of us, three YMCA women and five soldiers went to Mont Saint-Michel, a monastery in a secluded spot on the sea coast, its picturesque ruins bombarded by the British in the twelfth century, and again during the French Revolution. Nearby was the old Roule Fort, near the sparsely populated ancient town of Saint Vaast Hougue, looking just as prehistoric.

At the most north-western point of France is the entrance to the English Channel, near the small town of Saint Vaast Hougue, just eighty-eight miles across the channel from the British Isles. On the peninsula, we stopped for dinner in the town of Cherbourg before making our way back to Brest.

When we returned, a company of

Figure 16. The YMCA secretaries and troops that went to monastery at Mount Saint-Michel. **Top:** (1) Bright, (2) Green, (3) Robinson, (4) James, (5) Stephenson. **Bottom:** (6) Kathryn M. Johnson, (7) Hunton, (8) Curtis.

colored soldiers passed through the camp with a young Belgian boy they had adopted as a mascot. They had altered uniforms to fit him, taught him to sing in English, and tipped him with what ended up being three hundred French francs. With this money, the young boy hoped to get aboard one of the boats taking colored soldiers back to the United States. He walked up and down the dock, but no one would allow him aboard. That night, he returned to the empty barracks alone and he cried, having no one to care for him, no place to go, and no place to sleep.

One of the soldiers brought him to me. I asked him about his home. He told me that a troop of German soldiers had come to his farm in

Belgium, killed his mother and his sister, and captured his father. I asked him where he was when this happened. He said he was outdoors playing. I asked him what he did after the Germans left the farm. He said he couldn't do anything but cry. Later, when the soldiers came along, they took him with them.

The farm in Belgium belonged to him; he was the only one left in his family. He'd lost his identification papers somewhere along the way, but I was sure someone from his village could identify him and secure the homestead, so I took him to the camp commander and told his story. The camp commander took the boy to Brest and turned him over to the Belgian counsel.

During our conversation about the young boy, the camp commander asked me to speak at the Brest "segregation camp." These segregation camps were established adjacent to camp hospitals, and cared for patients with venereal diseases. This one was integrated, both white and colored enlisted men, and officers with ranks as high as Major. Unlike the camp at St. Nazaire, the camp at Brest was surrounded by beautiful gardens, and contained guards instead of barbed wire. I didn't know what to say to such men. I thought I should cancel, but the commander persisted, saying that many of the women who visited the camp were show women, and that the presence of a good woman would help their morale, so I agreed to speak.

Several days after speaking at the segregation camp, the commander told me there were four hundred and eighty-seven women in the camp, mostly from the Red Cross and YMCA, who opted not to attend because they were embarrassed to be seen in that audience.

On August 4, 1919, we left Camp Pontenezen for Paris. We had visited many places of interest during past trips to this beautiful city, especially Champs Elysees, the most beautiful street in the world. At one end is the Place de la Concorde, formerly the place where the French revolution started and where Queen Antoinette was guillotined. At the other end is the Arch de Triomphe, built to honor Napoleon.

The "Church of the Madelaine," a marvelous piece of architecture, rests fifteen minutes farther down the Champs Elysees. This beautiful church has no windows and is surrounded by statues of the Apostles. A few minutes' walk brought us to the Garden of the Tuileries, known at one time as the playground of the kings. We stopped at the Hotel Wagram, on the Rue de Rivoli, overlooking this famous garden.

The Louvre, said to be the world's greatest art gallery, is located at one end of the Garden of the Tuileries. When we first arrived, we couldn't tour it because sandbags protected all the entrances, but after the war, it re-opened to the public. *Venus de Milo* seemed to be the center of attraction for all visitors, her radiant smile, as natural as could be on a statue.

We planned on visiting the Luxembourg galleries, which houses many famous and quite expensive paintings, some painted by an American artist of color—the son of Bishop Tanner of the A.M.E church. His paintings were purchased by the French government and exhibited at the Luxemburg. He spent his life in Paris, though he always retained his American citizenship. France gave him the chance to develop his phenomenal artistic talent, unlike his own country, due to his color.

One day, I took the train to the Luxembourg galleries. The coaches were filled, and seats were scarce. At one of the stops, a white-haired French woman hopped on, looking for a seat. Traveling with us was a black Senegalese officer, who politely rose and offered her his seat. She gladly accepted, but before she sat down, she gave him a gracious bow and kissed his black hand. Being a colored American, I couldn't help taking note of the incident and thought to myself, *If that had been in the United States, someone would've probably set a bomb under the coach.*

We took a day to go to Fontainebleau, forty miles by train from Paris. Fontainebleau was the seat of royalty for seven hundred years, the place where Napoleon and Josephine spent their married life. Four kings were born there, and two died within its walls.

The Palace of Versailles, just at the edge of Paris, is famous for its ornate fences, spacious grounds, lakes, and fountains. Also, the Petit Trianon is located there, where Marie Antoinette lived before her execution. Her luxurious surroundings blinded her to the poverty of the people, so much so that when she was told they couldn't buy bread, she retorted, "They can't! Let them eat cake!"

This famous palace also houses the Hall of Mirrors. Dazzling mirrors cover every inch of wall and ceiling. The floors are beautiful, with wood so polished that it, too, sparkles. There's another room called the "Gallery of Battles," its walls covered with detailed paintings of battles fought by France throughout her long history.

On one of our Paris adventures, we invited Mme. Hirol, my hostess from Challes Eaux. She had never seen her own capital city. I took her to the church of the Madeline in Paris, thinking she would be interested in its architecture. She wasn't much interested in the structure of the building, but bought and lit a candle, holding it as she offered a silent prayer. *How beautiful*, I thought, even though it was demonstrative of the profound sadness felt by many French people.

Upon our return to Challes Eaux, Mme. Hirol remained but one night. A telegram brought her news of serious illness in a family member, calling her home. I never saw her again.

The colored soldiers of World War I produced an enviable record. There were several colored regiments called "Pioneer Infantry," all fine and upstanding men, ready to work or fight.

Croix de Guerre and Palm Medals of Honor

The highest morale of the American Expeditionary Forces was in the 802nd Infantry. Two thousand soldiers in one unit of the 802nd spent nineteen months in France, more than any other unit either white or colored.

Only colored regiments were cited for bravery by the French. They were decorated with the "Croix de Guerre": the 369th, 370th, 371st, and 372nd. The 372nd received the "Croix de Guerre" and the "Palm"—the highest honor of its kind given by French armed services. They were the first of the American Expeditionary Forces to receive such an honor.

The 369th Regiment was the first to reach the Rhine River. They served one hundred and ninety-one days on the front lines, five days longer than any other regiment. One hundred and seventy-one men received citation cards for exceptional gallantry in action, even though they had less training than any other regiment prior to going into action.

The French demonstrated no prejudice against the colored soldiers. I was in Paris when some of the great post-war celebrations occurred, but not one colored American soldier was seen marching with the American army. The black Senegalese were everywhere in evidence with the French troops; French law forbids discrimination due to race or color.

Figure 17. Victory parade, Paris, 1919.

I was also in Paris when the Peace Conference of World War I was in session. A Japanese member introduced a resolution, declaring the equality of the races. It was defeated by American and British votes. This was published in the daily papers and commented upon with bitter disapproval. The white American soldiers tried to carry racial prejudice to France. When a group of white American soldiers registered at a hotel, they would protest to the manager if any colored soldiers were there. At Brest, when colored soldiers were seen visiting French homes, white soldiers would stand outside and watch for them to come out. The colored soldier would be beaten or even killed when he left the next morning. We often got messages that Camp Pontenezen was closed until further notice because ongoing of race rioting.

The white American officers tried to enforce a color line. The following is a copy of an order issued to the colored 804th Infantry:

Warcq, France
March 20, 1919
Enlisted men of this organization will not talk to or be in the company with any white woman regardless of whether the woman solicit their company or whether the women are prostitutes or not.
BY ORDER OF CAPT. BYRNE

The order below was issued concerning the YMCA huts, one of which had a sign above its door: *No Negroes Allowed:*

S.O.S. Troops
Rimaucourt
There are two YMCAs, one near the camp for white troops, and one in town for colored troops. All men will be instructed to patronize their own "Y."

The antagonism between the white American soldiers and the French was profound. The Frenchmen were referred to as "frogs." Why? I don't know, but I have overheard several explanations. First, because of the French consumption of frog legs, then, the misinterpretation of the French flag and its "fleur-de-lys," which to some, resembled a frog.

On more than one occasion, the white American soldiers used the term to insult the French. While at St. Nazaire, an American soldier came to our hut to borrow an ice-cream freezer—there just happened to be a French lady with me at the time. As he left, he turned and said, "I can't bear a French frog."

"Now, be careful," I said. "This French woman who stands here with me is an interpreter and speaks excellent English."

He left, covered in shame and confusion.

On another occasion, I was on a train to Paris, sitting in a compartment with two cultured French women, both spoke excellent English. There were several American soldiers on the train, and while the three of us were engaged in conversation, a white American soldier came to the door. Evidently, he had been standing a long while and his nerves were worn to a frazzle. He looked at me as if he wanted to ask a question.

Finally, he said, "Is that seat taken?"

I said, "No, come in."

He entered quietly, but before he sat down, he began to vilify the French people. "I hate a French frog," he said, and proceeded to exhaust his vocabulary in abusive language against the French. Finally, I intervened. I told him that the two French women spoke excellent English and had understood every word he said. He was embarrassed, but the damage was done.

I returned to the leave area, and a few days later I received a letter from St. Nazaire, telling of another race riot.

The French realized that colored soldiers were not vicious and didn't have tails. A French girl entered a restaurant with a colored soldier. While they were dining, several white American officers engaged in profane and vile conversation directed at the French girl. The girl's brother was an official in the restaurant and understood English. He opened fire on the white officers. Troops had to be brought in to stop further escalation. This was relatively common whenever colored and white troops were together in non-combat situations.

The interaction between French civilians and white American troops was at best bitter, approaching adversarial by the time the American Army left France. At the Paris headquarters, I spoke with a YMCA official who said they were trying to get the American soldiers home as rapidly as possible, because, "The French people are tired of them!"

As the Summer of 1919 ended, we prepared for our departure from France. Mr. W. S. Wallace of Denver, Colorado, the YMCA Regional Secretary at St. Nazaire and later head of Field work in Paris, wrote me the following letter expressing appreciation for the work I had done at St. Nazaire:

Before your return to America, I wish to have an expression regarding the work you did while you were in St. Nazaire.

I remember very distinctly how you took hold of the educational work in Camp 4, and developed it, and the large number of classes that you handled, teaching the boys their first rudiments in Reading, Writing and Arithmetic. Aside from that, your work in the library was certainly such as to meet unqualified endorsement.

I trust that back in the states, you will still be permitted to go on with your same work.

Miss Anne Watson, Regional Director of Women's Work, gave me the following letter of introduction, addressed to Miss Helen Miller of the Paris Women's Bureau:

"This will introduce to you Miss Kathryn Johnson, who comes in with release papers to report to you Monday morning. I cannot speak too highly of the work of Miss Johnson, as she came into a hut where there had never been a woman before, and made it a home for her men.

She and her coworkers have brought a splendid influence at Camp Pontanezen. Miss Johnson has initiative and splendid ability for YMCA work. I am more than glad to have had her come to our camp."

Chapter Seven

Back Home to the States

"Now and then out of the void flashed the great sword of hate…and thus, in the land of the color-line, I saw the shadow of the veil. Surely, there shall yet dawn some mighty morning to lift the veil and set the prisoned free."

—W.E.B. Du Bois

AUGUST 4, 1919, COLORED YMCA workers, nine women and four men, leave Brest for Paris. The barracks and YMCA buildings are empty, the soldiers finally on their way back to America.

Figure 18. Segregated on the Steamer T.S.S. Noordam heading back to U.S.A. from France.
First row: (1) Hunton, (2) Childs, (3) Williams, (4) Stevenson.
Second row: (5) Wilkinson, (6) Wakinson, (7) Brown, (8) Rochon, (9) Reinert, (10) Earlie, (11) Johnson, (12) Ativeli.
Third row: (13) Grimes, (14) Kathryn. M. Johnson, (15) Scroggins, (16) Wilkins, (17) Shorkins, (18) Dums.

On August 8, following an all-night train ride, we arrived in Bologne. It was seven in the morning when we were taken aboard a small boat and then boarded the ocean steamer *Noordam* of the Holland-American Line. The ship, chartered by the YMCA, carried several Red Cross workers, Army officers and a few women and children from Holland. We set sail, and two days later the steamer anchored in Plymouth, England. We remained quietly in the harbor until Monday morning when several more passengers boarded. The boat left the harbor and headed southwest across the Atlantic. As evening approached, the thought of sleep overcame us; looking for our quarters, we came to realize the sleeping rooms were segregated.

Forewarned is forearmed and to prevent segregation in the dining hall, we decided to spread out and select our own seats. We sat at tables where there were no people of color. I chose a table and took a seat. Immediately, a woman across from me said with great fervor, "What are you doing here? You're trying to get away from your race."

I replied, "Doesn't every worker have the privilege of sitting where they please in the dining room?" I hurried through the meal and went to the head of the Women's Division. I told her the story and asked if segregation in the dining room was their policy, *Was that woman sitting across from me right?*

The answer was, "Why, yes, you don't think we're going to treat you like the French people treated you!"

I was choked with anger, but said nothing. What could one do? I felt like challenging her to a duel.

At the next meal, colored workers, Chinese officers, a Japanese officer, and an East Indian in civilian clothes were all put in separate rooms. The three foreign men were seated at my table, and as I looked at them I thought, *How brazen of white people to mistreat and disrespect people of color, yet fail to understand why the world's darker people don't like them.*

106

As we continued west across the Atlantic, a whale started following our ship. One of the seamen said it was a sign that a storm was coming and, sure enough, a day or two later we were hit by a violent storm. Waves rolled and dashed, the ship rising on the waves like a giant steam monster, cresting, then diving into the water leaving the propeller spinning in the air. The ship's frame shivered, her timbers creaked as, again, she would climb another mountainous wave. It took us fourteen instead of the usual ten days to make the trip.

Shaken from both prejudice and storm, I was very happy to arrive in the States. I received the following letter from Mrs. B.F. Langworthy of Evanston, Illinois:

The New York office has told us of your return from the work in France, and I want to tell you how warmly we appreciate the splendid service that you have given to the YMCA, and our boys in Europe.

I realize that I can never know the hardships and fatigue that you have undergone, but I know that your joy in the work has been so great that you have already forgotten all of that, and will carry with you always the memory of the magnificent service at the time of America's most critical need.

There were approximately 11,500 volunteers serving the AEF as regular militarized YMCA workers. After returning to the U.S., most scattered to the four corners of the country and the world. However, there were a few determined to collect and organize records that would document our work overseas. We wanted to preserve (for future generations) the historical and social data concerning the colored troops and workers. We reached out to other workers to collect the information needed to tell a full and accurate story of the experiences of both colored YMCA workers and soldiers during their time in France.

Several weeks later the War Historical Bureau, at our request, sent an appeal to all overseas secretaries, requesting that each chronicle his or her location and official position on Armistice Day, November 11, 1918.

Many replies were received, but there were hundreds that didn't respond to what we thought was an important historical endeavor.

Several months after returning home, I received the following letter:

It will greatly help those who are preparing the official history of the "Y" if it's possible for us to give a vivid and exact picture showing the distribution of our workers throughout France, England, Italy, and Siberia at the end of the hostilities.

You will be rendering, therefore, a real service if you will send me immediately a statement of your whereabouts on the enclosed card. If you were not overseas on Armistice Day, please say so on the card.

E. C. Carter, Lately

Chief Sec'y, AEF, YMCA

Yes, I could tell Mr. Carter exactly where I was on the day the Armistice was signed—I was at 118 Rue Villas Martin, St. Nazaire, France at the home of Mme. Nirol, the gracious French hostess whose home, I, and others of our group, lived. Mme. Nirol was a very lovely woman who knew no "color line." When I left her home, I expressed regret. She replied, "Pur quoi vous parte avec moi, Mademoiselle?" (Why do you part with me, Miss?) At the time, I was leaving St. Nazaire on my way to the 'Leave Area' at Challes Eaux. I could have remained with Mme. Nirol but preferred to continue providing services for the colored troops awaiting transport home.

When the whistles began to blow on Armistice Day, I left Mme. Nirol's house and went into the streets where crowds were milling up and down, bands were playing, and American soldiers were celebrating, happy at the thought of going home. The French people had little joy. Every house looked like a place of mourning. The women wore black in honor of their lost sons, husbands, and fathers. The women had been doing the arduous work of tilling the soil, carrying baggage, and harvesting crops. Much of France was desolate, whole towns and villages destroyed, farm fields ravished, families decimated. Railroad stations were overwhelmed with refugees fleeing to Southern France trying to escape the Germans. Mothers and children were in front carrying all the family's earthly possessions that were either tied up in sheets or bagged, not sure where they were going, simply trying to save their lives.

Yes, I knew exactly where I was on Armistice Day, 1918; however, in the history of the "Y" as proposed by Mr. Carter, I wondered what would be said, if anything, about the colored "Y" workers and the colored soldiers they served. What would be said of them? Would history be as silent, as disparaging, as forgetful about the achievements of colored people as it had been in the past?

In this horrific war, one hundred and fifty thousand colored soldiers and ninety-seven colored YMCA secretaries participated. Nineteen of the secretaries were women. Three—Mrs. Addie Hunton, Mrs. Helen Curtis, and I—had been in France since June of 1918. The other ninety-four arrived in March of 1919; they were delayed, not because of logistics, but because we carefully welcomed French women to our camps, so they could fraternize with our colored soldiers.

Because we knew the story of the colored soldiers in the war and because we knew that their story would not be included in any books written about the war (unless a person of color were to write it), Mrs. Hunton and I decided to write that story as we had seen it. We decided to call our book *Two Colored Women in the A.E.F.*

But before we could concentrate our attention on writing the book, we found ourselves caught up in another controversy.

The Birth of a Nation

At about this time, *The Birth of a Nation*, a play filmed by the late D. A. Griffith, was scheduled to be shown at the Capitol Theatre just off Times Square in New York. At the time, it was the largest movie playhouse in the world.

This play was slanderous towards colored people. It opens with a young white girl by a spring. A man of dark complexion approaches her and a chase begins. The girl runs screaming through the woods and finally jumps to her death over a precipice. Her body is found by the white neighbors…and then enter the Ku Klux Klan. They burn a cross. The lynching is not shown, but the dead body of the colored man is seen swinging from a tree "the next morning."

The National Association for the Advancement of Colored People published one hundred thousand circulars in protest:

STOP THE KU KLUX KLAN IN NEW YORK

The Birth of a Nation *exalts the infamous Ku Klux Klan which has been publicly accused of voting to blow up or burn Negro school houses in 1941. The film distorts and falsifies history.*

Georgia—Governor Dorsey of Georgia called the attention of a sheriff to the accusations against the Ku Klux Klan in connection with the terrible mistreatment cases in Georgia.

Florida—The Ku Klux Klan tried to terrorize Negroes out of voting in Florida in the election of 1920. Many Negroes were killed in the election day riots at Ocoee, Florida.

North Carolina—Governor Bickett of North Carolina called the revival of the Ku Klux Klan in 1919, a, "desperately wicked appeal to race prejudice." He said: "The scheme is transparently impossible, so plainly a gold brick proposition that ordinarily the inmates of a school for the feeble minded could not be induced to part with their coin for a certificate of membership in such a soap bubble.

"But running through the whole scheme is a wicked appeal to race prejudice. There is a hark back to the lawless time of the Civil War, and there is paraded before the mind of the readers the terrors of those dark days. The very name that is written on the fears and the prejudices of our people. Such an appeal is desperately wicked. There is no need for any secret order to enforce the laws of this land, and the appeal to race prejudice is as silly as it is sinful. Just now all of us need to be considerate and kind in

our dealings with the Negro. The best and the wisest men of both races are working to strengthen the ties of friendship and peace, and lay a broad and deep foundation for an enduring peace and prosperity for both races.

"I call on all men who do not desire to throw their money away to have nothing to do with this wildest of wild cat schemes, and I call on all true patriots to frown down on any and every attempt to capitalize race prejudice into cash."

South Carolina—The report of the investigation by Congress, into the activities of the Ku Klux Klan after the Civil War in South Carolina, where the scene of the, "Birth of a Nation," is laid, said, "That in the nine counties covered by the investigation for a period of approximately six months, the Ku Klux Klan lynched and murdered thirty-five men, whipped two hundred and sixty-two men and women, otherwise outraged, shot, mutilated, burned out, etc., one hundred and one persons. It committed two cases of sex offenses against Negro women. During this time the Negroes killed four men, beat one man, committee sixteen outrages, but no case of torture. No case is found of a white woman seduced or raped by a negro."

—The best white papers of the South are openly opposing the reviled Ku Klux Klan.

—Do you know that the Ku Klux Klan is not only anti-Negro, but anti-Jewish and anti-Catholic?

—Are you going to allow Ku Klux Klan propaganda to be displayed in the movies of New York City?

Published by
The National Association for the Advancement of Colored People
70 Fifth Avenue, New York

We had yet to take off our overseas uniforms when we were called and asked to appear in uniform to distribute circulars in front of the Capital Theatre at 1645 Broadway. Several uniformed soldiers also joined us for the protest. We wore sandwich boards protesting the Ku Klux Klan propaganda. We were instructed to say nothing if we were arrested.

Figure 19. *New York Times* photo of protest of "Birth of a Nation."

I was approached by a plain clothes policeman who showed his star and asked me to give him a copy of the circular. Then a man in uniform came and told me I was under arrest. I looked around and saw that Mrs. Helen Curtis and Mrs. Laura Rollins were also being arrested. Two men were also arrested—Mr. E. Franklin Frazier, now a noted author and sociologist, and Mr. Rollins, the brother-in-law to Mrs. Rollins. With a noisy crowd following us, we were taken down Broadway to the police station.

Miss Mary White Ovington, mother of the NAACP, Walter White, Jack Nail, and an attorney named Popel were arrested but, fortunately, had money to bail out. We were in custody for about an hour before being taken to night court. The women could take a taxicab, but the men were taken in patrol wagons.

The women were placed in a large cell previously occupied by twenty-one Japanese men picked up in a gambling raid. There were backless benches in the cell for us to sit on. But I just couldn't be still. I must have walked many miles during the three hours I was waiting.

People walked up and down the corridors and wondered who we were, saying, "What are they? Bolsheviks?" About one o'clock in the morning, we were taken into the night court. We were asked if we wanted to start the war over again. I was glad the war was over, but hated the prejudice facing us in our native land.

The women were found guilty and placed on parole, but the men had to pay $200.00 bail. The case was appealed to another court, which also found us guilty. However, a higher court reversed the decision, because the circulars were educational, not advertising.

The day after our arrest, every daily paper had the story. The Civil Liberties Union wrote us and offered their services. The Capitol Theater, in New York, returned all the money for the sold-out house and cancelled their presentation of *The Birth of a Nation*.

All of this happened from June 7 to June 10, 1921. *The Crisis*, issue dated December 1921, ran the following article:

THE LIBELOUS FILM

It will be remembered that Miss Kathryn M. Johnson, Mesdames Helen Curtis, Laura Rollceck, and Messrs. Edward Frazier and Llewellyn Rollock were arrested last June for distributing hand bills attacking The Birth of a Nation. The NAACP undertook their defense. They were given suspended sentences in the magistrate's court and appealed their cases. Judge Talley, of the Court of general Sessions, has just reversed their convictions, saying:

"In the opinion of this court, the defendants were well within their rights in distributing the circulars in question and the complaint against them should have been dismissed. I hold that the ordinance in question was never intended to prevent the lawful distribution of anything other than commercial and business advertising matter, and the circular in question does not come within that category."

"It would be a dangerous and un-American thing to sustain an interpretation of a city ordinance which would prohibit the free distribution by a body of citizens of a pamphlet setting forth their views against what they believed to be a movement subversive of their rights as citizens.

This is not only a victory for the NAACP, but for freedom of speech as well, and it was won by two colored attorneys, Aiken A. Pope and James C. Thomas."

Sometime after this occurrence, I was sent by the Brooklyn Branch NAACP, to see the president of the Trustee Board of Brooklyn's historic, Plymouth Church of Pilgrims on Orange Street. The Plymouth Church, a well-known northern Underground Railroad Station led by Rev. Henry Ward Beecher, a minister and avid abolitionist known for holding "mock" slave auctions for his congregation demonstrating the evils of slavery. (One such auction was held in 1860 to gain freedom for a nine-year-old bi-racial girl named Sally Maria Diggs. Bringing the little girl to the pulpit, appealing to his congregation, they raised enough money to buy her freedom. Sally Maria later married an attorney and became Mrs. James Hunt.)

We wanted to have a mass meeting in the church. Imagine my surprise when the chairman said: "Well, now we have Plymouth Church all repaired and cleaned up nicely since the fire and colored people want to use it. Who is going to clean it up after they get through with it?"

I had returned to the U.S. from France to the revival of *The Birth of a Nation* and immediate immersion into protest, arrest, trial, and appeal. And the Plymouth church incident certainly didn't put Mrs. Hunton and I in the frame of mind needed to write a book about the history of colored soldiers in World War I France.

Somehow, the manuscript was completed and many publishers were interested, but also concerned that publishing our manuscript describing the interaction between French women and colored soldiers, the non-racial tone of French culture and the prejudice the colored soldiers experienced from their white brothers in arms, would instigate race riots. So, we approached the Brooklyn Eagle Press, used by the NAACP to publish *The Crisis* magazine. The book was reviewed and well received.

Here are just a few of the reviews:

"Mrs. Hunton and Miss Johnson have done an important piece of work in giving to the world their experiences with the A.E.F. So far as I know, this is the first intimate and authentic account of the life of the colored soldier who fought for his country in France. The book is not only a good narrative but is educational and contains many a bit of information, many an anecdote which must make the colored ex-soldier consider it as a guide book to memory. Of course, for the stay at home, it is indispensable.

Though clearly not written as propaganda, we find in these pages, propaganda of the most effective sort. The dispassionate account, tempered by a sort of marveling sadness that such things could be of the needless, foolish humiliations, and distinctions which our boys were forced to undergo in France, leaves an indelible impression. If seas of blood cannot wipe out prejudice, what can? Yet the tone of the book is never despair.

From the standpoint of generations to come, a different arrangement of the pictures might have been wished for; but even as they are, they are valuable."

—The Crisis

"Of the many war records written by men and women of almost any age, there are scarcely any that present both so courageous and so honorable and at the same time so pitiable a story as this story of the two-colored women with the American Expeditionary Forces.

Sir Phillip Gibbs did not know, or perhaps he did when he gave such a title as, "Now It Can Be Told," to one of his after-war books that he was encouraging the truth in many minds to step out of its lair of prejudice and privilege. Well, war has always proved itself to be a nasty thing; and the World War, with all its glimmering garments of idealism, has proven itself to have been a beastly thing.

A foolhardy young American has recently attempted in the guise of fiction to tell the truth of what was endured by the doughboy. He is being called all sorts of things in some quarters. But the chorus of approbation of the truth he tells is too strong to make the carping cries of the opposition to count for much. Unfortunately, there will be no such controversy about what these two-colored women tell of the treatment accorded the colored troops by their fellow countrymen, as they all fought Mr. Wilson's flowery phases for the salvation of human liberty...."

—The Boston Transcript

"The Hunton-Johnson collaboration is a worthy addition to the valuable works on the world fight; and what is more, it is written much more interestingly than the average world war history."

—Brooklyn Daily Eagle

"There are some moving passages in the record, and some memorable word pictures."

—The New York Globe

"For they also sketch the history of the negro soldier in France—many, patient, efficient, heroic, whether as combat troops, or Service of Supplies Units, or in the terrible task to which they alone of all Americans were assigned- that of digging up the American corpses that had been dead for months, and burying them again in Romagne. Here will be found a tale of heroism fit to rank with any in the records of the ages."

—The Negro World

"The story is so interestingly told that it contains the elements of several movie scenarios. There is pathos, humor, tragedy, and some extremely clever situations depicted."

—The Billboard

"The cause of bitterness remained, however, and pursued them through France. The race prejudice of the white Americans. Such at least is the indictment set forth in detail, in a book entitled, "Two Colored Women with the American Expeditionary Forces."

—Current History

Such press reviews as these brought in a great many sales. However, I knew the book could not and would not get to the mass of colored people, where it was needed most, unless it was taken to them personally. I had learned this during my years of travel for the NAACP. On May 15, 1921, I bought a Ford coupe and began going through New York, Brooklyn, and the surrounding cities speaking to colored people and showing the book. I soon decided to travel the country and distribute what I came to call the "Two-Foot Shelf of Negro Literature."

Chapter Eight

The Two-Foot Shelf

"I believe in God, who made of one blood all nations that on earth do dwell. I believe that all men, black and brown and white are brothers, varying through time and opportunity, in form and gift and feature, but differing in no essential and alike in soul and the possibility of infinite development, especially do I believe in the negro race: in the beauty of its genius, the sweetness of its soul, and its strength in that meekness which shall yet inherit this turbulent earth."

—W.E.B. Du Bois

IT WAS APPARENT THAT IN the colored community, there was a thirst to learn whatever they could about the history and accomplishments of our people. In 1909, Charles E. Elliot, Harvard University's president, was doing well selling the fifty-volume collection of classic literature called the "Five Foot Shelf," and this gave me the idea.

I collected a small library of books on Negro history and literature, and, adding those to my own work about the colored soldiers in World War I, I called it the Two-Foot Shelf of Negro literature. I priced the collection at $25.00 and set out to help colored people learn something about themselves. I carried the books with me so that they could be deliverable at the time of sale.

Figure 20. Kathryn with her Model T Ford and her "Two-foot Shelf" of Negro
literature, 1921.

The winter of 1921 I lived in Brooklyn, where I tested my plan before moving on to Manhattan, New Rochelle, White Plains, and a few other New York towns. After some success, I set out to work New Jersey. During the week, I left my car in Newark and used the subway to go to and from Jersey City, except on Sunday mornings—that's when I drove to the smaller New Jersey towns.

When I arrived in a new town, I looked for colored churches and asked to speak to their congregation. I had my Two-Foot Shelf of Negro Literature with me so everyone could see it. I rarely had more than five or ten minutes to share my message of Negro achievements, which was usually time enough. In New Brunswick, I sold four sets of books at $25.00 each, and delivered them that morning.

How gratifying and valuable this initial experience was, traveling about, meeting and talking with some very fascinating people, all surprised that a woman would take on this responsibility, but all the same, greatly interested in the educational cause I sponsored. Many understood the need to know the achievements of their own race and the impact ignorance of such would have on their family and community. As I spoke with people, I realized how important my task was, and this realization was motivational.

Deacon James Lassiter

A meeting with Mr. James Lassiter, of Madison, New Jersey also supported the importance of my mission. A graduate of Hampton Institute, he was the patriarch of a fine family, Deacon and Chairman of the Board of trustees of his Baptist Church, and profoundly interested in the education of his race. He invited me to spend the night at his home after hearing my presentation. He had a large plot of land filled with fruit trees, flowers, and shrubbery. In the summer, people came to enjoy his spacious lawns and rest in his comfortable lawn furniture. He was very interested in the work I was doing and wanted his, and other, children to have an opportunity to learn more than he had about their own race. I thought Mr. Lassiter exemplary of so many in colored communities all over the country that are thirsty for a knowledge that, until now, was not available.

Since slavery, colored people have been systematically kept uneducated through laws prohibiting the education of Negroes, inadequate teacher training programs, because there were no schools (or only poorly maintained schools), due to intimidation and segregation. Many, realizing the importance of education, have overcome these obstacles through their own perseverance, using literacy as a means of conquering these injustices. One such person lived on the highway traveled by King George's troops that was meritoriously named King George's Highway.

Mr. Lewis

Mr. Lewis was born in Virginia and remained illiterate until he remarried after the death of his first wife. His second wife read stories that fascinated him. He did all the household errands, so that his wife had more time for reading. She eventually taught him to read the Bible and this knowledge opened a new world, leading to his calling to preach. He didn't believe that ministers should be salaried, so he earned his living working in an ammunition plant.

He loved nature and could describe to perfection any species of snake or other animal that made its home in the mountains of Old Virginia. He could also describe in detail the feathers of different birds and even imitate the twitter of their songs. He had no education, except through his wife, but his wealth of knowledge regarding nature was both wonderful and amazing. I visited their home on many occasions.

After months of travel with my Two-Foot Shelf outside of the New York area, I eventually returned to the more remote areas of Staten Island, where people were reading and praying by the light of coal oil lamps. I spent a night with Reverend Mrs. Florence Randolph, who, against all odds became pastor of the Rossville A.M.E. Zion Church and then one of the first women to attain deaconship in the A.M.E Zion Church in Staten Island before going to Liberia and the Gold Coast of Africa to minister and teach.

There are stories that demonstrate the power of prayer. Stories that inspire us to do more, moving us in positive directions and affirming that what we are doing is right. It was when I ventured back outside New York to Plainfield, New Jersey where I experienced one of those moving stories.

Mrs. Alexander and Other Noteworthy Women of Color

In the winter of 1922, it was Sunday afternoon when I arrived in Plainfield. I had some difficulty finding a colored church. By the time I found one it was nearly benediction, but the good pastor was kind enough to let me speak. During my talk, I emphasized the negative impact of illiteracy and the injustice of the color line, and that conduct, not color should be the measure of manhood and womanhood.

As I spoke, I noticed a large woman in the choir, whose face beamed with intelligence, her expression showed an appreciation for what I was doing. After the benediction, she walked up and asked if I had dinner plans or a place to stay until evening services. I replied that I did not. She invited me to her home. This was the beginning of a long and friendly relationship.

Mrs. Alexander was a native of Tennessee, was quite well educated and had taught school in her home state. It was there that she met and married her husband, Reverend Alexander. After being married for some years, Rev. Alexander's eyesight began to fail and she learned for the first time that, as a boy, he'd had a farming accident, a piece of lead had gotten into his eye and was never removed.

He was called to Plainfield to pastor a Baptist church. His congregation seemed to think a great deal of him while he could see. But, he developed severe eye pain and his sight started to fail; he could no longer read the sermons. The congregation started making negative comments. He decided to have an operation to remove the foreign piece of lead, relieve the pain, and hopefully improve his sight. The choir gave him $100.00 for the operation.

He went to New York, where he underwent eye surgery. This relieved the pain but did not improve his sight. While in New York, the congregation in Plainfield declared his pulpit vacant. When he returned, he had no work and no place to live.

His wife sent him to live with his sister in Virginia, and sent their two children to her sister in Tennessee. She then hired herself out for domestic services at five dollars a week, a fair wage at the time. Every other week she sent the money to her children, and on alternate weeks, sent money to her husband. She kept no money for herself, as she received meals and clothing where she worked. She went to church only at night, because she wore men's shoes and didn't want her friends to notice.

When Rev. Alexander returned, she began helping him prepare for evangelistic work. He did very well as a blind preacher, enabling them to start saving money. They saved a substantial amount, inspiring Mrs. Alexander to want to buy a home, but the Reverend objected bitterly. He felt he would always be a burden upon her and was afraid for her to be without money. But, she persisted and finally they made a down payment, moved into their new home and all seemed to go well until they faced financial difficulties.

They were unable to keep up with the mortgage payments. Eventually, they received a notice of eviction. Frantic, she opened her Bible and began reading. She got down on her knees and prayed to God with all the fervor of her heart. While kneeling, she received a psychic flash—the name of a man whom she had heard of, but never seen. She arose from her knees and from the fullness of her heart wrote the man a letter.

The next evening when she came from work, she opened the door and called, "Children, is there any mail?"

They answered, "Yes, Mama, there is a letter."

It was from that man. She was to meet him in his home at eight o'clock that night. Hurriedly, she ate her dinner, dressed herself and her little girl and, at twenty minutes to eight, left for the appointment.

A Japanese butler met her at the door, then showed her to the library. Promptly at eight o'clock the gentleman of the house entered. He spoke kindly and shook her hand. He inquired as to her obligations, then wrote two checks—one for the mortgage and one for her immediate obligations.

She was overwhelmed and scarcely able to express herself, but managed to say, "Well, it's wonderful for you to do this, but what arrangements can be made to repay you?"

He replied, "Take it and the Lord bless you. My money is to help the worthy, and there need not be any refund."

When I visited Plainfield, she was still living in that house, a two-story structure, its mortgage satisfied. As she listened to my plea for her help in bettering opportunities for colored children, her face brightened up like the dawn of the morning; after that, her home was mine.

I spent the end of the winter in Brooklyn, continuing to visit towns in New Jersey, telling my stories of Negro accomplishments and spreading my message of academic inclusiveness for all.

My Travels Along the East Coast

In the Spring, I picked up my car from Newark and took it to Brooklyn on the Staten Island ferry, avoiding New York traffic. I spoke in Long Island on a couple of Sundays, and secured speaking engagements in Flatbush, Flushing, Coney Island, Freeport, and Hempstead.

Over the next two winters, I stayed on the East Coast visiting Wilmington, Delaware, Washington, D.C., Baltimore, Maruland, Richmond, Petersburg, Norfolk, Phoebus, Portsmouth and Danville, Virginia, Raleigh, Durham, Greensboro, and Winston-Salem in North Carolina.

In most cities, the response to my message of education and inclusion was encouraging, but in Baltimore, the city that enacted the very first mandated residential segregation law, the colored community was hard to reach. It was 1923 and Baltimore still had earmarks of slavery, unlike Washington D.C., where thousands of colored college graduates had re-located and found employment, many with Government agencies.

I met Georgia Douglas Johnson, the colored poet and playwright in Washington, and found much pleasure in her company. The following is one of her poems:

TREASURE

When you count out your gold at the end of the day
And have winnowed the dross that has cumbered the way,
Oh, what were the hold of your treasury then-

Save the love you have shown to the children of men!

In Richmond, I came upon the tomb of Jefferson Davis, the President of the Confederate States of America and took a snapshot of it. The inscription on his tomb read: *Blessed are they who are persecuted for righteousness sake, for such is the Kingdom of Heaven.*

Strange that he should have thought it right to hold human beings in slavery.

Richmond was the home of the only female bank president in the United States, a colored woman, Mrs. Maggie Walker. She was also the leader of a fraternal organization named the Independent Order of St. Luke.

Then I met another very accomplished woman, Mrs. Janie Porter Barrett, who started a school for the rehabilitation of delinquent colored girls. The school was founded about ten miles out of Richmond. Mrs. Barrett was well liked and attracted the help of several white female organizations. With that support and some financing from the Virginia State Federation of Colored Women's Clubs, she purchased a farm outside of Richmond, allowing her to start the Industrial School for Colored Girls. She struggled to keep the project going, but realizing the schools value, the State of Virginia came to her aid by constructing several buildings and supplying her with much needed financial aid.

In Raleigh, North Carolina, I visited Shaw University. I stayed there for two weeks trying to secure a speaking engagement. Finally, Mr. Peacock, the school president, allowed me to speak to the student body. I must have hit a responsive chord, because the engagement turned into pandemonium, students clapping and cheering in a riotous manner. I later found out why.

I had spoken against racial discrimination and segregation. At the school, were several white teachers from New England supported by the white Baptist church. They refused to eat with or live in the same dormitory with colored teachers. This infuriated the student body; their cheers were in response to my highlighting those and other discriminatory practices.

In Raleigh, it was difficult to get approval to speak at the Episcopal College. It had become general knowledge that I traveled for and represented the NAACP. The president of the school was afraid that if he allowed me to speak, he might lose his position. Finally, he found his courage.

The following day, I drove forty miles to Durham with two teachers from the Episcopal College. They were quite knowledgeable about the socioeconomics of the colored community there, and helped me make several contacts in Durham's "Black Wall street."

Durham was the home of North Carolina Mutual Insurance Company. Founded by Mrs. Hattie Wooten, the company was said to be a million-dollar concern. Mr. A.M. Moore, president of the board, was in the process of creating a library for colored people, something sorely needed, as people of color were not allowed in the public libraries.

The next day, I started the fifty-mile drive to Greensboro. I had to travel over a long muddy road, making my car take on the appearance of a mud turtle. Accustomed to doing things for myself, I stopped at a water hydrant and began washing my car. Several people, some of which were students from the Greensboro colleges of Bennett and A&M, stopped to watch, some even offered to lend a hand.

Several days later, while touring the campus of Bennett College, I met the president of the College, and we chatted. He told me how glad he was that I had washed the car where the students could see me—that many of the students thought it a disgrace to work with their hands while in college. I thought this a residual of their observing of white people, who had servants to do such things, especially those from the more affluent areas of the South.

I drove out to Palmer Memorial Institute, a colored school of higher learning, built from the ground up by Mrs. Charlotte Hawkins Brown. The Institute was started in a rural Congregational church, eleven miles from the nearest city, a location that had no plumbing and no running water.

Its parsonage was a leaky frame structure, where Mrs. Brown slept. The roof leaked so badly that she had to move her bed from place to place when it rained. The main building was a nice brick structure with four large pillars in the front. Mrs. Brown would often say, "This building was built by faith and prayer," and "The mortgage note is due, but can't see any conceivable way to pay it." She told me that on one of the mortgage due dates, a car drove up while she was on her knees praying, the passenger got out and gave her the exact amount of money she needed at the time.

Ms. Brown was on a mission, teaching the rural colored how to build homes, hoping to get them out of the huts and shacks they had inhabited since slavery. She also hoped that such skills would enhance their self-esteem, self-worth and the value of their community.

I left Greensboro and headed for Winston-Salem, the epicenter of "tobacco growing." The city was at the base of a long steep hill, the odor of tobacco pungent as I drove into the valley below.

One of the state normal schools for colored was located just outside Winston-Salem. There were two owner operated colored banks and several other colored businesses located on paved streets, but in the colored residential community the streets were so muddy and rut filled that we could scarcely drive over them.

A colored physician, Dr. C.C. Lee, at 611 E. Fourth Street, purchased a home in Winston-Salem on the edge of a white neighborhood. As soon as he moved into his home, many of the white families moved out.

A riot started in Dr. Lee's neighborhood after a colored man got into a physical altercation with a white man. Shouting blame on the colored man, the unidentified white man was picked up and taken to the hospital. The white population getting wind of this, broke into the hardware store and pawnshop and stole weapons. After killing four or five colored people, the mob turned towards Dr. Lee's home, threatening to burn it to the ground, hoping to drive Dr. Lee and his family out of the community. It was about ten o'clock at night, and Dr. and Mrs. Lee, their two children and Dr. Lee's mother, secured the house.

Mrs. Lee got down on her knees, praying for help. Dr. Lee went to the kitchen to pray, preparing himself to die; he had three guns.

The mob continued to riot, cursing and swearing, some not more than fifteen years old, and having no experience with guns, one of their own was accidently killed and another shot in the foot when a weapon misfired. Finally, a white neighbor of Dr. Lee's came out and asked the mob to desist, emphasizing that Dr. Lee and his family were good neighbors, and that he did not want to see them hurt. Evidently, there had been an illness in this man's family and Mrs. Lee had gone over and offered her services. It was two o'clock in the morning when the neighbor finally mustered up enough courage to come out in defense of the Lees. This ended the riot.

The highway from Winston-Salem to Danville, Virginia was mud free, well paved, and smooth, making my journey to the home of the Langhorne sisters incident free. As I approached the home where Lady Nancy Astor and her sisters lived, I found myself thinking, *What a great state of preservation and what a beautifully landscaped street.* But, in the colored areas of Danville, the streets were muddy, had no walks and were void of landscaping. I spent ten days in Danville, trying to develop a plan that would increase governmental efforts towards paving those streets.

The muddy road to Richmond was about as bad as any road could possibly be. The drive, tiring as I dodged crevices in the muddy terrain, crevices so deep that I was concerned about getting stuck. I saw a white couple working a field and pulled over to talk with them. Commenting on the rough drive, they said it was, "the worst road in the world." I agreed with them.

After seventy-five miles of this muddy road, the car suddenly went dead, coming to a complete stop at the base of a hill. I got out and walked up the hill, hoping to find help. Fortunately, I found a repair shop and, with two repair men, returned to the car.

The men checked the engine and tapped this and that, but the car still wouldn't start. Unable to find the trouble, I started to become concerned, when suddenly I looked up and coming out of a corn field was a tall, thin, lanky person, looking more like a corn stalk with feet than a man. He walked up to the car and touched something on the motor. "Here's your problem," he said. The metal piece that held the timer in place was broken. He mended it the best he could, and added, "This should get you into town, maybe three miles, and in town you'll find a Ford supply station."

I got to town and sure enough the supply station was there, but they didn't have the part I needed. The attendant pointed across the street to a Blacksmith shop, saying, "He'll make a part for you." I went to the shop. The blacksmith made the part I needed and I was on my way.

I arrived in Richmond a little after midnight, paralyzed by fatigue. I put my muddy car in Mrs. Walker's garage and didn't look at it for three days. I had a wonderful visit with these women, but never did make headway getting the worst road in the world fixed.

Traveling with Dr. Bessie Tharps

I met Dr. Bessie Tharps in Richmond. She mentioned a good friend in Providence, Rhode Island. As she spoke, I sensed she had a desire to visit the East again. We agreed to share the ride North as far as Providence. Her friend was Miss May Tefft, a former teacher who had encouraged her to pursue her medical degree when she was but an

130

undergraduate at Hertshorn College. She eventually became Dr. Bessie Tharps, after finishing her training at Boston University in 1916.

There were only a few restaurants that would serve colored people in the South, so we filled the back of the car with canned goods and decided to buy perishables, such things as bacon and eggs, along the highway. While in France, I used a sterno kit; I kept the kit and we planned to use it while on the road. We'd spread our steamer rug under the shade of a tree, cook our meals, rest for a while, then get on our way.

Dr. Tharps asked to stop in Lexington, Virginia to visit Dr. Dabney, a classmate of hers. We had a pleasant visit and started on our way to Alexander, Virginia. We spent Sunday in Alexander, giving me time to visit with some friends in from Ohio, then we moved on to Washington, D.C., then Baltimore.

As we drove through the heavy traffic in Baltimore, we noticed a car following us. We slowed, letting the car catch up enough to see the driver. It was a man. He followed us through traffic all the way to the edge of the city. At that point, he drove up next to us. We stopped, he rolled down his window, and said, "Hello there, Miss Johnson, I knew that was you. I saw that French bag on your running board." It was Captain Dental, whom I had known in France. We reminisced briefly, exchanged contact information, and moved on.

We stopped, to eat and rest just outside Baltimore, at the base of a hill. We saw a carload of people coming down the hill fast, the driver not seeming to notice the bridge at the bottom. He lost control of the car, ran off the road, and crashed into a tree.

Dr. Tharps left her meal and ran down the hill to see if anyone was hurt. The driver seemed okay, but Dr. Tharps asked if there was anything she could do. The driver said, "No, the car is all torn up, but that doesn't worry me. All I want are my wife and children." They, too, were unharmed. Assured that the family was okay and needed nothing else, we moved on.

We spent the night in Philadelphia, then drove on to New York City, where we spent four nights in Brooklyn. While there, we took a trip up the Hudson River to the Y.W.C.A. summer camp about twenty-five miles from Camden.

It was dark when we arrived and unknowingly passed by the two-story camp house. We attempted to turn around and backtrack, but had to maneuver the car over a railroad track and up an incline. Just as we were crossing the tracks the engine stalled. This happened three times, but the third time a train, that was on its way to Atlantic city, whizzed by, just missing the car. Shaken, Dr. Tharps got out of the car and walked back to the framed camp house. In the meantime, I loosened the brakes and let the car roll backwards down the hill; I was afraid to try and turn the car around. Our near-death experience hung with us the entire time we were at the campsite.

We left the YMCA camp on our way to Providence, and then drove through Greenwich, Stamford, and Bridgeport, Connecticut. In Bridgeport we spent a rainy night. The next day we made it to Providence and Dr. Tharps left to visit her friend, Miss May Tefft. I parked the car on the top of a steep hill and proceeded to walk a short distance to nearby Brown University, where I continued to explain the reasoning behind my Two-Foot Shelf of Negro Literature.

August 10,1923, Dr. Tharps remained in Providence while I went on alone to Boston. I found the Bostonians quite interested in the socio-academic cause I was promoting. The schools in Boston were not segregated. In fact, Maria Baldwin, a colored person, was principal of Agassiz Public School where Harvard professors sent their children.

The Epicenter of the American Revolution…or Was It?

Boston, the epicenter of the American revolution, where Crispus Attucks, the ex-slave who spent twenty years at sea after escaping slavery, died at the onset of the war. He was shot at the Boston Massacre in March

1770 and is considered the first casualty of the revolution. John Boyle O'Reilly, an Irish poet and author, read a poem at the dedication of the Monument to Crispus Attucks. The following are just a few stanzas:

Where shall we seek for a hero
And where shall we find a story;
Our laurels are wreathed for conquest,
Our songs for completed glory.

But we honor a shrine unfinished,
A column un-capped with pride.
If we sing the deed that was sown like seed,
When Crispus Attucks died.

All honor to Crispus Attucks,
Who was leader and voice that day;
The first to defy, and the first to die,
With Maverick, Carr and Gray.

Call it riot or revolution,
His hand first clenched at the crown;
His feet were first in perilous place,
To pull the king's flag down;

His breast was the first one rent apart,
That liberty's stream might flow;
For our freedom now forever,
His head was the first laid low.

Shall we take a sign this negro slave,
With unfamiliar name—
With his poor companions, nameless too,

Till their lives leaped forth in flame?
Yes, surely the verdict is not for us
To render or deny;
We can only interpret the symbol—
God chose these men to die.

Boston was also the adopted home of Georgia-born Roland Hayes, a colored Lyric tenor and composer. He was not there but his mother still lived in their humble dwelling. When I asked someone for directions to a laundress, a woman answered, "Roland Hayes's mother lives right across the street, there."

Her very successful son had taken great care of her, but she continued her laundry services, washing and ironing, not always for money but for poor colored students who needed help. Her son wanted to take her to France, where she could get a taste of real "freedom" before she died, but she refused.

I met a man by the name of McGirt, who ran his own bicycle repair business. He was originally from Savannah, Georgia, where he found his passion for bicycle repair. One day he saw a white man throw away what seemed to be a perfectly good bicycle. He went to the dump pile, retrieved the bicycle, took it home and made the necessary repairs. After finishing the repairs, he offered the bicycle to the same man that had thrown it away. The man refused to take the bike from Mr. McGirt, a colored man, so he sold it to someone else, thus starting his business of repairing and selling used bicycles. His business grew to the point that he had to employ others to assist him.

There were other colored enterprises operating in Boston; however, the colored communities continued to frequent white businesses because of a fear of reactive segregation. They ate in places in which they couldn't work, enriched large merchants by patronage for which they got nothing in return, and elected people to office who promptly forgot them. This ongoing nightmare of segregation closed the door of opportunity for themselves, their children, and their communities—especially the children, whom they worked and sacrificed to educate, suffered in turn because they found no outlet for their hopes and aspirations. This is a place where abolitionists thrived prior to the emancipation but now colored communities were at best marginalized, unable to find meaningful employment outside of domestic work.

I didn't feel that white business or social enterprises had invited integration in the schools or workplaces. They hadn't in other large cities, and they hadn't in Boston!

Paul Coffee: The Richest African American

With Dr. Tharps as my traveling partner once again, we arrived in New Bedford, Massachusetts an old whaling town, on Saturday, August 23,1923. It was raining hard and continued to do so four days until late the following Tuesday morning. This was the town where a colored captain named Paul Coffee owned six whaling vessels, and was considered the richest African American of his time. Coffee was also in favor of re-settling ex-slaves to Sierra Leone, sailing there in 1815 with the intent of starting a settlement. This was also the town where, in 1838, Frederick Douglass found sanctuary after his escape from Maryland's bondage,

There were now colored teachers, as well as other professionals in New Bedford, but they were not accepted professionally or socially. I spoke to a young colored female teacher, who was starved for professional companionship beyond a business association with co-workers, all of whom were white except for four. The four non-whites were much older than she, so she found it hard to fit in. She spent a lot of her free time wondering whether she should continue teaching. Should she stay simply to show the parents and the school staff that colored teachers are as human and competent as others? Should she go to a colored school, where she might find a more supportive and accepting social environment with people of her own race; where she could be around people who understood and sympathized, rather than ostracized a person because of their skin color?

What a tragedy, this color problem. How can one feel part of the great scheme of Christian civilization when it withholds the act of being kind; when it crushes the spirit of one of his fellows just because her eyes are brown, her hair is black, and her face is dark.

I found similar scenarios in all the coastal towns of Connecticut and Rhode Island. These areas were historically freedmen havens and, until emancipation, had maintained the underground railroads to freedom, but reversals after reconstruction had remained. Freedom had taken a back seat to Jim Crowism.

Newport was the home of a very successful hotel and catering business owned by George Downing, a colored man who was instrumental in desegregating Newport schools. A grand old town with narrow streets and ancient dwellings, and sidewalks so narrow that people had to walk in single file. The wealthiest people frequented this resort city, spending summers in magnificent homes that faced the nine-mile ocean drive, circumventing the island. These houses sat far back on large manicured lots, adjacent to high fences, surrounded by mature shrubs and trees—such that passersby saw little of the grounds, their entrances, beautiful driveways with signs declaring: Private Entrance.

Occasionally, one might catch a glimpse of these beautiful buildings up close, but full views are only seen from distant vantage points. It seemed that each owner has tried to exceed their neighbor with the amount of money they spent on their homes.

I left my car in a garage owned by a colored mechanic, and spent several very pleasant days with a Baptist minister and his family before moving on to Providence. We took a ferry in Newport that dropped us off Quonset, Rhode Island, a short distance from Providence, then after spending two days there, we drove eighty miles to Hartford.

We arrived in Hartford, just as the lights were coming on, but could see that Hartford was a clean city with well-maintained, paved streets. The colored community appeared to live well. Many owned beautiful homes, but there were only a few colored nurses, and no colored teachers, postmen, firemen, or policemen. I found one grocery store owned by a Mr. Murray, a native of Virginia, who told me that the colored community was awake intellectually, anxious for improvements, and seeking new opportunities.

We discovered an old friend and schoolmate from Wilberforce in New Haven. He was the pastor of AME Church, and kind enough to offer the hospitality of his home and church, making it possible for us to spend a bit more time venturing out into the surrounding communities.

Many in New Haven were employed by Yale University, which provided much of the livelihood and social activity for the city. And, even though the colored community lived in non-segregated neighborhoods, and even though there were some colored business interests, most were domestics.

We discovered much the same employment situations in Bridgeport and Stamford. In Stamford, probably the most beautiful town in New England, the colored community, though segregated residentially, lived in beautiful homes on paved streets. I recall quite well, a stately looking residence at 52 West Broad Street, sitting back upon a very spacious well-kept lawn, fenced in by luxurious thorn less hedges.

There was a colored orphanage in Stamford, run by trained nurses and maintained by reliable housekeepers. I also found two colored churches, small but with a thrifty and enterprising congregation. I felt that one could find peace and contentment in Stamford's colored community.

There were many small towns along the Boston Post Road between Bridgeport and Greenwich, such that I hardly realized I had left Stamford until I reached Greenwich, about a thirty-minute drive.

In Greenwich, the streets were wide and tree shaded with magnificent homes surrounded by beautiful lawns; there were also paved roads leading into the country, where the wealthy had magnificent estates.

We moved on to Englewood, New Jersey by way of the Broadway-Riverside Drive through New York City. We reached Englewood after driving twenty miles up a winding road through the Palisade mountains. To our delight, our little car made the entire distance at high speed.

Englewood, was a town built on hills, another resort area for the wealthy. It was a quiet country town with many large beautiful homes, but these homes had no addresses and were on unmarked streets. The homes were located based on the name of their wealthy owners. This caused difficulty finding the homes where colored people worked; they would tell us that Mr. Smith lived over a certain rich owner's garage. This meant very little to a stranger and not much to the inhabitants of Englewood. I got the sense that even though Englewood's colored community lived in "colonies," they lived comfortably.

We went to Philadelphia by way of Lincoln Highway, but fatigued, we had to stop in Trenton overnight. The next day, we had to detour considerably because the Lincoln Highway was under repair. The roads were good and we entered Philadelphia while still light. The streets were cobblestone until we reached Broad Street, where we were welcomed by a view of the statue of William Penn, the city founder.

While there, I spoke to congregations about the upcoming anniversary of the Emancipation Proclamation, signed on January 1, 1863, and how all persons, white and black, gathered in Boston's Fanuel Hall awaiting the coming message. When it finally came, there was wild rejoicing throughout the city and people remained in the hall until well after midnight, singing, "Free At Last." But, some in the South didn't receive that message for several months and, as a result, we found some not celebrating the Emancipation until as late as August and September. How it would be wonderful if all colored people of the country could agree on one day of celebration, and how it should be to us what July Fourth is to the nation—a time of great celebration. The history of it should be handed down to future generations through such celebrations.

Mrs. Annie Blackwell

One of my longtime friends, Mrs. Annie Blackwell, wife of Bishop Blackwell of the A.M.E. Zion Church, died suddenly during my stay. I had talked to her only two days before and she had been well. She had left me in her house reading the newspaper, while she went out to run errands. That was the last time I saw her alive. She was a woman who had meant much to me during our many years of friendship. She gave encouragement and hope to everyone she encountered. Her quiet, everyday Christian life was above criticism. She worked incessantly for her church. She was head of the Home and Foreign Missionary Society for her denomination. When she took that position, there was only two thousand dollars in the treasury. Within four years, she brought that number up to forty-nine thousand.

She had planned to establish a school in Liberia, West Africa and was planning to take a trip there, but she died before she got started—a school had already been erected in Liberia in her name. She was a woman of very fine character, and I'd always stopped to visit her. Sadly, I couldn't say my goodbyes, but I wrote her obituary. Because of that, I felt some relief. I haven't felt at home in Philadelphia since.

Shortly after Mrs. Annie Blackwell's death, I drove to Washington City by way of Delaware through Baltimore. I took a boat down the Potomac River to the Tidewater section in southeast coastal Virginia. I drove off the boat at Norfolk, where I spent the winter. There were few paved streets in the colored sections, mostly mud and ruts everywhere. An enterprising group in the colored section had purchased nice busses and were running a transportation system, because Negroes were not allowed to use the public transportation system and, by design, there were no colored section routes.

One day I looked out the window and saw colored children coming home from school in the middle of the day. I asked, "Why?" I was told the school was celebrating the birthday of Robert E. Lee, the man who had led the Confederate Army to keep them in slavery.

I spoke in Portsmouth, Newport News, Phoebus, and Hampton, then drove up to William and Mary College in Williamsburg. There was a small community of colored people, but they were not welcomed or allowed to attend this old historic school of higher learning. I also went out to Jamestown, where the first, "twenty black slaves" landed initiating the institution of slavery in America.

History books tell us that these "twenty black slaves" were the first black men in this country. I have learned since that black men occupied and developed a civilization in America long before Columbus. I continued my work and travels through New York and Pennsylvania, then one Sunday I picked up the New York *Sunday Times* and found the review of a three-volume set of books, Africa and the Discovery of America. The books were written by Professor Leo Wiener, head of the Department of Slavonic Languages and Literature at Harvard University. The review excited me. I decided to investigate these books. What I found was so interesting and profound.

140

Chapter Nine

Africans in America before Columbus

"No archaeologist, no historian, no philologist will be more startled by the data collected in this book than I have been in their discovery. While I, to a certain extent, foresaw the end toward which the presence of Africans in America before Columbus must ultimately lead in the social and religious orders, I did not allow myself in my first two volumes to be influenced by any such consideration..."

—Leo Wiener

Africa and the Discovery of America, Vol. III

LEO WIENER WROTE THREE EARTH shaking volumes, proving trans-ocean migration of African people prior to Europeans. He was born in Russia on July 26, 1862, and died in Belmont, Massachusetts in 1939. He was educated in Minsk at the Polytechnic in Berlin. He migrated to the United States and worked in a cotton mill in New Orleans. He then gained a teaching position at Odessa, Missouri and later a professorship at the University of Missouri. In 1901, he went to Harvard University, first as an assistant professor, and then, in 1911, became the head of the Department of Slavonic Languages and Literature at Harvard, where he authored several academic text books and was a regular contributor to German, Russian, French, British, and American philological periodicals.

His greatest academic and editorial achievement was the twenty-four-volume compilation of Count Tolstoy's works. He wrote, "Mayan and Mexican Origins" in 1926 and contributed various etymologies to Webster's, New International Dictionary.

Between 1919 and 1923, this learned scholar produced a work in three volumes called, Africa and the Discovery of America. I was in New York when the book review appeared in *The New York Times*. I immediately wrote Professor Wiener, asking if I could include his volumes in my Two-Foot Shelf of Negro Literature. He replied to my request by letter, stating that the treatise was so scholarly that colored people would not appreciate the works. I decided to contact the publisher. A few days later, I was in Philadelphia at the publishing house of Innes and Company. I acquired several sets, added them to my Two-Foot Shelf and put them in a few homes and libraries.

The printers told me about the difficulties Professor Wiener experienced trying to get the volumes published. After spending years researching this masterpiece of academic literature, he could not find a publisher willing to print the work, even though at the time he was academically well-known and respected. A benefactor from Boston came to his rescue, advanced funds for the publication, saving the information. However, printing companies don't market books; they just publish them, so only a thousand copies of each volume reached the public.

I believe many literate African Americans would have been interested in these volumes, but only a few could obtain copies. They are now practically lost to the world, but I will quote a few lines to give you, the reader, an idea of how this information could have had an impact on lessening the suppression of African Americans in America.

The late Leo Wiener, quoted the following from Antonio De Mendozo, in the first volume of his, Africa and the Discovery of America:

"The twenty-fourth of last September I was told that the Negroes had elected a king and had resolved to kill all the Spaniards. All the country was to rise, and the Indians were also in the plot. I did not put any faith in it because it was a Negro that denounced this conspiracy to me; however, to assure myself of the truth, I ordered some servants to go out that evening and mingle with the Indians, so as not to be recognized by them, and to observe if anything suspicious was going on, for I did not wish to be taken by surprise, if by any chance the facts were true. Indeed, I picked up in this way many threads of the conspiracy. I immediately had the one arrested whom the Negroes had chosen for their king, and the chief conspirators. I immediately told the Spaniards in the mines and in the country to be on their guard and keep an eye on the Negroes."

This part of the manuscript was quoted directly from long-forgotten documents stored in the Vatican, describing events surrounding the 1537 Negro uprising in Mexico, eighty-two years before the "twenty black slaves" landed on the coast of Old Virginia in 1619.

Professor Wiener's manuscript reads as follows: "In the year 1537, the Negroes wanted to rise up in the City of Mexico and the instigators of this rebellion were hanged."

The manuscript includes a picture of a Christian church with a Negro hanging from the gallows, a picture Prof. Wiener reproduced.

As further quoted by Prof. Wiener: "Those who were arrested confessed to their participation. About two dozen of them in the city, and in the mine of Amatepec, whither I had sent Francisco Vazquez de Coronado, were quartered. The Indians brought me the soiled bodied of four Negroes and of one Negress, because I had ordered them brought dead or alive."

Mortal punishment by hanging or quartering were the murdering ways of the Spaniards and other European aggressors at that time. There is an old Spanish fort in the oldest city in America, St. Augustine, Florida. On the grounds of that fort is an above-ground dungeon, a cement structure with no windows, where prisoners were drawn and quartered. The prisoners were fastened to a flat board and drawn to the dungeon where they were cut into four pieces.

Quartering was a grotesque and torturous punishment imposed on these Negroes for trying to develop a kingdom of their own. Prof. Wiener goes on to say:

"There were several foci from which the Negro traders spread in the two Americas. The eastern part of South America where the Caribs are mentioned, seems to have been reached by them from the West Indies. Another stream, possibly from the same focus, radiated to the North, along roads masked by the presence of mounds, and reached as far as Canada. The chief cultural influence was exerted by a Negro colony in Mexico. From here their influence pervaded the neighboring tribes and, ultimately directly or indirectly, reached Peru."

The above-mentioned statements are not the only evidence discovered by Prof. Wiener. He also uses etymologic and Botanic evidence that proves the presence of Negroes in the Americas long before they were brought to Jamestown as slaves, and indeed long before Columbus's voyage to America.

In the first volume of his work, Prof. Wiener says, "I shall show that the Negroes have had a far greater influence upon American civilization than has heretofore been suspected." He proceeds to elucidate that influence and its supportive evidence.

In Chapter One of Volume I, he discusses Columbus's first letter, describing the West Indies Islands. Columbus describes one of the islands as particularly beautiful, stating: "This whole coast and the part of the island which I saw is all like a beach, and the island is the most beautiful I ever saw; and if the other islands are very beautiful, this one is more so."

Further on, Columbus discusses the discovery of a pair of "male and female" islands. These islands were quite a distance apart, reachable only by boat. One island was inhabited only by women and the other inhabited only by men. The men visited the women in May of each year and stayed three months. The children born were divided based on gender, girls went with the women and boys went with the men.

The name of the island inhabited by women was etymologically Arabic, and the West Indian word for "gold." The Arabic word connection was found throughout the island vocabulary. Prof. Wiener traced these words back to Africa via Arabia and supports the supposition that Africans brought these words to this area many years before Columbus stumbled into what for him was a "new world."

It is not only the islander's language as documented by Columbus, Prof. Wiener also found in Columbus's writings foods that were indigenous to Africa.

Carrying food aboard ships for long voyages was quite a problem in Columbus's time. When he arrived in Haiti, he began to examine vegetables growing on the island and exploring other islands for much the same reason—provisions. On November 4, 1492, he entered the following note in his log book: "These islands are very fertile and are full of "mames," which are like carrots but have a chestnut flavor."

The "mames," says Prof. Wiener, "from what follows below, are unquestionably the "Yams," and per the Spanish historian Oviedo, who wrote the controversial chronicle about the Spanish colonization of the Caribbean more than thirty years after Columbus, the yams were an African plant.

The peanut is another root vegetable transplanted from Africa, and Prof. Wiener points out:

"When we turn to Africa, it may be shown that over a vast territory the Arabic appellation (for the word 'peanut') spread southward as the name for 'peanut,' showing conclusively that the peanut must be an Arabic importation into Africa; and as the Negro word derived from the Arabic source lies at the basis of the Brazilian word for the same plant, it is clear that it must have been imported from Africa to brazil."

In the United States, Prof. Wiener pointed out that the American Negro uses the word "goober" and "pinder" for the peanut. Both appellations, states Prof. Wiener, are from the Kongo language "which shows that the Negro brought with him the knowledge of the peanut from Africa and did not acquire it here."

Examining the use of shells and beads as money, Prof. Wiener also traces the presence and influence of the African in America and concludes: "For the present time, this much is certain, the tiny gold beads of Peru, the necklaces of Castillo del Oro, are of African origin and belong to the same trade activity as the wampum belt."

If the African Negro was in America before Columbus, the question is: how long before?

There were people in the Americas before the American Indian. These people occupied a region covering what is now the United States, extending down as far as Central America. They dug copper from the region around Lake Superior; they worked in copper, silver, and gold; they tilled fields, built cities, and had governments. They left unremovable records of themselves in thousands of "mounds," great earthen structures as city sites, monuments, or possibly burial or ceremonial grounds. They were the "Mound Builders." When Columbus discovered America, the Indians were living here either unsuspecting or having long forgotten the significance of these mounds. The mounds remained just where the ancient Mound Builders had placed them, but are now camouflaged by ancient trees. Thousands of them stand in the state of Ohio. One in Adams County, Ohio in the form of a snake extending a thousand feet with a 164-foot earthen egg at its mouth. Another near St. Louis, Missouri covers eight acres and is ninety feet high.

These mounds, Prof. Wiener points out, bear great resemblance to those built by the natives of the African Sudan, and relics taken from them resemble the natives and the animals of Africa; beautifully carved pipe bowls picturing elephants and other animals found only in Africa; carvings of human heads resembling nothing but the African.

"In 1883, an article appeared in the journal, *Scientific America*, in which a reporter asked an aged Indian what his people knew of these ancient graveyards. He answered: "Me know nothing about them. They were here before the red man."

In America, Prof. Wiener tries to point out that "we have lived unknowingly in an ancient world." On the banks of Paint Creek, one mile from Chillicothe, Ohio, a "head carved from compact, red sandstone" was found. It is six inches at its greatest length, by five inches in height, with a broad, flat base. Several other artifacts have been found at various points on the surface in the same area. In the character of their material and style of workmanship, they sustain a close relationship to stone idols found in the states of Tennessee and Mississippi. One of these idols was discovered some years ago in the Grave Creek Mound of West Virginia.

Prof. Wiener says: "The human figure found in Virginia has a squatting attitude with its elbows drawn back and its hands resting on its knees. It's thirteen inches high by six and a half inches broad, the material and workmanship are identical with the one described above. Another stone idol was found on the banks of the Scioto River in Ohio. The headdress was the same as on the figurines found in the mounds."

A terracotta head was found in a cemetery near Nashville. Quoting from Prof. Wiener: "It is distinctly that of a Negress."

In 1887, H. L. Johnson a collector of antiquities, found a large marble or crystalline lime stone carving of a head in a mound on the Wallace farm near Clarksville, Tenn. The head was broken from the body, but the features of the face were distinctly African.

On Page 171 of Prof. Wiener's Volume I are illustrations of four carved heads that came from different mounds. Each face has what are called striations—small grooves thought to represent wrinkles or possibly a kind of tribal identification. These grooves run from the nose to the arm. Two of the carved heads have five each, a third has grooves around the mouth that may represent whiskers or mustaches. There are also what appear to be tattoo markings. One of the illustrated heads comes from the H.L. Johnson's collection in Nashville; one from Miami County,

Ohio; and several from the Missouri mounds. They all had striations around their mouths and cheeks, supportive of a common origin.

Another collector by the name of Charney picked up several terracotta masks from the Pyramid of the Sun in Mexico. One of them was Negroid, Prof. Wiener stating his "thick lips, flat nose and wholly hair proclaim his African origin."

Charney also gave Prof. Wiener a few drawings from his collection. There are several that are unmistakably Negro. Quoting Wiener: "One of these has wholly hair and two side knots. Another has a head adornment with three elevations; and still another has a knot with a rosetta design. A granite figure representing the head of a Negro with cross striations on the face is also reported from Vera Cruz."

These relics depicting African or Negroid heads show that Africans inhabited and developed a civilization in the Americas extending over a great part of the United States.

Tobacco pipes found in the mounds confirm this assumption. They are made like the tobacco pipes found today in Africa, and, per Prof. Wiener, tobacco smoking originated with the Africans. His volumes contain several pages picturing these pipes showing the similarity between those made in Africa and those found in the American Mounds.

The Denver Post dated Wednesday, March 22, 1950 printed a picture of an African head found in the southern Mexican jungle near San Lorenzo in the State of Vera Cruz. It was discovered in 1946 by a National Geographic Smithsonian Expedition. It weighed about fifteen tons and was too heavy to be moved; a plaster duplicate was made and displayed in New York's Museum of Natural History.

Scientist said the head had been there since the time of Christ, and that it was made by the people who lived in southern Mexico at that time. They mentioned nothing about Africa or why its features were Negroid.

In Volume III of Prof. Wiener's book, he says, "It is no mere accident that in 1862, a colossal granite head representing a Negro as found in the

Canton of Tuxtla and that at Teotihuacan, the oldest Mexican City of Temples, a number of Negroid heads have been found."

Prof. Wiener concludes: "There can be no question whatsoever of the reality of the statement with regard to the presence of the African in America previous to Columbus."

Chapter Ten

Touring the West and Far South

"For here in the east, we dream our dreams of the things we hope to do. And here in the west, the crimson west, the dreams of the east come true."

—Author Unknown

PROF. L. WIENER'S BOOK WAS a work of sound research supported by artefactual and photographic evidence. The need to disseminate the migratory history of Negroid people became a driving force in my life. The need to share this knowledge with my American brethren became a personal movement.

Figure 21. Kathryn with her new 1924 Model T Ford, on her way west.

In May of 1924 I bought a new Model T Ford and started driving Westward from New York.

I spent the first night in Yonkers, then continued up the Hudson to Albany, where I found a friend, an African Methodist minister who had served as a YMCA secretary with me in France. I spent the night with his family reminiscing about our times and travels throughout France and the great people we had experienced. The next morning, I left for Syracuse.

I came to a fork in the road right outside the city. There was no signage and it was starting to rain. Seeing a group of men standing by the roadside, I asked them which road would take me to Utica. One of the men turned and started toward the car, he was wearing a hat and long rain coat, he said, "This is the road; right this way and I'm going that way myself. I'll just get in and go right along with you."

I was a bit frightened, only two weeks before a woman on Staten Island had gotten stuck in an off-road ditch, got out of her car, started walking back to a filing station for help, and she was later found dead by the roadside. The man felt my apprehension and mentioned the dead girl, saying he wouldn't do such a thing.

He told me his name was Will Bailey, and rode with me all the way to Syracuse. When I stopped to fill the tank, I thought he'd offer to pay for some part of the fuel, but didn't. He must have enjoyed the free ride, though, because when I let him out in front of the YMCA, he offered to go with me again the next day.

I spent two months in Cleveland and then went to Chicago for the National Association of Colored Women biennial meeting. The meeting allowed me to renew my acquaintance with Mme. Ezella Mathis Carter, owner of a beauty culture business on the South side. She asked if I would go with her on her annual trip to visit her agents. I thought about it for a few days and told her I would, if she could arrange a corresponding lecture tour. Mme. Carter agreed and the planning began.

Mrs. Carter took the train down to Georgia. When I arrived at Waycross, Georgia, I rented a car from one of her agents. I was concerned about the muddy roads in Georgia and much of the South, so decided to leave my own car with my sister, Juliaannah, in Springfield, Illinois.

Leaving Waycross, we drove forty miles to Jacksonville, Florida and then several days later went to St. Augustine, the oldest city in the United States. We found a normal and industrial school operated by a colored man who, driven by his desire to provide an education to those denied such by the state, traveled all over the country raising money for his school.

We came upon an alligator farm run by a colored man. The skins, he told us, were used to make pocketbooks, belts, and other leather goods. He knew more about alligators than probably anyone else. He told us that alligators breathe only once every three hours and that is why they don't move unless provoked by hunger or threat.

I spoke in St. Augustine, and the next day drove down to Daytona Beach, an area made famous by Mary McCloud Bethune who started an industrial school for coloreds with only a $1.50 in her pocket and boxes for desks. She rented a "shotgun house" and found a few young female volunteers to wash and iron clothes. This was the start of a laundry service that eventually became popular, especially with white people spending winters in the resort area. In 1904, Mr. Gamble, of Proctor and Gamble Soap Company, visited Mrs. Bethune and asked where the school was located. She answered, "In my mind." He then helped to get the Daytona Normal and Industrial Institute started. Today, that industrial school is Bethune-Cookman College.

We drove south to Cocoa and West Palm Beach. In Cocoa, we arranged for a future speaking engagement. We spoke in churches in West Palm Beach, where colored people lived literally in the sand. There were few, if any, sidewalks or paved streets and their principle occupation was domestic service work in the Royal Poinciana and other hotels. They also transported tourists for sight-seeing trips using "Afromobiles," also called

Palm Beach Chariots. They were called Afromobiles because they were almost always pulled by colored people.

Once again education for colored children took second seat to the whims and comforts of white people. Between November and March, colored schools were closed so the boys could caddy for the tourists on the golf courses.

We moved on to Miami, and spent several days trying to digest what the colored population had to endure. The mail was delivered erratically and colored people could not use the main post office. There was one branch office in the "colored" neighborhood, there were no grocery or drug stores, and they were unable to grow vegetables or fruits in the sand.

The 150-mile trek from Miami through the Florida Keys to Key West took us six hours. Key West was a fishing village and home to one of the oldest Naval bases in the country, established in 1823 to combat piracy. There was a sponge fishery and turtle farm; some turtles were large enough to ride on. In Key West, Mme. Carter and I spoke at the A.M.E. Zion Church. The crowd was impressively large and appreciative.

We took the steam powered Governor Cobb boat and went to Havana, Cuba. Debarkation was delayed six hours, waiting for a New York train to arrive, originally due at 10:00 a.m., it finally arrived at four o'clock in the afternoon.

We arrived in Cuba at 10:00 p.m., and after our baggage was examined by customs officers, we found a taxicab, which, to our surprise, was a Ford.

Neither Mme. Carter nor I spoke Spanish, so we were challenged making ourselves understood. Just as I was recalling the challenges I had in small rural southern towns. A Cuban man overheard our poor attempts at Spanish and intervened with his broken English, asking us where we wanted to go. We had three addresses for potential quarters. After he hailed a cab, he sat beside the driver, directing him to the first address. We were disappointed because none of the locations had rooms available.

Then the Cuban gentleman directed the driver to a hotel. When we
arrived, he called a colored American porter over and asked where we
might find courteous lodging. He directed us to the Hotel Las Villas. The
manager greeted us at the entrance and we were treated with every
kindness. The Cuban gentleman got back in the taxi, lifted his hat, and
drove off without mention of fare or payment. What an experience!

Our room had no ceiling fan and no windows; we were on the third
floor, our only ventilation, the great open space above the room.
Somehow, we made it through the night.

We saw the president's residence and the Cuban capitol building.
Their "white house" seemed more beautiful than ours. We were driven
around the narrow streets of the old section, and the great boulevards of
the new section. The streets in the old section were so narrow that one
could almost reach out the car window and touch the walls. The sidewalks
were so narrow one person had to walk behind another.

The dead were buried above ground, like in tropical New Orleans. If
the rent was not paid, the bodies were taken out and placed in a large
cement enclosure with no roofs, covered only by a wooden door.
Someone had whittled the sliver cover off the door so you could peep in;
only sun-bleached human bones could be seen. The driver shook his head
and said, "Nobody sorry," meaning, it was a "Potter's Field."

We were taken back to our hotel by way of Boulevard Diaz where the
great equestrian statue of General Maceo was located. He was the Negro
general that saved Cuba during their war with Spain. The driver took us
through tropical gardens, stopped for a moment, got out and plucked a
flower for us. We appreciated that very much.

After two nights and three days in Havana, we returned via the
"Governor Cobb" to Key West and then via the Florida Overseas
Railroad back to Miami. On our way to Miami, we stopped at Long Key,
where all the white passengers had the privilege of getting off and going
to the dining room. We had no such privilege. Mme. Carter thought she

could get a handout at the kitchen window, but she was refused service, so she asked a porter if he would try to get something for her. They sent her a bean soup that had a lot of soup but not much bean, no spoon or other utensil. The "news butcher" (Train Boy), seeing tears running down her cheeks, gave her the fork from his lunch box.

We arrived in Miami, rented a car, and drove to Cocoa for the pre-arranged evening speaking engagement. We stopped in Ft. Pierce, where I slept for about an hour. We were told Ft. Pierce was not safe, that it was a nest for the Ku Klux Klan and very dangerous for any person of color. We were told to leave as soon as possible. We ate and left right afterwards.

On our way, we had several flat tires. The cement was so hot it caused the inner tubes to swell and burst. When we arrived, I was too exhausted to speak, so Mme. Carter took my place. She was a great speaker and full of humor. She created much merriment in her description of the beautiful highway along the Indian River, where she had seen spooks in the trees that shadowed us, and spirits in the water that sparkled in the moonlight; she gestured and shivered to show how frightened she was, and the audience roared with laughter.

From Cocoa, we went to Daytona Beach via Orlando. It was a better road, but we had to drive farther. We drove a mile over a sand bridge that encased the wheels up to the running boards. We were frightened at this but got through all right.

I spoke in Orlando on Sunday night at a local church. The pastor's name was Robert E. Lee Brayboy. I asked how he got such a name. He said his father fought under Robert E. Lee during the Civil War. His father and mother had not been married because of the anti-miscegenation laws, but his father had never had any other wife. His Father felt he could name his first son after the Confederate general if he liked. The minister further stated that he had found his father's will in his office desk, and he had left everything to his colored children.

When I went into the pulpit that evening, I saw several white faces in the rear of the church. On inquiry, I found out that they were tourists from Maine who had winter homes in Florida.

Mme. Carter, being born and reared in the South, was very much disturbed by them. I went down and told her that they were friendly but that didn't seem to console her. When I had finished my talk, I asked her, "How did I do?"

She replied, "Worse than ever...worse than ever." That night she didn't sleep; she remembered a race riot a few years before in a town not far away. A colored man had gotten up on a stump to express himself and the white people did not like what he had to say, so they drove the colored people out of their homes in their night clothes, burned their houses, and lynched a few. So, whenever she heard a foot fall, or dog bark, she said, "Miss Johnson, there they come. There they come!" When I inquired, who was coming, she said, "The mob. You can't come down here and talk like you did tonight without starting a riot." But nothing happened.

The next day we drove to Daytona beach, spent a night or so with Mrs. Bethune on her college campus, and then moved on to Jacksonville. On the way, we had to stop for a new inner tube, then three miles later the inner tube must have pinched because the tire popped and blew into some palmetto bushes on the edge of the road. With a thunder, the car landed on its wheel rim. I couldn't drive without a tire and the spare was damaged, so I had to find the tire that had blown off the car. Looking through the bushes, we found it and stuffed it with a gunny sack. Some white men stopped to help, laughing at our invention. Mme. Carter was afraid they wouldn't help me if they realized she wasn't my maid servant, so she sat on the running board of their car, slumping over, looking as ignorant and foolish as she could.

The tire carried us eleven miles to a repair shop where we purchased a new tire. The man at the shop laughed uproariously, saying he'd seen many things, but never a tire stuffed with a gunny sack.

Soon, we were in Jacksonville. This is where we spent the night. The next morning, we drove to Waycross, Georgia and returned the car to its owner. But, before doing so, we had to repaint it, tighten the tie rods, and buy new tires. Finishing that work made the car look and ride like new, the owner was quite pleased.

We stayed in Waycross for several days at the home of Mrs. Culbreath, then went on to Atlanta where we planned a three-week stay. We spent that time with Rev. A. A. Mathis, Mme. Carter's Father.

When we started back to Chicago, we boarded the train at night. We were sitting in the "Jim Crow" car, when a colored minister, whom we both knew, came in and said, "Mme. Carter, I have a berth and I think I can get you one too."

Mme. Carter was afraid to take the berth, but the minister insisted. The conductor assured her it was safe. We took the berth but the conductor's assurances didn't resolve Mme. Carter's concerns—concerns that kept her from sleeping, expecting someone to come in and assault us. When we got to Chicago, she looked, as tired as though she had sat up all night in the colored coach.

I spent two months in Chicago before going to Elkhart, Indiana where I spoke at the Booker T. Washington Settlement House—a social service institution, founded and operated by Mrs. M.A. McCurdy. There were few such settlement houses for colored and those few served increasing numbers of colored immigrants from the South.

From Elkhart, I went to Detroit, arriving at about the time the Sweet case was in the courts. In 1925, Dr. and Mrs. Gladys Sweet moved from Gladys's parents' home to a house they purchased from a white family in an all-white neighborhood. The white neighbors were up in arms that a black family had moved into their area. Concerned about violence, Dr. Sweet recruited nine men to stay at the house—some were relatives, some were friends and some were colleagues. Worried about potential violence, the police chief assigned men to guard the house from outside.

A mob gathered and, according to witnesses, the police entered the Sweet home and threw up the shades, saying it was so they could keep an eye on the inside as well, except now the mob could see to shoot into the house. Someone in the mob, either an adult or teen, threw a rock and broke a window. Shots rang out and two of the mob were hit, one died. The police arrested everyone in the Sweet house, including the fourteen-month-old baby. Handcuffed to each other, they were taken to jail, charged with murder, and held without bail. Initially, Judge John Faust was assigned the case and refused bail for all defendants, but he suddenly died and was replaced by Judge Murphy. Murphy was a young liberal judge who released Gladys Sweet on ten thousand dollars bail; the money was put up by her parents. With representation and backing from the NAACP and Clarence Darrow, all defendants were acquitted.

I spent an entire month in Detroit speaking in Jackson and then Grand Rapids to their branches of the NAACP. In Benton Harbor, I spent a night with my mother's friend, Tamara Holland. At seventy-seven years old, she spoke with clear recollection about my mother and their many years in Darke County as friends and neighbors. I often remembered hearing my Mother speak of Tamara. While sitting at Tamara's kitchen table, she repeated over and over, "You don't know how much I loved your mother."

I drove to Gary, Indiana from Benton Harbor. Years before I had organized a branch of the NAACP there. After my presentation, I drove to Chicago for a short stop over and then went to Bloomington, Illinois. It took longer than expected because I got off on the wrong road and had to backtrack twenty miles. It was night, the roads were not well paved, and I had two flat tires by then, but kept going. I was too tired to worry, so I drove into the city on the rims. I was expecting to meet Dr. Eugene Covington at the Wayman African Methodist Episcopal Church, but when I arrived the church lights were off and no one was there. It was quite a while before Dr. Covington arrived, but I was eager to talk with him, since he was the main reason their NAACP branch had been organized several years before.

I was unable to speak in Bloomington because of an epidemic of smallpox. It was late 1925 and the Bloomington city officials were requiring certificates of vaccination for all those attending public gatherings, even in churches. Dr. Covington told me there were nearly 150 cases of small pox in Bloomington.

The following day, I left Bloomington and drove to Springfield, Illinois. I spent two days with my sister, Nancy Jane, and her husband, Oliver Singleton. Upon leaving, Nancy went with me to East St. Louis, where she met with friends and I spent the night. The next day, I went on to St. Louis. I sold twenty books to the St. Louis Board of Education, then drove to Carbondale to visit a colored high school, where the students were quite interested in my message and work.

I drove on to Princeton, Indiana crossing the Wabash River on a hand-operated ferry, and then to Evansville, Indiana and Louisville, Kentucky by way of French Lick, Indiana. One could sense a difference as soon as we crossed into the South, where the schools for the colored were neglected. As I spoke with the local people it was obvious that knowledge was not well disseminated. Then I was on to Nashville, Tennessee by way of Bowling Green, Kentucky, where I was taken across the Cumberland River on another hand-operated ferry.

Nashville is an educational center. There were four colleges: Central Tennessee College, operated by the Methodist Episcopal Church, North; Roger Williams College, operated by the colored Baptists; The A&M State College, under the auspices of the State of Tennessee; and Fisk University, a congregational school. I spoke at all of them, receiving the greatest response and applause from the students at Fisk University.

The Bethlehem Center at 1417 Charlotte Avenue in Nashville, was initially a social service center for African American women and children, modeled after Chicago's Hull House. It housed a kindergarten, a well-baby clinic, sewing classes, and recreational programs. I spoke there in December of 1925, and after my presentation a lady approached me saying she wanted to donate a piece of land for an orphanage for colored children. Miss Mathee Nutt, then head of the center, went out to see the land with me. Miss Nutt was quite pleased with the location and took the responsibility of establishing the proposed orphanage. That land eventually became Camp Dogwood—the first camp for African American children in Tennessee.

Mme. Carter joined me in Nashville on January 21, 1926. She delivered a series of lectures on business development at Roger Williams College. Afterwards, we set out for Tuskegee Institute in Tuskegee, Alabama. We stopped in Columbia, Tennessee—at the recent scene of the shameful 1946 race riot. We drove over a mud road detour where the wheels sank up to the hubs; we crossed a swollen stream where the water lapped the timbers of a temporary bridge; and we lost our spare tire but finally got into Athens, Tennessee looking like mud turtles. We filled our tank and drove another eleven miles to the edge of the Tennessee River. We ended at a spot where lights shown out over the water and waves lapped the shore making the river look more like a sea, but there was no bridge. We saw a ramp and after a wait that seemed eternal, a ferry came over and took us aboard.

We spent the night in Decatur, Alabama directly across the river from Tennessee, and the next day drove on to Birmingham, and then to Montgomery where we rested for the night. The next morning, we made our way to the State Normal School for colored students and spoke to their student body.

Tuskegee was only a few miles from there and we arrived in time for their farmers' meeting. From all over the state, the farmers came to hear George Washington Carver and other great scientists tell them how to grow better crops, hoping to save the economy of the South.

We stayed in Tuskegee for ten days, renewing old friendships and making new ones. We met Dr. Fred Stokes, head medical officer of the Tuskegee Veteran's Hospital. He was born in Darke County and was a good friend of my brother, Joseph. I took time to speak with quite a few veteran patients one afternoon and, later that evening, Dr. Stokes arranged a larger gathering and speaking engagement in their recreation hall.

One thing that greatly surprised me was a building on campus called Dorothy Hall. No colored person had ever been allowed to stay in that building, even though it was on the Tuskegee campus. Dorothy Hall was reserved for white visitors only. I thought, *How strange and ironic that segregation even reached the campus of an institution for colored people.*

Tuskegee was primarily teaching industries—skills that would assure self-reliance through farming and other trades. In fact, every other day, industry was the only subject taught, making it hard to get a liberal arts education. However, Booker T. Washington was very thoughtful in planning the courses available, determined to provide his students with a functional education for the time. Tuskegee may have been the first school to offer its students a "work-study" program, paying their working students eight-cents per hour.

The women of Tuskegee were housed either in Huntington Hall, built in 1900 from donations by the widow of Collis P. Huntington the railroad baron, or White Hall, designed by famed architect Robert R. Taylor and built in 1910. The dormitories housed only four women; they slept on cots that had mattresses filled with pine needles. These women worked in homes in the town and neighboring places, where they received $2.50 per week in salary.

Booker T. Washington, Founder of Tuskegee, was the world wizard of industrial education. He carried his message to the people, speaking from pulpits and platforms everywhere, using as his motto: "Work with the hands," and "Let Down Your Bucket Where You Are."

We then drove out to the rural sections just north of Tuskegee: Loachapoka and Notasulga. We found a large community of colored people. Many came to their local schoolhouse to hear us speak. We also met an older woman who happened to be a member of Mme. Carter's clubs. (One of the things these clubs did was to provide its members a proper burial.) This older lady lived back in a field and we had a tough time finding her. When Mme. Carter entered her house, I heard the old lady shout, "I've always wanted to see this good woman! I'm an old woman and when the sun comes up in the morning, I say, 'good morning sun,' because I don't know that I'm ever going to see it rise again, and when night comes, I say, 'good night sun,' because I don't know that I'm going to see it set again. Now I'm 'unfinancial' in the club but I have the money here in my stocking to pay my dues, because I want that club to buy my case."

The next day, we drove to Gizzard Point, Alabama, the birthplace of Mme. E. M. Carter, then went on to Albany, Thomasville, Alabama, and then Tallahassee, Florida. We spent several days at the Florida Agricultural & Mechanical College in Tallahassee talking to students and driving around the surrounding area speaking at churches.

We stayed at A&M College overnight and slept in one their dormitories. Just outside the dorm window was a large tree. Some of its longer branches had grown through and around several links of a thick chain. The college was located on an old slave plantation, and this chain was used to tie the slaves when they were about to be whipped or shipped. I took a snapshot of Mme. Carter holding the chain when suddenly she dropped it, saying that she had an overwhelming feeling of profound grief. I left the campus and went down to Rascal Square, historically an open salve market, but now a place where people from the rural areas drove in on ox-carts bringing fruits and vegetables to be sold at the open farmer's market.

We drove on to Lakeland, Ocala, Tampa and St. Petersburg. In St. Petersburg, Mme. Carter left me to look for an old friend and classmate from Moorhead College. We were on a narrow street, so I drove into an alley to get out of traffic. As I turned, I hit a board that pulled off a tire, causing the inner tube to bulge. There were a few colored men nearby and seeing what happened, they came over to help. Just as they arrived, two white detectives walked up, put out their hands and said, "Tell my fortune."

I said, "I'm no fortuneteller."

They looked at my New York license plate and said, "What are you doin' down here, anyway? Hard on your folk down here; guess we'll just take you down to jail. Open the back of the car. Got any whiskey back there?"

I showed them that I had only books, but they kept repeating, "Guess we'll just take you on down to jail—hard on your folks down here—what you doin' down here anyway?"

Mme. Carter came up and took the situation in hand. She soon convinced them that we were neither bootleggers nor fortunetellers. She was furious and said she never wanted to return to Florida.

We found a few wealthy colored people in St. Petersburg. Elder Jordan Sr. was one of them, who, after migrating from North Florida, bought a large tract of ground for eighty dollars before land prices soared. The land grew in value and a white man, who owned a smaller plot next to his, offered him $100,000.00. Elder Sr. used that money to buy land on what was then the outskirts of St. Petersburg. He built housing for colored families on that land, and bought eight brand new buses, each costing $10,000.00, and ran them from St. Petersburg to Tampa. The fare was 75 cents round trip. Elder Jordan Jr. later ran that bus line and other enterprises that were started by his father in response to Jim Crowism.

Between St. Petersburg and Tampa, Florida is the Gandy Bridge. It's said to be one of the longest automobile bridges in the world. It cost nearly two million dollars and was nearly three miles long.

In Tampa, the colored community lived in sand. One could hardly turn a car around in their neighborhood without getting stuck. It was disheartening to see their living conditions.

We drove another twenty miles to Clearwater, where we stayed in the first paper house I had ever seen. It was built entirely of paper, but was substantial and comfortable. Driving back to St. Petersburg we bought boxes of fresh oranges from vendors lining the highways and had them shipped home.

We spent a night in Ocala and the next morning spoke to the public-school children. From there, we drove to Gainesville to speak at the new Lincoln High School that had opened in 1923. The principal, A. Quinn Jones, a seasoned teacher and administrator, was the backbone of Lincoln High, encouraging many of the students to go to college and return to Lincoln as teachers.

We crossed the Suwanee River on our way to Live Oak, but stopped on shore to have our pictures taken. We spent two nights in Live Oak at the Florida Memorial College, which was founded 1879. The school didn't appear to be doing well financially as they had only three framed structures. If sturdy buildings were synonymous with school success, this was certainly not a very successful school. But the teachers and students were very enthusiastic; they sang with a zest and gathered around Mme. Carter and me, expressing much sorrow that we were leaving. We were as sorry to leave as they were to see us go. The same was true with the students at the Tallahassee A&M College. We spoke in churches on Sundays and to the student body on Mondays. On occasion, we were late getting started because the students had to go into the woods to get firewood.

On March 15, 1926, we drove to Thomasville, Georgia about sixty-miles, and then on to Moultrie, Georgia, where we spent the night with an old friend of Mme. Carter's. The woman was a widow and quite old, but her four rooms were beautifully kept. Her son had been principal of the school there but had died. His mother kept fresh flowers on his grave, had a tombstone placed, and the grave cemented over.

On our way back to Thomasville, I noticed the car roof had started to leak, so I got out and painted it with an anti-leak paint and it solved the problem. When we arrived in Thomasville, we spoke to a group of church women. The following morning, we spoke at an academy that was started by northern whites, then at the high school—where the principal bought a shelf of books.

We left for Albany, Georgia but stopped over in Camilla, where we both spoke. This delayed the Albany arrival until after dark. The next day, Saturday, we went on to Columbus, Georgia, where their two A.M.E. churches had a joint meeting for us. The following Monday night, Chaplin Thomas came and took us out to Camp Benning, where I spoke to the soldiers and found some old friends I had known from my time in France.

After I finished with my speech, the Colonel of the regiment came to me with compliments and bought a set of books. I later found out that he was a New Englander and knew no "color line." We also spoke at the Fifth Avenue School in Columbus—the first school for blacks in Columbus, opened in 1868. We sold a shelf of books there, as well.

On Tuesday, March 23, 1926, we returned to Tuskegee by way of Opelika, Alabama. Opelika was adjacent to a, "fall line," whose rapids provided energy to run its growing numbers of factories. We met some old friends in Opelika and discussed the plight of the colored community. Those factory jobs were for whites only.

When we arrived at Tuskegee, the State Convention of Social Workers was in session. Most of the speakers were white and spoke in generalities, while the audience was made up of both whites and colored. The woman that was presiding over the meeting tried desperately to connect with the colored audience, but failed as there was not one colored person on the program.

One man by the name of Caesar Simmons asked if he might say a word. Having helped establish NAACP branches in Oklahoma, he wanted to comment on the implications of segregation in the rail cars. Major Robert R. Moton, Tuskegee's president, who sat on the platform, arose at once and said, "Two minutes, please, sir, only two minutes."

Mr. Simmons made the only worthwhile comment the entire convention. He told them, if they were interested in doing something for colored people, they might use their influence to get the railroads in Alabama to put wash bowls and mirrors in the washrooms of the colored coaches. The next day, Mr. Simmons was threatened with job loss.

We arrived in Birmingham on the evening of March 24, 1926. I wore my brakes out coming down Red Mountain. Three miles' worth of that highway was a sharp and steady curve that had to be driven with great care to prevent driving over the edge.

Mme. Carter took a train to Atlanta to see her father. I stayed, visiting clergy. I stopped at the home of Rev. Hawkins, a West Indian black man. His family was wonderful and I could feel the mutual love and respect.

Birmingham is a city of iron mines; the owners provided education for their employees and paid better salaries than the city paid their public-school teachers.

I went to the commencement of the new Industrial high school, the one they erected for the colored people. The females in the graduating class made pastries for the white people on the platform. The boys had a "bootblack" stand to shine the boots of the white visitors.

The State Teachers' Association met while I was there, the platform crowded with white people. It leaked out that there was not a single accredited high school in the entire state for colored people. The process was separate for colored versus white schools and, to date, none of the colleges for African Americans had attained that accreditation from the Southern Association of Colleges and Secondary Schools.

The International Sunday School Convention also met in Birmingham while I was there. Preceding the convention an ordinance was passed to segregate the attendees. Four hundred colored delegates usually attended this convention—when word got out that they were to be segregated, only eight attended.

Mme. Carter returned from Atlanta, we started on our way to Huntsville, Alabama, planning to speak at the State Agricultural and Mechanical Institute for Negroes. It was rough traversing the road around the mountains, but when we arrived that Sunday, we spoke from the pulpits of several colored churches.

On Monday, we drove to the Miles Memorial College located in a serene spot at the foot of the Adirondacks, overlooking the Tennessee valley. Then to the Seventh Day Adventist School for colored. The Adventist school was the recipient of bond money voted on by the legislature and earmarked specifically for a much-needed school for the colored children—for years they had attended a school housed in an ancient, dilapidated building. The money was diverted and used instead for a white school.

We moved on to Nashville, where we visited a school for delinquent girls. The school was very regimented, the girls given duties just as in the boys' schools. Some of the girls were cleaning mortar off bricks and piling them in a corner. Some were washing shirts for five cents apiece.

When I returned to Bowling Green, Kentucky I spoke to the congregation pastored by Reverend Offutt—the same pastor that had hosted me at the beginning of this journey. The meeting was lovely and afterwards we drove thirty-five miles to Mammoth Cave. Mme. Carter was just too big to get through the entrance, but I spent two hours in this underground wonder. We descended 364 feet below ground and took a boat ride on the underground Crystal River. In some places, the river was thirty-five feet deep and twenty feet wide. We could see eyeless fish under the electric lights. Only part of the cave had electricity, so we had to carry lanterns. Many people trying to go it alone found themselves lost in this cave and were never seen again.

In one section of the cave, the passage way was cordoned off and protected by a wire fence. We could see an onyx stone said to be worth five million dollars. Stalactites hung from both the ceiling and stalagmites covered the floor. Tapping one of the stalagmites produced a sound much like a bell.

I was very tired after leaving the cave and suggested we try and spend the night in the town, but there were no accommodations for colored people, so we drove seventy-five miles to Louisville. We worked at staying focused on our driving as we traversed the very steep and dangerous mountain roads of Pilot's Knob. I had to turn off the engine and use it as a brake, pushing in the clutch when we wanted to slow down for curves.

We stayed with a schoolmate of mine in Louisville, then crossed the Ohio River to speak at a church in New Albany; afterwards, I sold a shelf of books to their The Read-a-Bit Club. We drove to Indianapolis, then Terre Haute, where we had dinner with a first cousin. We made our way to Danville, Illinois, after which, the emotional ups and downs of travel throughout the South, caught up with me. Exhausted, I had to stop. Mme. Carter took a train back to Chicago, but I stayed in Danville with the Pamplin sisters, getting a much-needed physical and psychological rest.

After a week with the Pamplin sisters, I drove to Springfield to visit with my sister, Nancy Jane Johnson. She was fourteen years my elder, which, I don't believe I've mentioned. Nancy Jane was a widow and wanted to visit relatives in St. Louis, so I took her with me. Nancy stayed in St. Louis and I went to Kansas City, where I stayed two months speaking at churches, high schools, and colleges. I spoke at Lincoln High School on the Missouri side, Sumner High School on the Kansas side, and Western University. I didn't venture any farther west than Leavenworth,

Lawrence and Topeka, towns where few colored people lived. It would have been difficult to find lodging, food, or a place to just stop and rest along the miles and miles of lone prairie highway. So, on June 16, 1926, I left Kansas City and its hills and drove back to St. Louis, picked up my sister, stopped in Springfield (so she could replenish), and we both took off for Chicago, stopping in Bloomington, where I spoke at two venues and spent the night.

Miss Mary McDowell, founder of the University of Chicago Settlement House, was in the audience at one of the Bloomington talks and contacted me, asking if I would be willing to speak in front of white audiences at various churches and clubs. The talk that impressed her so was as follows:

"There is no doubt of the great need for education of the white people through the distribution of literature concerning colored people. Two years ago, I heard Mr. William Alexander, National President of the international Commission, make the statement that he was a grown man with all the prejudices of a southern white man, before learning that Crispus Attucks was a colored man, and upon learning this fact, 'his respect for colored people increased one-hundred percent.'

"That a white man could grow up in the South or any section of this country and learn nothing about the black man except that he had been a slave, is shameful. Even more tragic is the lack of physical and psychological contact with people of color, due to the stigma of mental segregation.

"While traveling as a field worker for the NAACP, I realized an absolute need to find a remedy for the imposed ignorance. I remembered vividly the stultifying effect that text books had on my psyche as a child in the public schools of Ohio. I remember vividly the picture of the African Black man depicted as representing the whole of the Black race. Nothing said, except he belonged, 'to the most inferior race.' I balanced that with the memory of the book I found while at Wilberforce that disclosed with clarity the accomplishments of my people: "Men of Mark."

"My academic experience at New Paris High awakened a passion to teach colored communities, disseminating a message, reminding them of the injustices of the past,

170

present, and potentially the future. So, for five years, I drove around the country devoting myself to the enlightenment of colored people by pushing as many copies of the Two-Foot Shelf of Negro Literature into to their hands as I could. I accomplished this through public speaking and disseminating the message of literacy and knowledge. My intention was to stimulate an interest in learning about our people through that Two-Foot Shelf. This has been an arduous task, fraught with difficulty and sometimes danger; for I have driven north, east, and west, but also the South, the birth of racial ignorance and indignation, through Missouri, Texas, Louisiana, Virginia, North Carolina, Georgia, Alabama, and Florida.

"In all my travels, to all communities large and small, to all the towns and cities, I have found to a greater or less extent an awakening consciousness among our people, and in many places their response has been gratifying to the greatest degree. I have been able to place into their hands thousands of copies of different books, selected to offset the silence in academic and other texts regarding the achievements of colored people.

"In the same way my work has been done among colored people, it should also be done among whites. My method was to talk to ready-made audiences, hoping later to develop a program or curriculum that others might use. When arriving in a city, I would ascertain the number of colored churches and how many of these had congregations with a fair degree intelligence. I would visit the churches on Sunday, talking for ten or fifteen minutes at the close of services, often constrained, dependent on the good nature and interest of the pastor. I also addressed insurance societies, women's clubs, conferences, conventions, and many other audiences.

Working in this fashion, I have been limited in scope. I have had to stay in cities like Washington, Philadelphia, and Chicago for six to eight weeks, unable to reach most colored people due to lack of access. Access, limited by inadequate education, poverty, class prejudice, or the ubiquitous "color line." Those with the socioeconomic and academic advantages responded wonderfully, but those are the minority in the colored communities. Those that need to hear the message have been sparse in number, the message delivered to them is only bread cast upon water, hoping that it might be gathered after many days before lost to disintegration."

I think a similar plan could be worked out for the white communities of this country. I would develop a 'Bureau for the Distribution of Negro Literature,' an organization that would recruit speakers, develop itineraries and arrange for public addresses in churches, schools, and a variety of other public platforms—followed by magazine sales and distribution of printed matter, along with home visits for those in the audiences that expressed interest in purchasing books.

Dissemination of Negro literature by public libraries could be accomplished through personal efforts. Miss Florence Pamplin of Danville, Illinois was instrumental in getting their library to offer my Two-Foot Shelf of Negro Literature. In a recent letter, she said that they were very popular, such that a second set was needed.

The Dunbar club of Evanston purchased a shelf nearly two years ago and donated them to their public library. I was told that there was much interest in those books amongst the white community.

Tuesday, the fourteenth day of June 1925, I had the pleasure of driving from Lawrence, Kansas to the University of Kansas to deliver a "shelf" to their library. I did this, following a request from Miss Davis, one of the colored students attending the University. She wrote to Mrs. Myrtle Cook of Kansas City, Missouri who spoke before the City Federation Forum concerning the matter. The president of the City Federation, Mrs. Wood, put the matter into the hands of Mrs. Maggie Clay, the chairman of her Educational Committee, who succeeded in getting donations to the amount of $25.00, the price of the shelf. One woman gave $10.00, immediately after I finished speaking.

I succeeded in getting several book sets into the libraries at St. Louis, Missouri and Gary, Indiana. I think these are the only places where I made such an effort, focusing my attention on the rank and file in the colored communities, hoping they would purchase the books and of course read them.

In Louisville, Kentucky, there were two colored libraries where homeowners could borrow books. They purchased two sets of books per library, but hid behind the erroneous statement that they had several sets of my books in both of their library branches. The truth was they had only two sets of books per library, making them available to one out of ten or fifteen thousand people, leaving most the colored community ignorant about their own history and accomplishments.

One of the best ways of reaching those thoughtful, influential people in the white community was through book purchases by their colored servants. During my five years of driving around the country, when going into servants' quarters in white residencies, the colored servants said they were not just buying the books for themselves but were going to give the books to their employers or leave them where their employers would surely pick them up. I found those employed servants to be of above average intelligence and they could buy books because their living arrangements—their room and board taken care of by their employers. I also think that those servants exerted a greater influence among white people because of proximity. I found the servants to be very reliable in pushing the cause I was passionate about, preaching the accomplishments of Negroes.

There was another approach worth discussing; it concerned the philanthropic white person. The white people engaged in schools and social service organizations were often able to do a greater good by establishing a platform for self-education and awareness. While in Nashville, I met a white woman who showed me a small book called *Handicapped Winners*. She planned to give the book to white children, especially those at the Methodist Episcopal Church South, where she attended. She was chairman of the church's Board of Missions. Her book was about the many things colored people had accomplished. Some accomplishments I had no idea had occurred. She gave me a copy of the book. I added it to the Two-Foot Shelf. I started using that book as a basis for discussions with high school and college students.

I believe that an adequately financed "bureau of information," with a repository of books describing the true history and accomplishments of African and African American people would begin to highlight and resolve the ignorance and miss information about this subject for both white and colored people.

During the month of August 1926, I drove to Richmond, Indiana to attend the State Federation of Colored Women's Clubs. I detoured to visit my brothers, Jesse and Joseph, in Dayton and Columbus and returned to Richmond to meet up wtih Mme. Carter who had just come from the Carter Industrial and Benevolent Association meeting in Atlanta, Georgia.

Mme. Carter and I then went to the Darke County colored settlement; Wilberforce University; Columbus; and then Indianapolis, Indiana, where we attended the national Baptist convention. We drove to Chicago on September 15, so I could begin my speaking engagements for Miss McDowell.

My first speech was before the Women's Department of the Chicago Church Federation. I spoke at several white churches and clubs. They bought many books but I don't think their segregationist attitude was changed.

The segregationist attitude is best demonstrated by the language of Mrs. Oakley, the wife of the pastor of a Christian church. She was born in Lexington, Kentucky and moved to Cincinnati, Ohio. Unfortunately, Mrs. Oakley had a "typical" southern white woman's viewpoint, telling us how incensed she was when, in her early married life, her northern born husband got up and gave an elderly colored woman his seat. Her husband went on to talk about intermarriage. A member of their congregation had married a Filipino woman and was immediately ostracized by their congregation. Both the Filipino girl and her white husband were greatly hurt and eventually left the USA and settled in the Philippines.

174

When I spoke with Minister Oakley about this and the fact that I didn't believe colored people were represented fairly in educational text books, he replied that colored people hadn't done anything worthy of mentioning in those texts. I told him that many of the colored accomplishments throughout history had been recorded as done by white people. He simply said, "That should be corrected."

Mrs. Oakley then spoke about a troop of Jubilee singers that visited the small-town church, where Mr. Oakley was pastoring at the time. To her consternation, the troop could not find a hotel or private residence that would let them stay. She said she was angry and finally took two of the troop into her own home. She commented that she had never met two more cultured women.

I said I could not understand how Christian people could oppose the legitimate mixing of the races in their communities or churches, because as with the Filipino woman and white man, it brought mixing without benefit of clergy and caused suffering to the couple and their children. I also commented that many white men fathered children with their slave women and reared those children, sent them to college, and secured their futures by leaving them part of their estates.

Mrs. Oakley said she thought young people should be warned about social ostracism if they contemplated mixed marriages. I told her that such opinions should be corrected and not tolerated; that to promote prejudice in that way was not keeping with the will of the Almighty; that white people seem to want to sit in judgment of God, by saying:

"God, you made a mistake when you did not make everybody white; you should have made all people the same color as we are. You did not know what you were doing when you created the universe; you better let me sit awhile on your throne. I'll show you how to do things. I can make a much wider and better God than you have made."

Chapter Eleven

George Washington's Son
(Interracial Mixing During Slavery)

"No other women on earth have emerged from the hell of force and temptation which once engulfed, and still surrounds black women in America, with half the modesty and womanliness they retain. I have always felt like bowing myself before them in all abasement, searching to bring some tribute to these long-suffering victims, these burdened sisters of mine whom the world, the wise, white world, loves to affront and ridicule, and wantonly to insult.

I have known the women of many lands and nations—I have known and seen and lived beside them, but none have I known more sweetly feminine, more unswervingly loyal, more desperately earnest, and more instinctively pure in body and in soul than the daughters of my black mothers.

This, then, a little thing, to their memory and inspiration."

—W.E.B. Du Bois

THE DISCUSSION AT THE CHURCH with Mrs. Oakley about racial mixing and intermarriage, made me realize that I hadn't thought much about race mixing or its racial-socioeconomic implications, so I started researching the matter.

White men, who forced themselves on women of color during slavery, make an interesting and horrific chapter in American history. The fair-skinned people seen everywhere, classified as "black," are proof of miscegenation, coital relationships between the white race and races of color. In the state of Louisiana after the Civil War, there were so many shades of grey, that many of the leading families were, "tainted," such that a state law was passed declaring that all who were only one-eighth colored (Octoroon) would be considered white.

Many of those with mixed blood passed for white and secretly intermarried with them. Years ago, a man came to Chicago seeking employment, eventually becoming a foreman at a large company. Among the employees was a girl he took a romantic interest in. A courtship ensued and he asked her to marry him. She had a problem, a secret which she felt she had to disclose. She was colored, a fact not known at the company. When she told him that she was in fact colored, he jumped up happily, and said, "Thank the Lord, for I'm colored, too!"

I read a magazine article a while ago which featured the following story:

"A slave owner had two children born about the same time, one by his wife and one buy his colored woman slave. He was away at the time, and when he came home he strode into the colored woman's room and asked which of the babies belonged to his wife. The slave woman was nursing them both and they could scarcely be told apart.

While he was away the slave mother had had time to think over the matter. She knew her own baby would be sold to the slave trader, so she decided to give her own child to the master. Years after, when this child, a daughter had grown to womanhood and had married, the slave master gave the colored mother to his daughter for a maid. This suited them both nicely, but when there were grandchildren, two of them caught fire in the backyard where they were heating water in a large pot to wash clothes. The grandmother in saving them was so severely burned that she died, but not before she told the master that his daughter was her daughter and that his grandchildren were colored children."

Such stories reflect fact. Julia Greene, my maternal grandmother, was a descendant of General Nathanael Greene, the Revolutionary War general, through General Greene's illegitimate son, Gabrael Greene.

Upon hearing the story of General Greene from my mother, I found my school history books and read about General Greene's life.

Nathanael Greene was born in Rhode Island of Quaker parents. His father was a minister of the gospel, but Nathanael left behind the teachings of his father after going South to Virginia and the Carolinas. His father was bitterly opposed to slavery, but Nathanael bought land and bought slaves to work that land. In Simms's, "Life of General Greene," it reads: "He was compelled at a time of peculiar pressure in the moneyed condition of the country, to sell the land which he had bought in Carolina at an enormous sacrifice. His slaves were removed to his estate, which Georgia had given him. This was a beautiful place called Mulberry Grove, where he died in 1785 and was buried in an unmarked grave."

Figure 22. Ms. Annie Elizabeth Faucett, granddaughter of Thomas Jefferson, third president of the United States.

Another famous American figure that fathered colored children, some of whose descendants I knew, was Thomas Jefferson. When Jefferson was alive, Tucker Issacs, a German Jew went to Charlottesville, Virginia to paint the Jefferson home at Monticello. Playing in the Jefferson yard was a light-skinned, colored, teenage girl whom Tucker Issacs took to fancy. The girl was Thomas Jefferson's granddaughter, Ann-Elizabeth Fossett.

Tucker went to the master of the house and told him he would like to take the girl to Cincinnati and marry her, because he could not legally marry her in Virginia. Jefferson went to the yard and brought the girl in and told her that Mr. Issacs wanted to marry her. The girl cried and said that she did not wish to leave the Jefferson home. However, Jefferson persuaded her, stating he'd go with her and Mr. Issacs and buy them a home in Cincinnati. He also told her that he would send her whatever pieces of mahogany furniture she selected out of his Monticello mansion.

Tucker Isaacs married the girl and lived with her in Cincinnati, in the home that Jefferson bought for her. The pair had six sons and two daughters. When these children grew up, Thomas Jefferson bought them a farm about eight miles from Chillicothe, Ohio. Mrs. Dora Wilburn, the daughter of one of the Isaacs' sons, and thus the great, great grandchild of Thomas Jefferson, was living in my present home in Chicago for the past three years.

The colored grandson of Thomas Jefferson, Anne Elizabeth's brother, Peter Faucett, pastored the First Baptist Church in Cumminsville, one of Cincinnati's suburbs, for thirty-two years. When he died in 1901, he left the building to the congregation.

Closely connected with both General Nathanael Greene and Thomas Jefferson, was the Polish military engineer, Tadeusz Kosciuszko, who came to America to aid in the revolutionary cause. Kosciuszko served with General Greene and sadly witnessed the institution of slavery. In a letter to General Greene, dated September 2, 1782, he wrote:

Figure 23. Pastor Peter Faucett, Ann Elizabeth's brother and grandson of Thomas Jefferson.

I think somebody ought to inspect when the baggage comes to your quarters. I recommend to you, two negroes belonging to L. C. John Laurens, that they may have part with La Brasseur. They are naked and need shirts, jackets and britches, and their skins can bear, as well as ours, good things.

Kosciuszko had deep feelings about the infelicitous relationship between "Colonial Slavery" and the Revolutionary War. Kosciuszko's feelings for his fellow man, slave or not, was lacking in many of the Fathers of our country, but some of these empathetic feelings must have eventually affected Thomas Jefferson. For his services in the Revolutionary War, Kosciuszko was given a tract of five hundred acres of land, now referred to as Kosciuszko's Grant, on the Scioto River, the site of today's Columbus, Ohio. During his second visit to America, he made a grant of this land to his friend Thomas Jefferson, as follows:

I, Tadeusz Kosciuszko, being just in my departure from America, do hereby declare and direct that should I make no other testamentary disposition of my property in the United States, hereby authorize my friend Thomas Jefferson to employ the whole thereof in purchasing negroes from among his owners as others, and giving them liberty in my name, in giving them an education in trades, or otherwise, and in having them instructed for their new condition in the duties of morality, which may make them good neighbors, good fathers or mothers, husbands and wives, and their duties as citizens, teaching them to be defenders of their liberty and country and of the good order of society, and in whatever may make them happy and useful, and I make the said Thomas Jefferson my executor of this.

—T. Kosciuszko
Fifth day of May, 1798

The terms of the will were entangled in litigation and never carried out, except that Jefferson may have used some of the proceeds from this land to free his own slaves or perhaps some of this land was used by Jefferson to settle some of his great-grandchildren, the sons and daughters of Thomas Isaacs.

Whether it was Kosciuszko's influence of Thomas Jefferson or not, there must have been something that changed the mind of Thomas Jefferson and turned him against the cruel institution of slavery.

Another "great" American slave owner that had sexual relationships with his female slaves, was George Washington; he owned 317 slaves at his death. During his lifetime, he was convinced that slavery was wrong, partly because of the influence of his friend, Marquis de Lafayette, who wanted him to emancipate the slaves. He left his slaves to his wife, but in his will instructed Martha to emancipate them.

George Washington was nurtured in the institution of slavery, not only by his family but also by his church. I have been inside that church in Alexandria, Virginia and sat in the pew where Washington worshipped. I quote from Walter H. Mazyck's 1932 book, *George Washington and the Negro*, speaking about that church as it was in Washington's day and the services that were held there:

"A dull September sun reflected a shaft of light from the brass on the railing around the Lord's Table of the Parish Church one Sunday morning, as George Washington, not quite ten years old sat at Divine Service. His childish eyes roamed from the flickering flame of the white candles on the table to the black muzzles of the sober muskets, showing like so many dried twigs above the high pew stalls. Guns and candles and church were always intimately associated in his mind. The candles, it is true, might disappear on communion Sundays, but the guns were ever present.

"After the minister had announced in solemn tones, 'Here endeth the second lesson' he took into his hands a copy of the Virginia laws, and in the same solemn voice began to read, 'Whereas, the laws concerning Negroes and other slaves have not had the good effect by them intended for want of being duly executed, especially those laws providing that bit shall be unlawful for any Negro to arm himself with any club, staff, gun, sword, or any weapon of defense or offense, or to depart from his master's ground without a pass, to be granted only upon particular and necessary occasions, or to assemble at feasts or funerals; that no inhabitant shall suffer a strange Negro to remain upon his property above the space of four hours without examining him and his pass; freemen will not repair to divine services or other assemblies unless armed to prevent surprise attacks of slaves; and any slave caught off his master's plantation without a pass after dark will be dismembered.

Thus, on and on the minister continued through a list of barbarous laws and inhuman punishments which the feat of servile rebellion had forced into the Virginia codes, until finally he came to the end with the announcement that those who violated their provisions would answer to His Majesty's government to their utmost perils.

Through the reading of these proclamations twice a year, as the law required, at divine services, George and the children of his generation were taught that slavery was right. It was thus, too, that the means of controlling slaves were being revealed to them. They were learning that, 'To make a contented slave, you must make a thoughtless one. It is necessary to darken his normal vision, and as far as possible annihilate his powers of reason. The child was thus, nurtured in tyranny."

Quoting Mazyck's book still further, we find George Washington concerned over illness among his slaves:

"His diaries, ever terse, abound with references to his sick Negroes, and the steps taken for their care. On January 28, 1760, he, 'found the new Negro, Cupid, ill of pleurisy, at Dogue Run Quarter, and had him brought home in a cart for better care.' The next day he lamented the inroads of death upon his slaves: 'Darcus, daughter to Phillis, died, which makes four Negroes lost this winter, viz; three dower negroes, namely Beck, appraised to fifty pounds; Doll's child, born since, and Darcus... and Belinda, a wench of mine, in Frederick.'"

Concern over their illnesses was not George Washington's only slave related concern. Some states became known as, "slave breeding states," and without doubt the slave holder would save much time staffing his mansion with his own mulatto children, then sell them on the auction block if he felt it necessary. This was the slave owner's custom, and George Washington was a slave owner before he was general of the Army, or President and Father of this country.

It must have been hard for Washington to learn morality while living in a system where mulatto children grew in abundance and where the Episcopal Church in Alexandria kept guns over his head and read the Virginia Code twice a year, re-enforcing how the poor slaves must be treated. Of course, mulatto children were valuable. They brought the highest prices in the slave markets.

The drama that went on behind the scenes between the slave masters and the female slaves would, no doubt, fill many books.

On Page 71 of Rupert Hughes, *Life of Washington,* he writes: "Out of the little volumes that Washington decorated with his only autobiography, a few passages may be taken from their nestling places in print along-side his steel plate script. Here is one for the month of March 1771:

'Now the spring approaches, which will make the blood be stirring; but if thou cans't not live honestly, take a wife of thy own, for there is never anything got by wenching, but duels…And mistresses, like green peas at first coming, are only had by the rich, but afterwards they come to everybody!'"

This will give an idea of what he meant by the word "wench." Hughes continues: "The breeding of slaves was in the beginning of what it became later, one of the chief industries of Virginia. The services of the midwife were in frequent demand. She was usually the wife of Bishop, the old soldier whom the dying Braddock had turned over to Washington."

The slave women in this travail were known by first names and nicknames—Betty, Kate, Sue, Muddy Hole Kate, Catherine, Lame Alice, Negro Moll, House Alice.

Hughes continues: "It is pitiful to observe that these poor bonds-women did not even have last names. They were labelled like cattle by their pastures, or some deformity, 'Muddy Hole Kate,' 'Lame Alice,' 'House Alice,' who worked in the house."

Few of them had husbands, and Haworth writes that Washington apparently never cared whether they had or not: "He was a citizen of his time and environment."

West Ford was the name of one of George Washington's mulatto sons. I learned of this son several years ago. I was driving from Springfield to Danville, Illinois when I stopped at the Camp Butler National

Cemetery to visit with Major George W., a colored man who had gained his title by organizing a company in Kansas for the Spanish-American War. His father was my sister's family physician.

As Major and Mrs. Ford and I sat talking, he asked me questions about where I had been and how I was succeeding in placing my Two-Foot Shelf of Negro Literature. In telling him of stories, I mentioned Alexandria, Virginia where I had stopped once to visit with friends.

The Major's interest quickened. "Alexandria, Virginia," he said, "that's

where I first saw the light of day." He got up and went into another room and returned with a photograph. "This," he said, showing me the photograph, "is my grandfather, Mr. West Ford, who lived on a plantation next to George Washington's estate in Mt. Vernon. George Washington gave him the plantation. Mr. West Ford was George Washington's son."

Figure 24. Mr. West Ford, said to be the mulatto son of General George Washington.

I took a good look at the photograph he was showing me. I was struck by the resemblance between the photograph of West Ford and the many pictures of George Washington I had seen.

Major Ford's wife said that during one of her visits to Mt. Vernon she had found the picture. She said it had been published in a magazine in 1850. She had forgotten the name of the magazine but thought it might have been the *Century*.

I asked if I might borrow the picture, take it to Danville, and have a copy made. I told him I would send it back as soon as I had finished. Major Ford agreed.

When I got to Danville, I inquired about a photographic studio. I was directed to the Worshing Studio, Suite 204 in the Loof Building. Arriving at the studio, I found a man that was immediately interested. I held up the picture and asked him whom it resembled. He said without hesitation, "George Washington."

I mailed the original back to Major Ford, whom I never saw thereafter.

As of today's, date, May 14, 1952, Major George W. Ford has four living children. Virgil Ford, a chiropodist who lives in Springfield, Illinois, and three daughters. They live in Peoria, Illinois, Philadelphia, Pennsylvania, and South Carolina.

When I talked with Dr. Virgil Ford, he told me he knew about his family's ancestry, had seen the picture of Mr. West Ford—George Washington's son—but hadn't seen the picture in some time.

The story of George Washington's son could be told repeatedly. If the pains of tracing the ancestry of the many mixed bloods in this country was undertaken; the blood of many of the nation's most illustrious men courses through their veins, but often those descendants didn't fare as well as West Ford.

"With a harshness and indecency seldom paralleled in the civilized world, white masters on the mainland sold their mulatto children, half-brothers and half-sisters, and their own wives in all but name, into a life of slavery by the hundreds and thousands. They originated a special branch of slave trading for this trade; and the white aristocrats made more money by this business during the eighteenth and ninetieth centuries than in any other way."

—W.E.B. Du Bois

Frederick Douglass

The slave woman and her children often suffered greatly. I had a sewing teacher at Wilberforce University who was a slave as a child. Her name was Elizabeth Keckley. She was born in Old Virginia, somewhere near the East Coast. As a child, she wanted to grow up to be a dressmaker and during leisure times, practiced by sewing for her dolls. She became Abraham Lincoln's maid and the "modiste" of Mary Todd Lincoln, while the Lincolns were in the White House.

Growing up, she developed into a comely young woman and to use her own expression: her master "developed evil designs" upon her. She kept out of his way as best she could, but he finally caught her and beat her with the handle of a hoe until she submitted. She was in bed for two weeks recuperating from the beating. She became the mother of a son.

Frederick Douglass was the son of such a forced miscegenistic relationship. His master's name was Auld; Auld was also his father. Little Frederick did not fare well. As a small child, he slept in a tow sack and, often, the eastern shore of Maryland could be very cold. His feet were frost bitten from exposure. At night, he would get into his tow sack and crawl into a closet to get warm. He was often very hungry and would come out of his sack late at night and parch corn in the embers of the fireplace. One night, while he was trying to satisfy his hunger, his mother, who lived twelve miles away, came in the door. She had to walk that distance at night and return before daybreak so that she would not be missed, just to have a few minutes with her son.

Frederick Douglass said in his narrative that at night she brought him some cookies and took him upon her lap and fed him. For the first time he realized, that he was not only a child, but "somebody's" child.

Frederick's master whipped him once a week on general principle. Once, after he had grown up, young Frederick fought back. His master called for aid, but nobody came. Frederick escaped into the woods and after that his master left him alone.

When Frederick became a good-sized boy, when hungry, he would find his way to the window of his master's daughter and sing, *"A little talk with Jesus makes it right, all right..."* Miss Auld, his half-sister, would hear him and throw some biscuits out the window to appease his hunger.

Finally, he ran away from slavery and became a member and speaker for the abolitionist movement, traveling nationally and internationally, telling of the horrors and cruelty of slavery. William Lloyd Garrison often travelled with Frederick. When Garrison would introduce him, Garrison would describe him as a graduate of the institution of slavery, with his diploma written on his back.

The immoral intrusions by slaveholders upon the helpless slave woman often ended in terrible suffering for the children as well as the mothers; the children often sold from their mother's breast.

Chapter Twelve

The Student Girl's Center in Atlanta

"The school house was a log hut, where Col. Wheeler used to store his corn. It sat in a lot behind a rail fence and thorn bushes, near the sweetest of springs. There was an entrance, where a door once was, and within, a massive, rickety fireplace: great chunks between the logs served as windows. Furniture was scarce. A blackboard crouched in the corner. My desk was made of three boards, reinforced at critical points, and my chair, burrowed from the landlady, had to be returned every night. Seats for the children, these puzzled me much. I was haunted by a New England vision of neat little desks and chairs, but, alas, the reality was rough plank benches, without backs, and at times, without legs."

"I trembled when I heard the patter of little feet down the dusty road, and saw the growing row of dark, solemn faces, and bright, eager eyes, facing me."

—W.E.B. Du Bois

TRAVELLING OVER THE COUNTRY BY train and automobile made me realize the difficulties children of color must overcome to get even the most basic education, especially in rural areas. In Louisiana, even though the colored communities pay a large share of the parish and state taxes, few of the parishes have public schools for colored children; the same holds true for most of the southern states. Understanding this, Ezella Mathis Carter, who spent two winters travelling with me, visiting her agents and establishing benevolent clubs, decided to establish a center for young girls. A place where young colored girls could live and attend school in Atlanta, Georgia, their expenses covered by the benevolent clubs. These benevolent clubs or "Life Boat Clubs," collected dues and distributed money to those in the colored community that showed the greatest need, thus the moniker "benevolent." In 1926–27, Mme. Carter expanded the mission to include educational centers for rural girls.

Atlanta was chosen for the location of this Student Girls' Center, because there were four colored colleges within walking distance of the center:

Morris Brown College—Named after the second Baptist minister of AME Bethel church in Philadelphia, Pennsylvania.

Atlanta University—Sponsored by the First Congregational Church, visited by President Taft in 1898.

Morehouse College—Initially, the Atlanta Baptist Seminary, and later named after Dr. Henry L. Morehouse, of the American Baptist Home Mission Society.

Spelman College—Initially, Spelman Seminary, endowed by John D. Rockefeller, Sr. and named for his wife, whose maiden name was Spelman.

Spelman Seminary was founded by two white women, Ms. Harriet Giles and Ms. Sophia Packard, both from Maine. They started the school in the basement of the Friendship Colored Baptist Church. The colored community went to them to learn, but Atlanta's white community resented this endeavor, making the lives of those two East Coast women miserable, and eventually subjecting them to gunfire. Determined, they persevered and developed a wonderful curriculum and a beautiful school. Spelman College is now located on the historic spot of General George William Tecumseh Sherman's headquarters, where he organized his famous march to the sea, now known as the Savannah Campaign.

The colleges made a wonderful community, making it possible for the students to live in a culture where they experienced very little, if any, racial prejudice—unless they got on a streetcar or walked to city center.

190

Within Mrs. Carter's, Student Girls' Center, was the Giles Charity Club, an organization first formed by Mrs. Carter in Chicago, that took the initiative to buy a piece of property at 92nd High Street in Atlanta. There were several structures already on the property, a large building and two small cottages. The cottages were at the rear of the lot facing the alley, and the organization expected to get rental income from the cottages, helping to pay for the property.

The management of the property was left in the hands of a white real-estate firm. The monthly reports showed that the income from the cottages was going toward repairs for the main building, as opposed to the mortgage.

In the Fall of 1932, I drove to Atlanta to help Mme. Carter with the Student Girls' Center. A female friend from Chicago, who was on her way to Georgia, accompanied me. We went by way of Evansville, Indiana to Elizabethtown, Kentucky, where we spent the night. There was a meeting at a colored church that night. I decided to attend, hoping to speak to the audience, display my Two-Foot Shelf of Negro Literature, and possibly sell a few books.

The next morning, we got on our way, but by afternoon brooding storm clouds and hard rain overtook us as we reached the mountains of Nashville, Tennessee. The headlights of the eighteen wheelers blinded me as they came over the mountain road toward us. I stopped at a filling station and asked if there were any colored families in the area. The attendant gave us directions and we found a nice farmer and his wife that made us welcome in their beautiful home.

That night, I learned of the severity of the depression gripping the country and its impact on all communities. The farmer told me about families as far away as Detroit, seen walking along the highway barefoot, trying to get back to their southern roots. He told me of a man who ran out of gas and money, sold his perfectly good car for six dollars, continuing his way by hitchhiking, and he talked about a man who drove his last cow into Nashville and sold her for five dollars. These were white people, offering six dollars for a fine car, five for a whole cow.

Food was scarce, even at the farmer's house; yet, they shared what they had with us. My car's back seat was full of canned goods and cured meat, so we gave the farmer some, thankful for what he did for us.

The next day, the rain cleared and we continued over the mountains on our way to Nashville and then Chattanooga, where we went up the forty-five-degree incline to Point Park, where above the clouds, twenty-four hundred feet above the Tennessee River, the battle of Lookout Mountain was fought.

We drove the fifty-three miles to Calhoun, Georgia, where I stopped for a brief time to see the colored high school that the great African American tenor and composer Roland Hayes helped to build. He bought six hundred acres of land near town—the same six hundred acres on which he was born, and where the original white owner had held his father in slavery.

I also passed by the spot where just a year earlier, Juliette Derricotte, the past Dean of Women at Fisk University was involved in a fatal automobile accident. After the accident, she was taken to a hospital in Athens, Georgia, but died because she was refused treatment due to her color.

I finally reached Atlanta, where I spent the next eleven months helping to establish the Student Girl's Center. I did this willingly without compensation, supporting the work through lectures and sales of my books. I wasn't the only volunteer; many women of Atlanta rallied faithfully to lend a hand.

One afternoon, I drove eighty-five miles to Macon, Georgia, and then another eighteen miles to a two-teacher grammar school for colored children. The principal of the school lived in Macon and drove the eighteen miles to and from the school, Monday through Friday. The following day, I went with the principal on her way to school. Some twelve miles out we saw a young, colored girl walking through the mud in the opposite direction. I stopped and asked where she was going. She told me she was on her way to Macon to attend the high school for colored children. A little further on, I saw a school bus picking up white children. There was also a white high school in Macon.

The next day, I was scheduled to speak at the two-teacher school. One young girl I spoke with told me she had come a long way, across fields and through pouring rain to hear my message. I took a special interest in her because her shoes and stockings were so muddied she had to remove them at the schoolhouse. She told me her parents tried to keep her from coming but, hearing stories of my message, she cried until her parents agreed to let her come.

I spent the night in that rural community with a teacher that lived in the area. When we left the school, it started to rain again. There were no walkways, gravel paths, or paved roads, just mud. We had to cross streams on foot logs to get to her house—a four-room country shack with a leaky roof. The shack belonged to her father, the son of a slave. When the rain stopped, she took me outside to show me the property line, explaining that a white man owned the adjacent property. She told me that all his colored tenant farmers (land rental farmers) brought their stock and supplies to his farm and left with nothing, never able to cover the rents with their goods. The white man would inflate and change rental costs, take everything away from the colored tenant, and then cancel their agreement, letting them go with nothing. I asked why this had never been reported to the NAACP. She told me the colored people were afraid.

In the adjoining county, there was a white man that kept colored people in actual peonage. He got free labor through the legal system, from colored men picked up by sheriffs for made-up offenses. They'd be fined, and then unlawfully leased to the farmers in the county. Those that happened upon his farm looking for work were starved to the point of desperation, and having to steal food for survival, would then get arrested, appear before a judge, and get fined. The land owner would pay the fine, make them work the payment off on his land, then when they almost finished their time, he would starve them again, so they'd steal food and get arrested. It became a vicious cycle, many dying in this illegal peonage.

In Macon, I attended the trial of Angelo Herndon, a young colored man from the North who had led six hundred people, white and colored, to the county building in protest, asking for food. It was at the depth of the depression and many people were hungry.

Young Herndon was arrested and jailed, languishing in the Fulton County jail for three years. He was fed unwashed turnips just pulled from the ground, no doubt the cause of his worsening stomach trouble.

I listened to Herndon's defense, admiring his fearlessness in this Southern court, where a black man had no respect. The court decided against him, even with no supportive evidence. The case was appealed up to the Supreme Court, where the decision was reversed and Herndon was again, a free man.

I was overheard expressing my resentment towards white people that treat us like second-class citizens and worse. A graduate of Morehouse said, "Oh, don't say that; when I went to Morehouse the white teachers actually shook hands with me." I didn't realize until then that the decorum of the south forbade white people from shaking the hand of a person of color.

I recently spoke with a white minister who told a story about an experience he had in Atlanta. He was at a meeting and shook the hand of a colored person. He was summarily laughed to scorn by the white participants at the meeting.

The Atlanta winters were mild and, unlike the Midwest, temperatures never dipped below freezing. I spent many hours in the splendid library of Atlanta University, reading newspapers from around the country and borrowing books and magazines to enjoy later. There was no fear of racial mistreatment, as the only white people were teachers from the North and East, who came south to teach in what they considered, a missionary school.

During the latter part of my eleven-month stay, I noted that the buildings at the Center were in progressively worsening disrepair. I decided to investigate the financial health of the organization. This is when I discovered that the white real estate firm that was managing us, was reporting bogus billings for repairs that were never done. This deprived us of our planned rental income.

I enjoyed my stay at the Student Girl's Center, hoping that the Center might set an example for other Black Colleges and Universities to develop educational opportunities through collaboration with their colored communities. But because of the ongoing Great Depression, the misrepresentation of building repairs and bogus billings, the Center finally had to close its doors.

For a while we kept the project going, recruiting volunteers to take charge, but that fizzled out as finances further diminished. I started my return to Chicago, driving over Lookout Mountain and around Missionary Ridge, where I could see the Tennessee River and its great Moccasin Bend. I spent the night in Chattanooga and the next day drove across the Tennessee River, heading towards the Great Smoky Mountains, where I spent the day driving through tall pine trees that seemed to reach as high as the heavens. I went through the town of Monteagle, a town developed by mountaineers, in an area initially inhabited by the Cherokee Nation. The mountain was named by the Cherokees for the vast numbers of Golden Eagles that nested along its ridges. I drove 'round and 'round those ridges and cliffs that seemed to pierce the cloud studded azure sky, and finally down the other side over the fearful, mighty mile of road that claimed many an unaware driver. All day I drove through this breathtaking scenery, arriving in Nashville after dark.

I stayed at the A.M.E. Sunday School Union, a publishing house established in the late 1800s. The next day, I drove to Evansville, Indiana, where I rested for three or four days, speaking only once at their colored high school. From Evansville, I went to Terre Haute, Indiana and spent the night with a first cousin. Then I went on to Danville, Illinois and back to Chicago, where I put my car away, never to drive again. My spirit forever affected by the long, lonely trip, over those treacherous mountains.

Chapter Thirteen

Stealing a Nation

"Primarily, Africa is the land of the blacks. The world has always been familiar with black men, who represent one of the most ancient of human stock."

—W.E.B. Du Bois

MY ACTIVIST SPIRIT DIDN'T END at the U.S. borders. I kept in contact with many of my African Wilberforce classmates. Through their communications, I could keep abreast of the political situations affecting these colored nations.

In 1928, African Chief Benjamin Nxumalo, came to this country. Benjamin Nxumalo was from Poremersdorp, Swaziland, South Africa. He came here as a delegate for the African Methodist General Conference, scheduled to meet in the armory at Thirty-Third and Giles Avenue in Chicago, where the old 8th Regiment used to have its meetings.

Chief Nxumalo had another mission: he wanted a journalist from the United States to document Britain's exploitation of his country. Charlotte Manye Maxeke, a classmate of mine from Wilberforce, also attending the conference, was spending time at my home and, while there, she was visited by several conference attendees, including Chief Nxumalo. You might recall Charlotte's story from Wilberforce—a singer and choir member from Africa that was brought to this country by an Englishman for a nationwide singing tour.

Chief Nxumalo came back to my home again and again to visit Charlotte Maxeke, or so I thought. After several more visits, Chief Nxumalo finally confided his other purpose for coming to America. I was surprised when he told me that he felt I was the one to write the story of Britain's exploitation of Swaziland. I agreed to do so.

A few weeks after Chief Nxumalo returned to Swaziland, I received a large package filled with legal documents, that supported his contention that Great Britain, during its years of occupation, had pillaged Swaziland's natural resources without supporting its people. Britain then dissolved historic tribal borders, making whole countries disappear. The same thing was currently happening in Kenya, resulting in the Mau Mau's attempt to drive the imperialist out of their country.

Figure 25. Charlotte Manye Maxeke, Johannesburg, South Africa, circa 1934

It took me ten years to complete the pamphlet, "Stealing a Nation." My correspondence with Chief Nxumalo had to be carried out through a third person to circumvent South African British censorship. I had to send my mail to a mutual friend in Sophiatown, just outside of Johannesburg. My friend then opened the letters, put them in new envelopes, stamped them with "British" stamps and re-mailed them. All this effort, to keep the British secret service from discovering what Chief Nxumalo was doing. Swaziland was not a member of the Union of South Africa and was trying to stay out of that organization; but mail for Swaziland was routed through the Union.

Chief Nxumalo told me that he had to be very careful about what he said, concerned that he could be arrested, tried for treason, and shot by the occupying British. In review of his letters, it was apparent that he was quite afraid that something might happen to him before he could get his story to the world. Then on August 20, 1939, I received the following cablegram: *Advise Kathryn Johnson delay public activities on her latest publications. Writing airmail.*

The cablegram was sent by Mr. Xuma, a minister in the African Methodist Church in South Africa. Later, I received a letter from Chief Nxumalo written the same day as the cablegram:

Dear Miss Johnson,

I received both the pamphlet and your cable reading, "Sailing Holland America Line." Insist have immediate cable from you; being under the impression that you may in accordance with your cable have sailed. I have written to Bishop Gregg as follows: "Advise Miss Johnson her activities may spoil good chances." In my last letter, you will remember I said you should not do anything before receiving a copy of our petition we intend presenting to Parliament in England. Both the King and I are afraid that if you start a campaign in England before the presentation of this petition, the whole case will be prejudiced…the king has written Bishop Gregg in appreciation of your work. He advises that you should be as moderate as possible in your actions. Now that the dynamite has been exploded, you should write me through Mrs. Tantsi, Box 809, Pretoria.

A subsequent letter notified me that Chief Nxumalo was dead. The letter came from his daughter, Constance, who said he had died of heart trouble.

I completed the book, *Stealing a Nation*, and saw it through to publication. Captain Harry Dean wrote the introduction. In it, he explained my contention that Great Britain had seized an enormous amount of land belonging, by rightful ownership, to the Swazi people, "a tale which should bring a blush of shame to every righteous man's cheek."

I dedicated the book to: *All the people of the earth who are suffering from the imperialism and exploitation of the physically strong. Both at home and abroad.*

Under the guise of war, the same happened in Ethiopia.

Chapter Fourteen

The Race of Ethiopia

"Africa is at once the most romantic and the most tragic of continents. Its very names reveal its mystery and wide-reaching influence. It is the 'Ethiopia' of the Greek. And 'kush' and 'punt' of the Egyptian, and Arabian 'land of the blacks.'"

—W.E.B. Du Bois

IN THE EARLY 1930s, MUSSOLINI, with a million-armed man and an impressive but bloated air force, pompously strode onto the world stage. He had dreams of building an empire and one of the lands he coveted was the ancient nation of Ethiopia, the only independent kingdom of the colored race left on the continent of Africa. This piqued my interest and concern because it was just after my experience with Chief Nxumalo and Swaziland.

Prior to Mussolini, many attempts were made by great European powers to divide Ethiopia, but the country had survived because of its fierce army, its climate, and its deserts and mountains.

Secret Agreement

Over time, agreements between England, Italy, and France concerning spheres of influence and partitioning of Ethiopia were kept secret. These secret agreements were part of a great conspiracy, allowing these European nations to conquer and dominate the nations of Africa.

In a series of documents dated March 24 and April 15, 1891, as well as May 5, 1894, England agreed to recognize Italy's sphere of influence on a vast section of Ethiopia lying north and east of the Juda River, east of the 35th Meridian and east of Greenwich, except for the French territory around Djibouti and the English possession of Somaliland. Italy, in return, recognized England's claim to the west and south of this line, which ran east of the Nile River.

It appeared that England was making secret agreements with both France and Italy, agreements that gave both countries a sphere of influence on the same territory. The vast Harrar section of the eastern highlands of Ethiopia is one example where both France and Italy had agreements with England unknown to each, but understood by England. It became necessary for England to keep the agreement with Italy secret from France until May 5, 1894.

Meanwhile, there was a treaty of 1889 between Italy and King Menelik II, then king of Ethiopia; whereby, Italy claimed a full protectorate over Ethiopia. And there were agreements with England in both 1891 and 1894, where England recognized Italy's protectorate claim.

But there was a problem: the two copies of the Italian-Ethiopian treaty given to each country's representative, differed in text. The Italian copy made Ethiopia an Italian protectorate; the Amharic or Ethiopian copy left Ethiopia an independent state.

King Menelik II finally denounced the treaty and declared to the great powers of Europe that Ethiopia had no need of protection, stating, "She stretches forth her hands unto God."

The Italians attempted to invade and conquer Ethiopia but were soundly defeated by the forces of King Menelik II at the town of Adowa in 1894.

In 1934, when Mussolini began preparing for an invasion of Ethiopia, he was pursuing an old Italian dream—that for fifty years, Italy had been scheming to subjugate Ethiopia and take the rich resources from the mountains and valleys belonging to their people and country.

The pretext for the invasion of Ethiopia was the dispute over the town of Welwel, two hundred miles from the coast of the Red Sea, well within the Ethiopia's eastern territory (by area agreed or treaty with the English in 1897 and with the Italians in 1908).

Italian troops had occupied the town illegally for five years, and between December 14, 1934 and September 4, 1935, in preparation for the invasion of Ethiopia, Mussolini transported more soldiers and armament into the vicinity of Welwel—the troop count soaring to 300,000 men, and this did not include Air Force or Tank Corps. If troops mobilized but still in Italy were added to the above, Mussolini would have had a million men prepared to fight.

In an honest attempt to stop the impending conflict, Haile Selassie, then known as Ras Tafari, appealed to the League of Nations of which Ethiopia and Italy were members. Their avowed purpose was to guarantee the sovereignty of smaller nations in the face of invasion by larger powers. Articles one and two of the Covenant of League of Nations read:

1. Any war or threat of war, whether immediately affecting any member of the League or not, is hereby declared a matter of concern to the whole League, and the League shall take any action that may be deemed wise and effectual to safeguard the peace of the nations. In case any such emergency should arise, the Secretary-general shall, on request of any member of the League, forthwith summon a meeting of the Council.

2. It is declared to be the friendly right of each member of the League to bring to the attention of the Assembly or of the Council any circumstance whatever affecting international peace or the relations which threatens to disturb international peace or the good understanding between nations upon which peace depends.

On July 4, 1935, the anniversary of America's independence, Ethiopia presented an appeal to President Roosevelt, asking that he intervene to prevent an impending unprovoked invasion of its land by Italy. Along with the great European powers, America had been instrumental in the creation of the Kellogg-Briand Peace Pact of 1928, outlawing war. Both Italy and Ethiopia had also signed that pact. The United States Government, in its reply to Ethiopia, expressed concern for the maintenance of peace, but made no reference to its obligations under the Kellogg-Briand Peace Pact. The next day, July 5, citizens of the United States living in Ethiopia, about 125 in number, were notified to ready themselves to leave the country on short notice.

On September 6, 1935, the League Council decided to appoint a committee of five to make a general examination of the Italo-Ethiopian affair, hoping to find a peaceful settlement. The five-member council was made up of one representative each from Spain, Great Britain, France, Poland, and Turkey.

On September 25, suggestions prepared by the committee were submitted to the League Council. Ethiopia accepted the suggestions as a basis for negotiation, but Italy again refused.

On October 3, 1935, Mussolini invaded Ethiopia, starting the second Italo-Ethiopian War. The League of Nation's program of hesitation and procrastination had given Mussolini time to get his troops into Ethiopia, and with the use of poison gas, which left the poor Ethiopian soldiers writhing in pain and agony, he was able to bring them under subjugation before sanctions could have sufficient crippling effect to prevent his diabolical attempt to crucify a small nation that stood out for truth and justice, and, which followed to the letter, plans for its members to settle disputes, as laid out by the Covenants of the League of Nations.

The League was dominated for the most part by Pierre H. Laval, French Minister of Foreign Affairs. He was acting in part as spokesman for various fascist groups in France, and as a quasi "diplomatic" ally of Italy by siding with Mussolini, hoping to keep him on France's side, in case Germany decided to invade Austria. This developed into a sort of three-card Monty between France, Britain, and Italy, at the expense of Ethiopia. Laval and British Foreign Minister Samuel Hoare, secretly developed the Hoare-Laval Pact, that gave Mussolini Ethiopia. This diverted the League from the "plans" made in Geneva on that historic night in 1920 to a "program of deception" that forever discredited the League. When the Hoare-Laval Pact became public, it led to the final dissolution of the League.

The *Chicago Daily Times* published the following editorial:

A girl in Africa has sent a challenge to civilization which women will understand better than men. The girl is the daughter of Emperor Haile Selassie of Ethiopia. In the name of her people and humanity, she sent a telegram which was read before the British House of Lords. The telegram described the horrific sufferings upon the Ethiopians by poison gas.

The girl's protest reached London along with reports of the bombing of the city of Harrar, second largest city in Ethiopia, with a population of 40,000. It is an unfortified city a thousand years old. Last December, Ethiopia announced that Harrar had been demilitarized into a hospital center.

...Whether the victor be Italy or Ethiopia, the effect would be harmful beyond exaggeration to the League and all that the League stands for. The attempt that we have made in the post-war world to substitute peaceful settlement for the arbitration of the sword would have been frustrated. The small weak countries of the world would see the protection upon which they have been depending gravely endangered. The pacts that have been laboriously concluded for the greater security of Europe would be little more than scraps of paper...

Outside Europe, the reactions, though they may not be so immediate, will be no less deplorable. For a generation, we in Great Britain, and our friends in France have been engaged in a wise and generous policy of eliminating issues between the white and colored races. We do not believe in the inevitability of these color clashes. We have worked, not to dig a gulf but to build a bridge between Europe and Africa, and between Europe and Asia... A war that claimed to be a war between the white and black races would throw intolerable obstacles in this path of reconciliation and mutual understanding.

205

If the Italian people have complaints to make against the Ethiopian Government, let them make those complaints in the proper and regular manner. They will find the League ready to give full and impartial consideration to the case which they put before it. But these are issues that can be settled without recourse to war. Above all, they are issues that can be settled without a war which would inevitably lead to confusion in Europe, to the serious weakening, and perhaps destruction of the forces of peace and to the formidable unsettlement of the great colored races of the world.

The brutal war continued until Emperor Haile Selassie I was driven from his throne. He established a provisional government at Gore and fled to Jerusalem with his family. He stayed in Jerusalem a brief time and used it as a place of prayer. He then proceeded to Geneva, where he appeared before the League of Nations. His speech was a masterpiece, an historical record of the first magnitude. His majesty spoke in closing:

"…At the beginning, toward the end of 1934, Italian aircraft hurled bombs and tear gas upon my armies. Their effects were slight. The soldiers learned to scatter, waiting until the wind had slowly dispersed the poisonous gases. Italian aircraft then resorted to mustard gas. Barrels of the liquid were hurled upon armed groups. But this means also was not effective. The liquid effected only a few soldiers, and the barrels upon the ground were themselves a warning to the troops and the population, of danger.

"It was when the operations for the encirclement of Makale were taking place that the Italian command, fearing a rout, followed the procedure which it is now my duty to denounce to the world. Special sprayers were installed on board aircraft, so they could vaporize over vast areas of territory, a fine death-dealing rain.

"Planes rained destruction. Groups of nine, fifteen, or eighteen followed one another, so that the fog issuing from them formed a continuous sheet. It was thus that as from the end of January 1935, soldiers, women, children, cattle, rivers, lakes and every living thing were drenched continually with deadly rain.

"It was to inform the civilized world of the tortures inflicted upon the Ethiopian people that I resolved to come to Geneva. None other than myself and my brave companions in arms could bring to the League of Nations the undeniable proofs.

"The appeals of my delegates, addressed to the League of Nations remained without answer. My delegates had not been witnesses. That is why I decided myself to come and bear witness against the crime perpetuated against my people, and to give Europe warning of the doom that awaits it, if it should bow before the accomplished fact."

The Emperor went on to give in detail the repeated appeals he had made to the League. "I did not hesitate to declare that I did not wish for the war, that It was imposed upon me and that I should struggle solely for the independence and integrity of my people, and that in that struggle, I was the defender of the cause of all small states exposed to the greed of a powerful neighbor."

"In October 1935, the fifty-two nations who are listening to me today, gave me assurance that the aggressor would not triumph, that the resources of the Covenant would be employed to insure the reign of the right and the failure of violence."

"I ask those fifty-two nations not to forget today the policy upon which they embarked eight months ago, and on the faith of which I directed the resistance of my people against the aggressor whom they had denounced to the world."

"In that unusual struggle between government commanding more than forty-two million inhabitants, and having at its disposal financial, industrial and technical means which enabled it to create unlimited quantities of the most death-dealing weapons; and on the other hand a small people of twelve million inhabitants, without arms, without resources, and having on its side, only the justice of its cause and the promise of the League of Nations…

"Has each of the state members, as it was its duty to do in virtue of its signature appended to Article XVI of the Covenant, considered the aggressor as having committed an act of war, personally directed against itself? I had placed all my hopes in the execution of these undertakings. My confidence had been confirmed by repeated declarations made in the Council to the effect that aggression must not be rewarded and that force would end by being compelled to bow before right.

"In December 1935, the Council made it clear that its feelings were in harmony with those of the hundreds of millions of people who in all parts of the world, had protested against the proposal to dismember Ethiopia.…

"I was defending the cause of all small people who are threatened with aggression.

"…I assert that the problem submitted to the assembly today is much wider than merely a question of settlement of Italian aggression; it is collective security; it is the very existence of the League. It is the confidence that each State is to place in international treaties. It is the value of promises to small states that their integrity and independence may be respected and insured. It is the principle of equality of States on the one hand, or otherwise the obligation made upon small powers to accept the bonds of vassal-ship. In a word, it is international morality that is at stake.

"Apart from the Kingdom of the Lord, there is not on this earth any nation that is superior to any other. Should it happen that a strong government finds that it may, with immunity, destroy a small people, then the hour strikes for that weak people to appeal to the League to give its judgement in all freedom. God and history will remember your judgement."

Chapter Fifteen

African Sparks Fly in the Streets of Chicago

"Behold the sphinx in Africa! The bond of silence is upon her."

—Kelley Miller

BACK IN 1935, WHEN WE learned that the League of Nations would do nothing to prevent Italy from waging a war of aggression against the small northeastern African Kingdom of Ethiopia, we banded together through an organization known as the Chicago Society for the Aid of Ethiopia.

We met weekly to discuss the Ethiopian situation, trying to understand why the Kellogg-Briand Peace Pact was not invoked to stop the war. We sent medical and surgical supplies for the Ethiopian wounded. We planned a parade in hopes of drawing public attention to the Ethiopian injustice.

We couldn't get a permit for the parade, so we planned, instead, to meet for a demonstration

Saturday, August 13, 1935

I was arrested in the city of Chicago, at the corner of Forty-Sixth and Prairie Avenue and taken by patrol wagon to the jail at Forty-Eighth and Wabash Avenue. I was placed in a cell, set aside for incarcerating those of us trying to stage a parade.

Seventy-nine women were arrested that Saturday, five were colored and seventy-four white. Many of the white women didn't know why they were arrested. Some had simply been driving through the colored neighborhood, gotten out of their cars and gone into stores to do Saturday afternoon shopping. Some were changing cars at Forty-Seventh and Indiana; a few had never moved from their homes, still living in the neighborhood when the police invasion began.

Many, who knew nothing about the parade, resisted arrest and came into the cell with their heads beaten and bloody. Some had crying children and were trying to comfort them.

Every available space was taken. Some stood, some sat either on the floor or on the few available crude metal seats in the cell. To occupy our time, we sang, "John Brown's Body" and "Study War No More." A guard came to the cell area and threatened to turn a hose on us if we didn't stop the singing. Our songs floated out the windows, gaining attention of passersby, stopping traffic on the street below. One white girl stood on a bench and wrote high on a wall: *Black and white, Unite and Fight.*

After about four hours they began to let us out. I was the first arrested, dressed in my YMCA uniform that I had worn in France during WWI. I was wearing the Ethiopian colors draped over my left arm and a red poppy bought from a street vendor on Memorial Day to aid the disabled veterans.

"Are you a red?" the policeman asked, as he began his interrogation.

"No," I told him.

"What's that you're wearing?" he said, pointing to the red poppy.

I told him its significance and how I had gotten it.

He replied, with exaggerated emphasis, "Well its red, ain't it?"

He soon dismissed me without a booking.

I stood there for a while just listening to the way they addressed the white women. They were very abusive, scolding them for being in the colored neighborhood. Some of those women were helping us with our work, fighting the color line, just as we were. They resented being reprimanded for going where they pleased, whether the neighborhood was white or colored.

Monday, August 15, 1935

I went down to the police station at Eleventh and State to witness our trial. Our crowd was easily identifiable, heads bandaged, some on crutches, some in wheel chairs. One young man had to be lifted to a platform so he could speak.

The police stations in the colored neighborhoods were all full. The Wabash Avenue cell for men was so crowded, they could not sit down, having to stand all night.

We tried for two weeks to get Mayor Edward Kelly to give us a permit to parade in protest of Italy's War of Aggression in Ethiopia. This was the final day for permit approval and we sent a committee for the third time to try and get the permit. This committee was headed by a professor from the University of Chicago. Waiting at our assigned posts to get word, we were sure the permit would be approved. Instead of sending out the permit, they sent the police. Some estimated their numbers at seven-hundred and fifty. One woman, seeing such police mass, thought they were out to attend a funeral for one of their own. This mystified us. We thought perhaps it was because of the goodwill visit made by General Balboa in Summer 1933, with his fleet of airplanes flying in for the Century of Progress World's Fair. The city fathers made a great deal of this visit, naming a street, Balboa Street, just off Michigan Avenue.

We couldn't help but wonder if this authoritarian response, the mistreatment of those of color, all occurred because the Ethiopians belonged to the host of dark races of the world.

Ethiopia was one of the signatories of the Kellogg-Briand Peace Pact, which outlawed war, making it a crime. The United States was also a signatory of the Pact, and we felt that our government had an obligation to take interest, especially since the Pact was initiated by Mr. Kellogg, our Secretary of State.

The morning after our arrest, the *Chicago Daily News* carried the following article:

Three hundred persons, among them many white girls of school age, were arrested yesterday when they defied a police edict and attempted to parade on the south side in protest of the war on Ethiopia.

Lt. Make Mills, of the police industrial squad, said the demonstration was engineered by Communists and that many the girls seized said they attended of the University of Chicago or had just graduated from High School.

Police Use Clubs

Heads were thumped with night sticks and would-be demonstrators were carried screaming and fighting to patrol wagons as 750 police broke up the affair.

Center of the disturbance was at 47th Street and Prairie Avenue.

Most of the agitators carried inflammatory literature and banners with such signs as: Hands OFF Ethiopia, We want 500,000 Signers to Protest War and Force Congress to Act.

Cells at Wabash Avenue Police Station were jammed with 178 men and 79 women. The women attempted to sing the "Communistic Internationale," but desisted when told that the fire hose would be turned on them.

Thomas B. McKenna, Chicago Secretary for the League Against War and Fascism, was booked on charges of disorderly conduct and unlawful assembly, and freed on $25.00 bond.

His bond was put up by two attorneys from the Civil Liberties Union. Paul Darrow, son of Clarence Darrow, who appeared with them explained he was merely an observer but added his father had declined to appear in the case.

Hold 15 for Trial

Police announced all the prisoners would be released except about fifteen ring leaders, who would face charges similar to those McKenna.

The parade had been refused a permit three times by Police Commissioner, James P. Allman. Endorsers of the protest were announced on handbills as Professor Robert Morse Lovett of the University of Chicago, Dr. Arthur E. Holt of the Chicago Theological Seminary, and others.

Clarence Darrow said, in reply to the newspaper statement, "The Police Commissioner ought to know enough about the rights of American citizens to know that any group of them has the right to protest against the acts of a foreign nation."

Following is an excerpt from a letter sent out by the Corporation Council of the city of Chicago, giving reasons why they refused to grant a permit for the parade:

August 21,1935

In re: Permit for "Hands OFF Ethiopia" Parade.

…If the city of Chicago should grant a permit to use our streets for these avowed purposes, probably emphasized and aggravated by slogans on banners and placards, it might be deemed by Italy, with whom our nation is at peace, and our Italian citizens, as a hostile or unfriendly act and unjustifiable interference in or criticism of their affairs, and there is a danger that such a parade might precipitate a breach of the peace through racial feelings."

No doubt it was for these reasons that the Chicago Park District has refused to grant a permit to these people for a parade and open-air meeting in Washington Park….

"Therefore, under the provisions of Section 979, of the Chicago Code above quoted, and after investigation of all facts and circumstances and especially those appearing in the application and written correspondence, the granting or refusing of this permit is a matter which lies in your discretion.

Approved: Barnet Hodes, Corporation Council, Quinn O'Brien, Ass't"

Back on July 15, while we were agitating, and looking forward to a mammoth parade, New York had held a parade of five thousand. Following is a clipping from one of the New York newspapers:

One of the most effective parades ever staged in Harlem was that on Monday evening when over five thousand persons marched in silent protest against the League of Nations recognition of Mussolini's conquest of Ethiopia. Silently the long line of colored

213

patriots, waving flags as they went, trod along Harlem's highways in a procession
stretching as far as the eye could reach. Later in the evening a protest meeting gathered
a large sum of money to send to the League in session, cablegrams to urge the League
to disregard Mussolini's claims to Ethiopia.

Despite the resistance by the City of Chicago, The Chicago Society for the Aid of Ethiopia continued sending cablegrams to the League of Nations. It also sponsored mass meetings, collecting donations for food and medical supplies to send to the people of Ethiopia. People, who were being sprayed with poisonous gas that ate the flesh off their bodies, poisoned their water, and killed Ethiopian patriots and the livestock they depended on for subsistence.

The League of Nations Bias
January 1936
In the latter part of January 1936, Lij Tesfaye Zaphiro, the private secretary to the Ethiopian Minister of London, arrived at the LaSalle Street Station in Chicago, to represent the Ethiopian Government. He was met by a committee from the Chicago Society for the Aid of Ethiopia, and hoped to get assistance for his suffering people.

It was twenty below zero, the coldest weather the young diplomat had ever experienced. He was rushed without delay to the Congress Hotel, where even though he had reservations, was told they had no room for him. He was then taken to the Stevens Hotel, where he was met with the same rebuff.

The reservations at the Congress Hotel had been made by a local physician; however, the hotel authorities claimed no knowledge of such.

Mr. Zaphiro was First Secretary to the Imperial Legation, London, England, and was the master of several languages. He was a pleasing orator and gave some of the early history of his country.

Following, are some excerpts from his speech:

"Ethiopia has tried throughout the years to develop her country, and to make it a land which is worthy to be called an important one in the world; but she has continually met with various ones who do not desire her independence; but with God's help and duty to our policy she has stood free.

"...You, to understand the situation, must know something of the early history of Ethiopia.

"In 525 B.C., the Emperor of Ethiopia ruled over the land which combines the Sudan, parts of Asia, including Arabia and Italian, British and French Somalilands.

"In 700 A.D., we were attacked by Mohammedians, and they took much of our Arabian territory, and we were driven back to a smaller land space. For 1000 years, until the eighteenth century, we have been fighting continually....

"In the early nineteenth century, Italy tried to purchase a part of the land. The Italian Government took land from the trading company, gradually encroaching inland until they had obtained more and more land.

"Time, the magazine, chooses once a year a man whom they think has done the most constructive or outstanding thing. Even though Emperor Haile Selassie was a "Barbarian," last year he was chosen the greatest man of the year. You should be proud that a colored man heads the list.

"There is one question that lingers in the minds of the world's dark people: was it the Empire of Ethiopia that caused the disintegration of the league of Nations, or was it the color of the inhabitants of that little Nation?

"But meanwhile, three facts are salient. First, the British are so aware of the German threat that they consider that the League is almost working under the threat of war now and therefore will try to get the Germans to a new Locarno conference whether the Germans answer the British questionnaire or not. Second, the League council and the Poles, to whom the council has entrusted the matter, do not like doing anything serious if the Nazis jump Danzig. Third, the Italians do not really need to leave the League, since it has been proved to the hilt that they can remain in Geneva and get away with murder.

Chapter Sixteen

Volunteer Social Service Work in Chicago

"And may the evening twilight find me gentle still."

—Max Ehrmann

I RETURNED TO CHICAGO PERMANENTLY in 1933 and continued pushing my Two-Foot Shelf in the colored community, talking to audiences at every opportunity. Mme. Carter turned her home into a home for working women. She saw the financial injustice experienced by colored women, whose maximum weekly wage was about five dollars, not enough to pay for room rent, let alone clothing and food. Fortunately, those that worked as domestics, the only jobs available for colored women, generally got food where they worked.

In May 1934, Mme. Carter died before she could get the home developed and occupied. In her will, she named me as one of four beneficiaries; but there was an error in the document and the property was sold before a good deed could be made.

I rented the home for a while, trying to continue the social work envisioned by Mme. Carter. Finally, after a few years, I bought it. The Great Depression continued, but I tried to help young male students for several summers. I allowed them to stay on the first floor and in the basement.

These young men came up in the Spring from southern black colleges, Fisk, Talladega, Morehouse, Tuskegee, and Tugaloo, because after their winter semesters they had no money, and had to find work during the summer if they wanted to return to their schools.

In the 1930s, the Wabash YMCA was charging $3.60 per week for a room, a small amount, but those boys didn't have it. One young man named Williams was sent by a young medical student I had met a year earlier. I had a small room on the first floor and told Williams he could have the room for $1.75 a week. He was delighted, but said, "I haven't any money." I told him I could wait for the money.

The next day he went out, met a student that owed him a quarter and said, "Look here, fellow, got any money?" The other boy said, "I got two cents." Williams said, "Give it to me."

Williams went downtown and found a job at the Auditorium Hotel, making $5.00 a day. Then the following day, he came to give me his rent money.

Five students came up from Tugaloo College in Mississippi. I put them in a large basement room. They were young, thin, small and could sleep two to a bed, one at the head, the other at the foot. The fifth boy came in later and begged me to let him stay with his friends. I had run out of beds, but had an old army cot in disrepair. He fixed it, slept on it, and I charged him a dollar a week.

One day, I went down with my receipt book to collect the rents. When I came to the "army cot" boy, I saw pain flash across his face. He took out his knotted handkerchief, untied the knot and found a dollar in change. He gave that to me, saying that was all he had. I went upstairs, sat down, and thought about these boys, so limited in their opportunities and generally unable to find work; only certain jobs available to them because of their color. I sent for the "army cot" boy, asked him to clean the stairway, gave him something to eat, gave his dollar back to him and credited him his rent for the job.

After a month, they began leaving for Detroit. They had tried to get on as red-caps at the bus station, but unable, they found work on a boat at the Detroit pier. One of the five young Tugaloo students came to see me after their return from Detroit and told me about their collective struggle to live, all five of them.

The Schultze Bakery, at Fifty-Fifth and Wabash Avenue, sold bags of day old bread, cookies, and doughnuts for ten cents. Three of the boys would get up early in the morning so they would be first in line and assured a bag of bread. They'd get there by five o'clock, pool their money, buy some sausage and cook on the stove in their little apartment.

In the laundry room, they'd be naked to the waist, washing their shirts to hang on the clothesline. One young man named Porter James had a wife and son. His family was still in the South; he'd left them, trying to save money to go to the University of Chicago. He had been a teacher at the State Normal School in Alabama.

Porter asked if he could build a flat in the basement in exchange for his rent. We planned it and bought the lumber. He'd found a job as a red cap on the Chicago to Denver route, and after his route, he would work on the flat. This was the most profitable decision I'd ever made.

When Mr. James paid his tuition at the University of Chicago, he had a roll of five hundred-dollar bills from tips received on the train. When he counted out his tuition, all eyes were on him. He was the curiosity; the white boys paid with checks.

I have had many experiences with women who have come here through the years. Once I opened the door of the stairway to turn off the light and there at the foot of the stairs lay a human form—a woman. She told me she had just gotten out of the hospital, and the people she had been staying with would not take her back. She had tried the Y.W.C.A. and several other homes without success, so she slipped into the hallway behind a girl entering my building. Afraid that I would also turn her away, she lay down on the floor at the bottom of the stairway and covered herself with her coat.

I asked her to get up and come to me. Then I said, "Blow your breath in my face."

She said, "Oh, I don't drink."

I took her in for two to three days. She said she had work but had to wait two weeks before her first payday.

Another woman came to my building and asked if I'd let her stay. I asked if she had any money. She was well dressed and made a nice impression. I took her in, and gave her something to eat as she told me her story. Her husband had gambled their money away, and said he'd return when he'd earned it back. That was seven years ago. She stayed with me until we got money for a trip back to New York. The Jewish charities assisted with that. Upon her return home, she mailed me five dollars.

A radio artist found her way to my building. She was illiterate and had very little education but was a natural dramatic artist. I recognized her talents and potential, so I taught her how to read the daily papers and some easy books. She would then tell me in her own words what she had read and I would type the script for her radio show.

A promoter heard her broadcast and called the radio station. He offered her a hundred and thirty-five dollars a week as a secretary. He set a time for an appointment to meet face to face, but when he saw her brown face, he wouldn't even talk with her. She came home and cried for hours.

While organizing the home for women, I was asked to preside over a newly formed neighborhood club, ultimately named the John R. Lynch Model Community Council. I worked for the club for ten years. Our first project was to get the people in our precinct on the ballot for a local option election. The issue was the number of taverns on the forty-five hundred block of South Indiana Avenue. Another neighborhood club had tried to vote in a "dry block," the 4400 block of Indiana. Mrs. Nannie Jackson Myers had led that charge as the block clubs president.

We began our campaign to get the precincts in our community on the local-option ballot. Petitions had to be signed for each precinct, there was a minimum number of signatures needed, required by law.

The taverns were lawless, impudent cesspools of iniquity. They spewed out their wrecks of humanity between midnight and the early morning hours, screaming, fighting, and killing one another. There were three murders in just one week.

The language these drunken brutes used was vulgar, profane, and disgraceful. Neighbors could not sleep at night. These taverns made property ownership a burden, making, "living in peace," almost impossible.

We proceeded to get the signatures we needed for the petition, but not without objection. One woman was knocked down the stairs and her petitions taken. We had to print more petitions and repeat her work. We succeeded in getting about half a dozen precincts on the local option ballots.

The Anti-Saloon League contacted us, wanting to know if they could help; I went to see them. They wanted to know if I knew Paul Edward Thurlow, minister of the gospel and an attorney at law. They made an appointment for me to talk with him; he promised free legal assistance if needed.

The Tavern Owners' Association stated in their magazine, that they had a battle fund of $10,000.00 to defend their business. At the end of the 1940 election, we had won in most of the precincts, especially the 4500 block of Indiana Avenue.

The tavern owners took us to court. They accused us of duplicating and forging names on the petitions. Of course, none of that was true, but that was there strategy after every local-options election.

Mr. Thurlow came to our rescue. We went to court several times, but the tavern owners were never prepared and always asked for continuances; they wanted to wear us out, but we would not yield.

When the tavern owners, "Folded their tents, like Arabs, and quietly stole away," it renewed the neighborhood.

Our neighborhood club, the John R. Lynch Model Community Council, continued its fight for clean communities. We found that, "people wore the grass off lawns because they didn't want a hiding place for snakes." But some were ignorant of civic duties and, having very little civic pride, felt it was not their business to pick up papers.

Bishop Quinn

When I first came to Chicago to reside in 1924, I joined Quinn Chapel A.M.E. Church at Twenty-Fourth and Wabash Avenue. My interest in that church dated from the time I was told the story of Bishop Quinn.

Bishop Quinn used to ride through Darke County, Ohio on horseback, and always stopped at the home of my great-uncle, James McCown. William Paul Quinn was born in Calcutta, India and was of Hindu parentage. He was banished from his home because he took interest in the Christian teachings of a Quaker missionary woman. He left his home and landed in the United States. He joined the Methodist Episcopal Church in Baltimore, Maryland, but left because of color prejudice. He then joined the African Methodist Episcopal church and was made the first missionary to spread the gospel and build churches. His missionary area was the Middle West. He settled in Richmond, Indiana, a short distance from where I was born and where I first joined the church.

When he rode through Darke County, spending nights at the home of my great-uncle, he was constantly preaching against slavery, and was arrested time and again, detained for, "disturbing the peace." When speaking about the slave owners, he would often say, "May God forgive them; I never will."

Some of the stories told by Bishop Quinn and my Uncle Jimmie McCown, as they sat by the large fireplace on winter nights, have been passed down to me.

He went into St. Louis, Missouri, which was a slave market, and became so well-known for his opposition to slavery, that he was often escorted out of the city. He would conduct well attended anti-slavery meetings on the Missouri side of the Mississippi River, but it was dangerous for him to cross, so he stood on the Illinois side of the river bank, and preached across the waters to the congregation of people on the Missouri side. Eventually, this cross-river preaching born the St. Paul's A.M.E. Church in St. Louis in 1841.

I knew some of this history and gathered more from Dr. L.L. Berry's book, *A Century of Missions in the A.M.E. Church.*

I was a member of the Quinn Chapel A.M.E. Church for several years. It was then on State and Madison in what is now Chicago's Loop, later moving to its present location Twenty-Fourth and Wabash Avenue; it also served as a station for the underground railroad before the Emancipation.

The early bishops of the church were consecrated men who led exemplary lives, but as with many institutions, academic or religious, eventually some men who were dishonest, intemperate, and immoral crept in; one of these men was placed at the head of the Fourth Episcopal District when I was a member of Quinn Chapel.

A classmate of mine, Reverend Harry E. Stewart, paid off Quinn Chapel's long-standing mortgage. He realized that several people were making a living soliciting for the church, the money they made however was never turned in. When this thievery was stopped, the church became debt free.

Shortly after, the bishop started a movement to place a mortgage of $30,000.00 on the building. A committee of women asked me to lead a protest movement against the mortgage. I did; we called ourselves the,

Common Sense Committee, and were joined by some of the male congregation.

It was a known fact that the bishop handled church monies carelessly. We investigated and circulated our findings through printed material in protest to what appeared to be a system of graft.

At one time the, "Chautauqua," was held at Quinn Chapel, and $10,000.00 was collected for Wilberforce University. Only $1,000.00 ever reached the University.

The by-laws of the A.M.E. Church stated that charges against the bishop must be made through the presiding elder. That man was an appointee of the bishop, and he simply pigeon-holed the protest letters and the charges therein.

We wrote letters, sending one to each bishop, broadcasting them to various newspapers in the colored community. We received nationwide publicity.

We went to San Antonio, Texas, where the Bishop's Council was in session, hoping to bring the matter before them. Leaving St. Louis, we entered the Colored-Coach, knowing we'd be forced to when we crossed the Arkansas line, sometime that night. We found Rev. Williams, pastor of Wayman Chapel in Dayton, Ohio sitting there reading. He was sympathetic to our concerns, but told us we would never be allowed to bring the matter before the Bishop's Council; that we should have the charges printed and circulated.

He was right; the bishops would not allow us a hearing, so, we did as he directed and circulated the information, which created quite a sensation. On our return trip, Rev. Williams sat with us in the Colored-Coach, the bishops and ministers occupied the Pullmans they had chartered. He was afraid for our lives and wanted to protect us.

This bishop, the presiding elder, was later appointed to the Chicago Civil Service Commission in Chicago, influential in increasing the numbers of colored police officers, Reverend Archibald J. Carey Sr. died while under indictment for taking money in exchange for police positions, but was never convicted.

The Common Sense Committee grew into a layman's movement to fight corrupt practices in the church. One of the things we disapproved of was the after-conference bylaws changes influenced by ministers and bishops. Laws passed during the conference would be changed or eliminated altogether by the General Conference Secretary at the request of either a bishop or minister, this occurred after the fact and unbeknownst to the general conference.

Bishops get $8,000.00 a year plus expenses. They hold six or eight conferences a year, each lasting a week; the rest of their time is given to general supervision. Many preach every Sunday, and request the minister to ask the congregation to give a hundred dollars or more for the bishop's time. If the minister doesn't abide by the bishop's request, the minister is held responsible, and given less money the next time. This amounted to selling pulpits.

Bishop B.F. Lee, one-time president of Wilberforce University, would tell the congregation publicly, that he was paid and didn't want their money.

One summer while in New York, I was witness to a great uproar over money for a church mortgage. The congregation had collected $17,000.00 to pay off the church's mortgage. A General Conference was held in Detroit; their pastor was elected bishop. When the new minster came, the mortgage had not been paid and the money was gone. The entire congregation left this church, worshipped in a Seventh Day Adventist church, raised more money and bought another church, leaving the previous denomination completely.

I think the ministry has become enticing to colored men, who are so limited in their opportunities, have the gift of "expression," and become preachers, and because the congregations are so eager to spread Christianity, they will give the ministers their hard-earned money with no accountability. Under these circumstances, their money has been misused and wasted many times.

During my time at Wilberforce, the university was $100,000.00 or more in debt. Every year the ministers would come to the conference, and the bishop would solicit money. Women, who had washed and ironed to earn their money, would give it up willingly; yet, the debt never diminished.

When Charles Wesley, D.D. was elected president of Wilberforce, he put on a nationwide drive and the debt was paid off. The following commencement, the presiding bishop of the Trustee Board had him dismissed without cause.

A brief time later, Wilberforce put a $30,000.00 mortgage on the property, reasoning that they could not fundraise if it were known the school was not in debt. This was just a delusion and a snare.

The church is a spiritual organization and should not be used as a machine to get money. Money is necessary, but not at the expense of fraudulent activity.

The crux of the Christian church is contained in, "Ye must be born again." Nicodemus went to the Savior by night to learn what this statement meant. The Savior's answer was: "The wind bloweth where it listeth, and thou hearest the sound thereof, but canst not tell whence it cometh, and whither it goeth: so is every one that is born of the Spirit." (John 3:8, KJV). Many people who have not had this experience do not understand it. It is not expected to be understood; it is a psychic phenomenon.

I once attended a meeting in Paris composed of women from all over the world, trying to gain an understanding of why parents, wives, and relatives of soldiers received psychic messages when the soldier died. Parents would be awakened from sleep, suddenly knowing their son was killed. They saw him as he fell by the side of a great rock, or into a shell hole. The cry of agony would go up, "John is dead. I saw him fall!" A few hours later a cablegram would bring the confirmation.

Richard Singleton

My grand-nephew, Richard Singleton, was in the Second World War, the son of Mr. and Mrs. Walter Singleton of Kansas City, Kansas. He was blown out of his ship in the South Pacific. His mother knew immediately, and went upstairs. The children asked, "What's the matter, Mama?" She said, "Something has happened to Richard." They were inclined to doubt her statement, but she insisted. She could not eat; she could only pray. For twenty-three hours Richard was in the water. He swam to a rubber raft where there were three other men, one of whom was white. It was only big enough for two, so two hung on the outside and two stayed inside, and then they'd change places. Finally, after twenty-three hours a plane flew overhead, and they were rescued.

Richard was so exhausted that he went to sleep and didn't wake until he was in the hospital in Guam. When this happened, his mother got up and said, "Richard is all right now."

When Richard returned, he had a wiener roast, and invited his friends to the home. They talked about their social lives, school, and family. The color question came up and the boys talked about discrimination. After a while, they talked about how they hated white people. It was a general agonizing cry: "I hate white people."

In desperation Richard cried out, "Oh, don't say that! It was a white boy who saved my life!" Tears rolling down his cheeks.

The spiritual side of life is the foundation of the Christian church. Christ was a spirit. After his crucifixion, he was on the earth for forty days with his disciples, and without being seen.

In this crucial time, "It must be of the Spirit, if we are to save the flesh."

Dr. Andrew Gour

Still trying to understand and offset the silence of textbooks on the achievements of colored people, I traveled through the Great West, Des Moines, Omaha, Denver, and then fifteen hundred miles to Portland, Oregon, Tacoma, Washington, Seattle, Vancouver, British Columbia, Berkley, Oakland, San Francisco, Los Angeles and down to Tia Juana, Mexico. Everywhere I went, I spoke to groups and congregations, giving ten-minute talks as my health would permit.

I was aging and feeling ill, when a most unusual thing occurred. A woman named Mrs. Loretta King came to visit and was very interested in my story. She had been a teacher in the Chicago schools. She had an aunt who belonged to a prayer band on the city's west side. I gave her two dollars and asked her to put my name on the prayer list.

Four weeks later, Miss Sarah Sabolsky, the head of the Victory Business School on South Parkway, telephoned me, wanting to know why I hadn't been around. I told her I lacked the strength, and was hardly able to climb to the second floor.

She replied, "You go to Dr. Andrew Gour in the Kimball Building. He will help you."

I made an appointment. He is an osteopathic physician and a pioneer in natural healing. He placed me on the table and began manipulating the bones of my spinal column. I had driven through the country for ten years. And, many times, while in these rural country areas, far from help, I had flat tires, making it necessary for me to take care of that very difficult task. The vertebrae of my spine had slipped and were affecting my nerves, causing chronic pain and fatigue in my upper back. Under his manipulations, the fatigue resolved. I had a cough, which was chronic and un relenting, too. Within a month the cough disappeared, and I haven't had a cold in over two years.

I have since been strong enough to attend the State Convention of the National Association for the Advancement of Colored People, which met in Springfield, Illinois. I had the privilege and honor to lay a wreath on Lincoln's tomb. The following is my address at that event:

Abraham Lincoln, We Honor You Today

In the name of the State Convention of the National Association for the Advancement of Colored People, we honor you today. Not because you were one of the greatest presidents we ever had, if not the greatest; not because you were one of the most honest men; you were so honest they called you, "Honest Abe." But we honor you today because you were the great "Emancipator of Slaves."

Much mischievous propaganda has been abroad to the effect that you were not interested in freeing the slaves, but only in saving the union. This came about because of what you said in your letter to Horace Greeley. You said in substance on that occasion:

"My main purpose is to save the Union; If I can save it by freeing all the slaves, I'll free all the slaves; if I can save it by freeing half the slaves, I'll free half the slaves; If I can save it by freeing none of the slaves, I'll free none of the slaves."

This mischievous propaganda ends with these words, and leaves out the statement which follows immediately:

"But I would not have you forget my oft expressed desire that all men everywhere might be free."

Mr. Lincoln, you were right in saying that your main purpose was to save the union; had you freed the slaves without saving the union, they would have been immediately re-enslaved.

In a great speech delivered in this very city of Springfield, Illinois, you showed your attitude on the question of slavery. It has come to be known as the "House Divided Speech." In this address, you made the statement that, "A house divided against itself cannot stand; this country cannot exist half slave and half free; it must either be all slave or all free."

Your friends came to you the night before you delivered that address and said, "Mr. Lincoln, if you deliver that speech on the morrow, and include that statement, you will not be elected United States Senator." You replied, "I would rather deliver that speech and include the statement, and not be elected senator, than to leave it out and be elected senator."

On the next day, you went forth and delivered the speech, and included the great house divided statement; you were defeated for United States Senator, but four years later you were elected President of the United States.

The Civil War came. You were elected president a second time, and in your inaugural address you made the statement:

"Fondly we hope, fervently do we pray, that this dread scourge of war shall speedily pass away; but if it should continue until every drop of blood drawn by the lash shall be paid for by one drawn by the sword, then must we say with the psalmist that the judgements of the Lord are true and righteous altogether."

The Civil War gave you a chance to issue the Emancipation Proclamation. You could not have done this as president of the United States; you had no constitutional right to do so; but you had the right as commander in chief of the armies.

With this instrument, you "struck the shackles from four million bodies, and the fetters from four million souls."

The Proclamation was written on the twenty-second day of September 1862, and issued on the first of January 1863. A great crowd had gathered in Faneuil Hall in Boston. This city had at one time allowed slavery. Crispus Attucks, the man who shed the first blood of the Revolutionary War, ran away from Massachusetts slavery in 1750; he went to sea and stayed away from his native land; but returned in time to be the first martyr of the War of 1776.

Phyllis Wheatley was purchased from a ship that brought slaves from Africa, and anchored in Boston harbor.

But slavery was abolished in Massachusetts in 1780.

Boston afterwards became the center of the abolition movement; thousands of colored people lived there, whose friends and relatives were in the bondage of the mouth.

The great crowd that had gathered in Faneuil Hall, in Boston, to hear the Emancipation Proclamation held its breath, as the great document's wording began to come over the wires. It was midnight. The last momentous words were as follows:

230

"And upon this act, sincerely believed to be an act of justice, warranted by the Constitution upon military necessity, I invoke the considerate judgement of mankind, and the gracious favor of Almighty God."

When the name of Abraham Lincoln was called as the signor, the audience jumped to its feet with a mighty shout.

It was the happiest hour in history. William Lloyd Garrison must have been happy, because he had been dragged thru the streets of Boston at the hands of a mob, because he had fought slavery. Wendell Phillips must have been happy, because he had reached the heights of oratory in his defense of the slave. Charles Sumner must have been happy, because he had been beaten over the head with a gutta-percha cane, because of a speech he made in the United States Senate on behalf of the slave.

But the happiest people were those who had escaped from slavery and those whose friends and relatives were being liberated by the great document. Frederick Douglass was known as a graduate of the institution of slavery, with his diploma written on his back; he was at the meeting; perhaps he led the rejoicing crowd.

They shouted all over the streets of Boston, from midnight until the break of day. "Free at last, Free at last," until the heavens reverberated with the great jubilee. It must have been like the time when the morning stars sang together, and the sons of God shouted for joy. They shouted and sang, and wept; it was the greatest exhibition of human emotion ever expressed in the history of mankind.

And yet the great proclamation that brought about this ringing of joy bells almost to the ends of the earth, has no place in the tomb. Neither is it included in the history text books of the United States.

In the name of the Illinois State Convention of the National Association for the Advancement of Colored People, I call upon the citizens of the State of Illinois to have the Emancipation Proclamation placed in the tomb; and I call upon the Publishers and Educators of the United States to have it placed in the history text books.

Abraham Lincoln, we honor you today,
EMACIPATOR OF THE SLAVES and MARTYR TO THE CAUSE OF FREEDOM.

231

Delivered by: Kathryn Magnolia Johnson for Negro History Week, 1953.

Epilogue

"But what of black women? ...I most sincerely doubt if any other race of women could have brought its fineness up through so devilish a fire."

—W. E. B. Du Bois

Kathryn Magnolia Johnson died on November 13, 1954. In her last will and testament dated September 1953, Kathryn spoke of her service as one of two colored women that served in WWI France, about her travels, her work with the NAACP, and the Ezella Mathis Student Girl's Center. She mentioned the many scrapbooks, pictures, and diaries she'd created chronicling her life's work—Kathryn wanted those materials distributed to her grandnieces and nephews that would appreciate them most. In the final disposition, most of her collection went to her nephew, Dr. Roscoe Singleton.

Kathryn's cape, cap, and uniform worn during her service in France were given to my father, Kuroki Bertram Gonzalzles, her great nephew, and grandson of Nancy Johnson, one of Kathryn's older sisters. As the family historian, much of the collection was given to him by his Uncle Roscoe. Over a twenty-year period, he organized Kathryn's many documents, articles, and pictures into several binders.

Kathryn's books were donated to the George Cleveland Hall Library, including the three volumes on "Africa and the Discovery of America" by Leo Wiener.

Kathryn was survived by her last remaining sibling, William H. Johnson, as well as a host of nephews, nieces, and cousins. The funeral services were held at 4136 S. Michigan Avenue, Chicago, but she was interned at Oak Ridge Cemetery in Springfield, Illinois.

Kathryn had no children of her own, having never married; however, she did have a love interest, Mr. Milton Josiah Smith. He is listed in the 1910 North Dakota census as a lodger with Sarah and John Smith. Kathryn visited Grand Forks, ND in 1909. She doesn't mention Milton in her diaries, but letters from M.J. Smith to Kathryn are part of the collection.

In a letter dated September 8, 1909, M.J. writes: "*Dear, I miss you so much. It is very lonesome here without you, especially as I wish for you in the evening at the time, just at 11:00 p.m., when you used to give me one of the sweetest kisses on earth.*

"*Dear, I just can't forget it, neither do I wish to, but I cherish the memory, which inspires the hope for a more perfect happiness in the future. I think of you very often, my dear, and sometimes I wonder if you are really true and will remain faithful to me.*"

The letters start in 1902 when Milton lived at 453 East 35th Street in Chicago. In that first letter, he states: "*Association, my Dear, is a great thing. I mean between the sexes. Had we not been associated as we were, we never would have loved, or I never would have loved you. But to know you, means to love you. You are so sweet, lovable, and gentle and, at the same time, you seem to have a right conception of life.*

"*I must close now, Dear. You need not answer until you hear from me again; for I will leave the city shortly for Iowa. So be sweet and just imagine that you are giving me one of those sweet kisses.*"

Milton couldn't afford to go to college in Chicago where the tuition per semester was $200.00, so he moved to Iowa, where it was more affordable.

The long-range relationship seemed to fizzle by 1917. This letter is dated April 8, 1917: "*My Dear Kathryn—Yours rec'd and found me getting along not so well. I've been here in St. Paul for the last two months and did not write you because I felt it best for your interest as well as my own that we cease correspondence.*"

In follow-up letters from Milton in June and December, it appears that Kathryn was not willing to give up so easily. In the last letter dated December 28, 1917, from Minneapolis, MN, Milton writes:

"You ask in the letter you wrote in Sept., if I didn't want you to come out and spend a week or two with me. I don't think it is a good plan nor a wise one for you to come out here to see me like that. You see I am not in bed sick. In fact, no one knows that I am not well if I don't tell them, and for you to come would make them think that we were not just right and then there would be those who would talk. Then, besides, I would not like to trust myself with you. Although I have the best wishes for you and your welfare, I think it best for you to stay away. We may meet someday and enjoy each other's companionship, for a little anyway.

Oh, by the way, I asked you to send me my ring in the letter I wrote you. I shall expect it when you write me."

The letters to Kathryn stopped in 1917. In the later part of 1917, Kathryn received three letters from Milton's brother, Dr. C. A. Smith, a physician living in Argenta, Arkansas. It supports the contention that Kathryn did not want to end this relationship. On October 1, he states:

"You can't imagine how I appreciate your kindness towards him (Milton). You are one in a thousand that would continue to love a man after they find out he is sickly and can't take care of themselves. I only wish that he had married you when he was well. I am sure he never would have been in the condition he is now in, and that you would have made him such a sweet wife."

On October 5, Dr. Smith writes:

"I trust my brother will soon be well as he said he is improving. Don't mention to him that I gave you his information."

In a last letter to Kathryn, dated October 10, 2017, Milton's brother states:

"You asked me what I thought you should do about him. Well, I think as he has asked you to forget him, and he is sick as he is, and perhaps shall be as long as he lives, and as he truly loves you as I believe he does, I think it would be best for you and him both, for you to forget him."

No other written communication transpired between either Milton J. Smith or his brother. Kathryn volunteered to serve in WWI France in the Spring of 1918.

Kathryn was a prolific writer, not only publishing several books, pamphlets, and poems but articles for newspapers and magazines. Her collaborative book with Addie W. Hunton, *Two Colored Women with the American Expeditionary Forces*, was listed in the 1921 New York Times Book Review. She wrote articles praising Jesse Binga, Amanda Smith, and other inspirational and historical figures. Kathryn published a piece on the emancipation, stating: *"It would be a fine thing if all colored people of the country could agree on one particular day, and have a nation-wide celebration on that day each year."*

Today, Emancipation Day is celebrated on April 16, the date Abraham Lincoln signed the "Compensation Emancipation," rewarding the criminal rather than the victim, i.e., the slave owner was compensated in exchange for releasing his slave(s).

When a teacher in New Orleans asked her if Mr. Douglass was white, Kathryn published an article trying to rectify that erroneous belief, followed by a book about Frederick Douglass that was widely distributed.

In 1920, Kathryn published an editorial called "Clean Government" in the *Chicago Tribune*, voicing her concern about Mr. Oscar De Priest, who took the place of alderman Martin B. Madden, who had suddenly died in office. Kathryn knew of De Priest's indictments for graft, accepting kickbacks from gambling houses and taverns that plagued the colored neighborhoods. Kathryn was concerned that this man would further damage the families of her community. She followed up with another editorial entitled "Part of the Fat," exposing the "doorbell pushers" men that were on the city payroll for simply going door to door during election time and telling people how to vote. Kathryn asked the hard question: *"Why do taxpayers have to pay political dead heads for promoting their own selfish graft-filled interest?"*

In the December 15,1927 issue of the *Chicago Tribune*, Kathryn published an article questioning the lack of support for the Fourteenth Amendment. She opens with: *"Representative Tinkham of Massachusetts has a resolution for the enforcement of the Fourteenth Amendment in states in which suffrage is restricted. The constitution requires that where the right to vote has been abridged congress shall reduce the representation of such states in the house of representatives. It is not enforced. Congress itself has nullified the constitution."*

If Kathryn were alive today, she would have written that same article.

In 1935, Kathryn, along with other members of The Common-Sense Committee, and the Committee on Publicity, wrote an open letter to the Delegates of the General Conference in Chicago asking them to please investigate their candidates: *"If a man is a libertine, drunkard, or thief, do not impose him on the people."* How fitting even in today's political representatives.

Kathryn's writings demonstrate an emerging trend, from social and literacy activism to community and political activism. In 1940, Kathryn ran on the Republican ticket for the first Congressional District of Illinois. On that ticket under the heading, "Representative in Congress, First Congressional District" were: William E. King, Patrick B. Prescott, Kathryn M. Johnson, Benjamin W. Clayton, Richard E. Parker, Carl A. Hansberry, G. Blake, and Oscar De Priest. Kathryn was the only female on a Republican ballot of over 100 candidates for various governmental offices. Kathryn didn't win that election, but she must be considered a trailblazer for women in modern day politics. In 1940, women weren't respected in the in the male-dominated working world, even today nearly 120 years after the Nineteenth Amendment, we still see gender discrimination in all forms.

On June 25, 1941, President Roosevelt signed Executive Order 8802, creating the Fair Employment Practices Committee (FEPC). The order banned racial discrimination in any defense industry receiving federal contracts by declaring *"There shall be no discrimination in the employment of workers in defense industries or government because of race, creed, color, or national origin."* The order also empowered the FEPC to investigate complaints and act against alleged employment discrimination. In 1945, as a member of the Council for a Permanent FEPC, Kathryn along with other members of that committee, met with Congress, supporting fair hiring in federal jobs for African Americans.

Kathryn's activism didn't stop at the borders of the United States. In 1920, Kathryn received a letter from William T Amigen, Superintendent of Missions for the National Baptist Convention, Foreign Missions Board. In that letter, Rev. Amigen asked for her help in raising funds for the families of Liberians that were living in abject poverty. This is his letter, dated March 7,1920: *"The problem here is very large and complicated. Men, women and children in deplorable condition. Naked, barefoot, eating bugs, snakes, and monkeys. No God in their lives. While much has been done here, the work seems hardly begun."*

Kathryn's brother, Dr. Joseph L. Johnson, was the American Minister for Liberia at the time, and wrote Kathryn telling her about the lack of medical care available, even to those Americans stationed in that African country. He wrote his wife asking that she collect and send medicine for a leg wound he had sustained that had subsequently become infected. There were no antibiotics available in Monrovia, Liberia, only soap and water as an external germicidal and, whisky as an "internal antiseptic."

Kathryn launched a fundraiser in New York to collect clothing and medicinals to send to Liberia.

In 1937, during the Spanish Civil War, she collaborated with Paul Robeson, Langston Hughes, Richard Wright, and other prominent African Americans to raise money to help the families of Spain. A flyer sent out to request donations read: *"For a Fully-Equipped Negro Ambulance in Spain. Send this Ambulance Aboard the American relief Ship for Spain, sailing in September. When you help women and children in Spain you help defeat Mussolini and avenge Ethiopia."*

The League of Nations' refusal to act on behalf of the African nation Ethiopia after its invasion by Italy's Mussolini was a cause that Kathryn championed, one which sparked riots in the streets of Chicago.

Kathryn braved the dangers of war, volunteering to serve with the YMCA in WWI France, pushing literacy, she expanded the minds of colored troops, set up libraries, reading courses, arranged cultural excursions and took care of the spirit of the colored soldiers.

When Kathryn returned from France, she, once again, had to face legalized discrimination known as "Jim Crow." Blatant in the South, these laws impacted every part of a civilized society. Every venue of learning for Negros was impacted, especially schools and libraries. Kathryn loaded her Ford Coupe with her "Two Foot Shelf of Negro Literature," comprising fourteen books, and started her journey. This was the collection:

The Negro in Our History
Carter Woodson

The Negro
W.E.B. Du Bois

Negro Poets and Their Poems
Robert T. Kerlin

Two Colored Women with the American Expeditionary Forces
Addie Hunton and Kathryn Johnson

Unsung Heroes
Elizabeth Ross Haynes

The Life of Frederick Douglass
Booker T. Washington

The Souls of Black Folks
W.E.B. Du Bois

The Education of the Negro Prior to 1861
Carter Woodson

The Gift of Black Folk
W.E.B. Du Bois

The History of the Negro Church
Carter G. Woodson

Bronze
Georgia Douglas Johnson

The Heir of Slaves (Bursting Bonds)
William Pickens

The Negro Literature and Art
Brawley

In addition to the above list that encompassed the center of her "Two Foot Shelf..." Kathryn also offered, *Life and Works of Dunbar, Story of My Life and Works* by Booker T. Washington; *Africa and the Discovery of America* by Leo Weiner; *Negro Orators and their Orations* by Carter Woodson; *The New Negro* by Locke; *Color* by Countee Cullen; *Homespun Heroines* by Hallie Q Brown; and *The Negro Mind as Reflected in Letters during the Crisis* by Carter Woodson.

Kathryn also sold children's books; *Charming Stories* by Floyd, *The Upward Path* by Ovington and Pritchard and *Boy's Life of B.T. Washington* by Jackson.

Mary White Ovington, cofounder of the NAACP, wrote an article, entitled "Selling Race Pride for Negroes Up and Down the United States." It was published in the 1920 *Boston Christian Science Monitor* and in1925 in *The Publishers Weekly*, New York. By happenstance, Mrs. Ovington was walking to the railroad station near New Jersey, when a Ford Coupe drove up and stopped. Ovington, in her words, *"hastened forward to greet an old friend who offered me a lift to Newark."* Ovington goes on to say, *"Katherine Johnson, part white, part Negro, part Indian; all alert American, was wearing her Y uniform that she had worn for fourteen months in France, and as we drove along she told me what she was doing."*

Kathryn: *"I am trying to awaken race pride, to show the colored people that they have contributed much to America's civilization and that they have reason to be proud of their many great men. That the loose-mouthed buffoon of the cheap magazine and the vaudeville stage is the only type that the white world will recognize."*

White terrorist organizations like the Klu Klux Klan, pervasive in the south, intimidated those she was attempting to educate. Kathryn, nonetheless, persevered, hiding in churches and homes. And, even though she was afraid, she continued to be a champion for Negro literacy.

Kathryn comments in her diary that *"One of the most undesirable conditions incident to touring the country is that I am alone most of the time. I have taken precautions, however, not to drive at night, unless I can get someone to go with me."*

The first bookmobiles documented in the United States were in 1890 and 1904. They were mule-drawn wagons, first reported in Fairfax, Virginia and Chester County, South Carolina respectively. In 1905, a librarian for Washington County, Maryland developed one of the first American book wagons. In 1920, Sarah Askew Byrd was credited as one of the early developers of the bookmobile, driving her model T Ford to deliver books in rural New Jersey. Even though colored libraries in the Northeast were established in the early 1800s, after the 1896 Supreme court decision, Plessy v. Ferguson, allowing for separate but equal legalized segregation, most public libraries did not allow Africa Americans access. Kathryn recognized this and should be credited with establishing the first colored bookmobile. In the NAACP's 1950 magazine covering their Illinois State Conference there is an article entitled, "The NAACP Bookmobile." In that article, Kathryn M. Johnson is credited with being *"The owner and motive force of the NAACP bookmobile,"* continuing with, *"To Miss Johnson bringing information to the people is a familiar story. For eight years in the '20s, she toured the United States in a Ford, carrying a two-foot bookshelf of Negro literature."*

Kathryn spoke about race, and published articles in support of the need to enlighten the white population to the culture and accomplishments of Negroes. Her most recognized book, "Two Colored Women with the A.E.F." written in collaboration with Addie W. Hutton, was well received and caught the attention of President Warren G. Harding in 1921:

My Dear Miss Johnson,
The President has read with appreciation your letter of October 28 and he asks
me to thank you for your courtesy in sending him a copy of your book.
Sincerely yours,
Geo B. Christian Jr.
Secretary to the President

After their book was published, the bond between Addie Hunton and Kathryn Johnson fell into disrepair. Their collaborative on the book, *Two Colored Women with the A.E.F*, was featured in the June 2, 1921 New York Times Book Review section, but on October 2, 1922, Addie Hunton wrote Kathryn a blistering letter accusing her of financial dishonesty and threatening liable. Their friendship dissolved forever.

Kathryn probably inherited her courage, activism, and quest for adventure from her ancestors. The adventurous nature of Daniel McCown, her great, great, great Grandfather on her mother's side is one example. He travelled from Scotland through India and finally to pre-revolutionary America, at a time when most people rarely left their village or town. In the Virginias, Daniel and his Hindu wife bore one child, Archibald, who married a colored woman at a time when it was not just unacceptable but illegal, showing the courage to do what was in his heart, rather than what was deemed socially acceptable. Kathryn did what was in her heart, what she felt was right, rather than what was acceptable for her time. Even after the emancipation, the vestiges of slavery continued to work against literacy and education in colored communities, but Kathryn was fearless in her pursuit of education, academic achievement, and social justice for the colored communities throughout the nation and the world.

What inspired Kathryn Magnolia Johnson's self-confidence and determination, what motivated her to continue academic advancement at a time when availability of Negro education was sparse, unpopular, and discouraged? What made her risk physical harm and potential death to help her community? I believe it was family and faith.

The underpinnings of Kathryn Magnolia Johnson's pursuits stem from her upbringing in Darke County, Ohio, a place strong in family history, values, faith, and racial equality. Kathryn's unique family history dating back to the 1750s, was replete with diversity. Even though unacknowledged, her great, great grandfather on her grandmother's side, General Nathanael Greene, a hero in the Revolutionary War, had an illegitimate son, Gabriel Greene, with a captured Cherokee woman. Kathryn knew of her families' diversity, making discrimination even more confusing, asking, "Am I African, Hindu, White or American Indian?"

Probably more confounding was the exodus of her brothers and sisters after her mother, Lucinda Jane, remarried a man of dark complexion. This caused everyone to face injustices in their own community—that skin tone was directly related to worth, darker skin meaning less value. Kathryn defended the rights of all people of respect.

The quest for learning, her fearlessness, righteousness, and the urge to teach others was part of Kathryn's makeup. Her pursuit and dissemination of knowledge, her life's work, as demonstrated by her literacy activism both here and abroad, deserves to be recognized by peers and mentors alike.

Kathryn, as member of The Young People's Society of Christian Endeavor at Wilberforce University, practiced her faith throughout her life. Prayer was her savior and support through times of fear and turmoil.

Kathryn graduated from the Normal and Industrial Department of Wilberforce and returned, later, for an additional degree. In a letter of reference written by Superintendent J.P Shorter, he said of her:

"This bears witness that Miss Kathryn M. Johnson, during her entire school life with us, has been an exemplary young woman, a faithful and conscientious student. She graduated from our regular Normal course in 1898 and after many excellent results as a teacher, returned and is now a member of the Senior Class of the Scientific Course.

"I cheerfully recommend her to any one, believing she will give the best results in any work she may undertake."

Kathryn's orations were demonstrative of mutual respect between races. In a letter following a talk at the St. Mark Methodist Episcopal Church on February 11, 1817, Pastor John W. Robinson wrote:

Dear Miss Johnson,

I heard your address on, "The Birth and Progress of a Race," given with stereoscopic pictures at St. Marks M.E. Church Sunday night. It gives me pleasure to recommend this message as instructive and inspiring. I am sure the address and pictures are such as will encourage the Negro and if they could be shown in the churches of white people as well, they would contribute to the mutual respect of both races. Wishing you abundant success, I am—

Yours for the Race,

John W. Robinson

In June of 1917, after a presentation at Quinn Chapel A.M.E. Church, the following letter from the pastor was posted:

Miss Katherine Johnson, delivered at Quinn Chapel, Chicago, IL, Thursday, June 7, one of the most thoughtful lectures I have ever heard in reference to our race. She has vision and a message of unusual merit, and with fine skill, puts them in possession of her hearers,

Respectfully Yours,

J.C. Anderson

Pastor of Quinn Chapel

Kathryn's activism was certainly buttressed by that first copy of *The Crisis* magazine; however, her writings support an even deeper self-motivation. In a December 1916 article in *The Half Century Magazine*, Kathryn's writes:

"That the establishment of legitimate and successful business enterprises is one of the surest and most immediate solutions that can come to the industrial and economic problems that are so vexing to the colored people today, has constantly impressed itself upon my mind during the four years in which I have travelled as Field Agent for the Crisis and the National Association for the Advancement of Colored People; and it has been impressed there until it has become one of my deepest convictions."

Kathryn ends the article with:

"This can be done by a cooperative get-together movement on the part of the colored people. Let colored men and women go into business; into every kind of business that is necessary to supply the wants of the people; let their places of business be so attractive that they will induce men and women of all races to trade with them; then let the colored people show them preference in their patronage. Help them to grow by telling their faults to them, and their virtues to the public; help to make them men and women of wealth; they may employ your boy or girl someday; or your boy or girl may marry in their families, and some of the money you have spent with them will come back to you, a thing that is not very likely to happen between your family and the white family whom you are now making rich by your patronage."

❖

Kathryn opens her narrative with the existential relationship between loss of her father at an early age and her determination and self-reliance. The role of the father has changed throughout the social history of the country. In the 1800s fathers were more involved with childrearing—John Demos, an historian on fatherhood, states this in an article published in the *Republican Herald* dated June 20, 2010:

"Fathers traditionally assumed a broad range of responsibilities defining and supervising the children's development and domestic control was largely in the hands of men, as wives were expected to defer to their husbands on matters regarding the children."

In that same publication, Scott Coltrane, an expert in the study of fathering and fatherhood, states:

"If you go back to the late 1800s, most Americans lived on farms. Most people's businesses were their homes and just provided a whole different social context for fathers to be involved with their kids. They were very involved with the education of their children. They were very involved with instructing them in various things, so they were around to be seen."

What impact does the loss of a father have on a daughter? When interviewing adult daughters that lose their fathers at an early age, the answers are very similar—tenacity, responsibility, empathy and compassion when warranted. One person summed it up by saying, "I had to teach myself to be a man."

W.E.B. Du Bois and Mordecai Johnson are well known for the famous phrase "the talented tenth," referring to those 10 percent of educated colored people that were to lead the 90 percent that were not. In the early 1900s, only 37/1,000 people in the United States had a bachelor's degree. That certainly makes Kathryn Johnson one of those talented tenth. However, as Ida B. Wells remarked, the chauvinism of black educated men made her somewhat invisible. Kathryn Magnolia Johnson deserves visibility and recognition for more than her and Addie Hunton's book, but for the impact she had on the lives of so many people she touched. The students at New Paris High School and Wilberforce, the girls at Sumner High and Shorter College, the thousands of people that found hope through her presentations for the NAACP, the colored soldiers she taught to read, and those she culturally enlightened during WWI, and the men and women that found inspiration in her Two-Foot Shelf of Negro Literature and the other books she sold throughout the country.

It is my hope that this autobiographical compilation will give Kathryn Magnolia Johnson the place in American and African American history she deserves.

Acknowledgments

I must start by thanking my late father, Kuroki Bertram Gonzalzles, who toiled for some twenty years collecting and preserving the history of our family. The foresight he had when deciding to name me as custodian of those records was a surprise. My father was aggressive in his research and meticulous in organizing the many documents and pictures other family members sent him.

I must also thank my wife, Miriam S. Gonzalzles, for her tedious work in transcribing Kathryn's diaries from the written to a word document, which made it so much easier to interpret. I must also thank her for reading the manuscript and pointing out errors in my construction.

Lisa Cerasoli of 529 Books and her editorial staff were exceptionally helpful in making sure I didn't suffer from TMI (Too Much Information). Lisa was patient and supportive to someone who has never written a book before.

Michael Bennett, PhD, deserves much praise for taking his valuable time to review the manuscript and write a forward that gives me more praise than I deserve. I thank him for his friendship, ideas, and the support he has shown me over the many years we have known one another.

Carol Neal, excellent photographic restoration specialist, who took what I thought were photographic disasters and turned them into very usable prints that are an intricate part of the text.

Lastly, Bonnie Fields, M.S.W., who took time to translate, French to English, letters to Kathryn.

Addendum

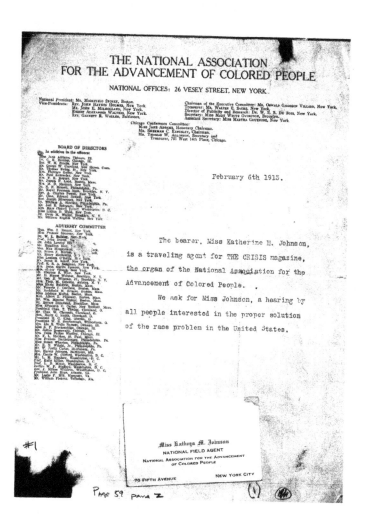

February 6th 1913.

The bearer, Miss Katherine M. Johnson, is a traveling agent for THE CRISIS magazine, the organ of the National Association for the Advancement of Colored People.

We ask for Miss Johnson, a hearing by all people interested in the proper solution of the race problem in the United States.

Miss Kathryn M. Johnson
NATIONAL FIELD AGENT
NATIONAL ASSOCIATION FOR THE ADVANCEMENT
OF COLORED PEOPLE

70 FIFTH AVENUE   NEW YORK CITY

E. B. DUBOIS, EDITOR-IN-CHIEF.   ALBON L. HOLSEY, BUSINESS MA

BUSINESS DEPARTMENT

THE CRISIS
A MONTHLY MAGAZINE

CIRCULATION   ADVERTISING
23,000   CIRCULATION
          TWENTY-SIX VESEY STREET.   MAIL ORDER

NEW YORK   August 18th 1912.

My Dear Miss Johnson:-

      I think you will understand the
bill if you remember that it includes not simply the copies which you have handled as traveling agent, but also,
the copies sent to Kansas City.

      It was alright to keep the unsold cop-
ies and use them on the trip.   I think when you come to
settle up, you will find no difficulty in understanding the
bill.   We would be very glad to have a remittance from you
at your convenience.

      We are sending to-day, 50 copies to
Columbia, and 100 to Meberly, and hope that they reach you
in time.

      We are writing to Mr. White to ask
him if he will act as our agent.

      Very sincerely yours,

      W. E. B. Du Bois

      Per- M & A.

Miss K. M. Johnson,
Columbia, Missouri,
General Delivery.

#2

DuBois, Editor-in-Chief.

ALBON L. HOLSEY, Business Manager.

BUSINESS DEPARTMENT

THE CRISIS

A MONTHLY MAGAZINE

CIRCULATION
23,000

TWENTY-SIX VESEY STREET.

ADVERTISING
CIRCULATION
MAIL ORDER

NEW YORK   August 30th 1912.

Dear Miss Johnson:-

Your Kansas City account is as follows:-

600	May	CRISIS---	$30.00
225	June	" ---	11.25
200	July	" ------	10.00
200	Aug.	" ---	10.00
			$61.25

From this must be substracted:-

330 May copies used for traveling and to be accounted

for separately---$16.50
Remittance------- 4.50
Returns, 88 June- 4.40
$25.40

Balance due----- 35.85

It may be of course, that there are copies of the
June, July and August issues to be returned. If so, that
will reduce the bill. I think that the trouble is that your
representatives in Kansas City have not remitted as you expected. We have heard from them only twice. Once they
sent in one subscription, (Aug. 26th) and once they sent us
a Money-Order for $4.50. To the above account must be add-
ed the following:-

330 May copies
June "
500 July "
August "
Subscriptions--------60 yearly
Received------------27 half yearly

I think this will make the matter perfectly clear. If
not write me. The mistake arose in our book-keepers getting
Your Kansas City and traveling accounts mixed.

We are attending to all of your requests in your letter
of August 26th.

Very sincerely yours,

W. E. B. DuBois
Per M.F.A.

#3

Page 64 part 2

TELEPHONE ⬤⬤ 5688

THE NATIONAL ASSOCIATION FOR THE
ADVANCEMENT OF COLORED PEOPLE

NATIONAL OFFICES—26 VESEY STREET, NEW YORK

National President: Mr. Moorfield Storey, Boston.
Vice-Presidents: Rev. John Haynes Holmes, New York.
    Mr. John E. Milholland, New York.
    Bishop Alexander Walters, New York.
    Rev. Garnett R. Waller, Baltimore.
    Miss Mary White Ovington, Brooklyn.

Chairman of the Board of Directors: Mr. Oswald Garrison Villard, New York.
Treasurer: Mr. Walter E. Sachs, New York.
Director of Publicity and Research: Dr. W. E. B. Du Bois, New York.
National Organizer: Dr. M. C. B. Mason, Cincinnati.
Secretary: Miss May Childs Nerney, Brooklyn.

BOARD OF DIRECTORS
(In addition to the above)

Miss Jane Addams, Chicago.
Rev. Hutchins C. Bishop, New York.
Rev. W. H. Brooks, New York.
Dr. C. E. Bentley, Chicago.
Mr. George W. Crawford, New Haven.
Mr. Thomas Ewing, Jr., New York.
Mr. J. Morton Jones, Brooklyn.
Mrs. Florence Kelley, New York.
Mr. Paul Kennaday, New York.
Mr. Joseph Prince Loud, Boston.
Mrs. Max Morgenthau, Jr., New York.
Dr. N. F. Mossell, Philadelphia.
Mr. Wilson M. Powell, Jr., New York.
Mr. Charles Edward Russell, New York.
Dr. William A. Sinclair, Philadelphia.
Dr. Joel E. Spingarn, New York.
Mr. Charles H. Studin, New York.
Mrs. Mary Church Terrell, Washington, D. C.
Miss Lillian D. Wald, New York.
Mr. William English Walling, New York.
Dr. O. M. Waller, Brooklyn.

May 22, 1913.

Miss Kathryn M. Johnson,
1002 East Springer Avenue,
Guthrie, Okla.

My dear Miss Johnson:

    Your very encouraging letter of May 13 was awaiting me on my return from the country yesterday. I do not dare, since a week has elapsed, send the literature you requested to the address you gave. If you will tell me where you wish it shipped, I will see that it is sent immediately.

    Will you let me know confidentially if the people making up the Muskogee Branch, of whom I enclose a list, are representative and if they will be militant and aggressive in the work. We find we have to be more and more careful in admitting branches as we are apt to get the wrong kind of people, particularly people who want to use us politically or otherwise. Our organization is now becoming so powerful that many would like to use its influence. Please let me know if you think these people representative, and I will regard your letter as strictly confidential.

    I had a very enthusiastic letter from Dr. Du Bois. He is delighted with his trip.

    With best wishes,

        Cordially yours,

        May Childs Nerney

#4

April 29, 1913.

Miss Kathryn M. Johnson,
   315 North 9th Street,
   Muskogee, Okla.

My dear Miss Johnson:

      Thank you for your letter of April 25 enclosing six dollars to cover six Association memberships. We are delighted at your success and congratulate you. I suppose we have your good efforts to thank for the Constitution which just reached us from Muskogee. Even before I got your letter I inferred that you were our good angel.

      Is it not nice that Dr. Du Bois is making his western trip. I know he is going to be successful.

      All the memberships that you send will be acknowledged directly. Do you not think you could use some of our annual reports for free distribution? I am sending you a sample under separate cover.

      Very sincerely,

      May Childs Nerney

J. E. Johnson	Mrs. J. B. Fue
W. Scott Brown	J. B. Washington
J. W. Sharpe	J. A. Roberts
John H. Escoe	Mrs. L. F. Fue
O. B. Jefferson	Mrs. G. A. Patrick
J. W. Gentry	Rev. H. T. S. Johnson
J. M. Lilley	W. E. Brown
J. E. Hart, M. D.	E. W. Brown
H. R. Edwards	J. H. Mosaley
Mrs. W. Scott Brown, Jr.	Dr. E. P. Brown
Mrs. G. L. Prince	Rev. M. P. Brown
Rev. G. L. Prince	T. E. Lightner
Rev. R. M. Perrin	J. H. Templeton
H. King	Mrs. J. R. Stewart
Rev. T. J. Magbie	C. B. Bryant
R. Pickens	
Rev. T. H. Tyson	
Mrs. R. M. Perrin	
Griffin T. Holman	
Dr. L. M. Banks	
F. Gaston	
G. H. Bell	
Rev. G. A. Patrick	
W. V. Gentry	
Rev. H. H. Edmonds	
Mrs. H. H. Edmonds	
J. B. Fue	

This was the first branch the N. A. A. C. P. Organized south of Mason & Dixon's line, I was its Judge, twenty three weeks ...

#6

THE NATIONAL ASSOCIATION FOR THE
ADVANCEMENT OF COLORED PEOPLE

NATIONAL OFFICES—26 VESEY STREET, NEW YORK

May 27, 1913.

Miss Kathryn M. Johnson,
315 North 9th Street,
Muskogee, Okla.

My dear Miss Johnson:

We have just received an applica-
tion from Oklahoma City to be admitted as a branch of
the National Association. I enclose a list of the
proposed members. Please let me know if they are all
right. Are any of them white?

With best wishes.

Very sincerely,

May Childs Nerney

Proposed Members of Oklahoma City Branch.

May 23, 1913.

Mrs. William Harrison	821 East 27th Street
H. C. Hawkins	912 East 4th Street
T. R. Debnam	814 East 4th Street
Mrs. T. R. Debnam	814 East 4th Street
David Wisener	814 East 4th Street
Mrs. David Wisener	814 East 4th Street
Mrs. Ladley F. Guy	907 East 3rd Street
Robert Jackson	224 East 2nd Street
Mrs. M. E. Littlepage	816 East 7th Street
W. H. Slaughter	327½ East 2nd Street
Mrs. W. H. Slaughter	327½ East 2nd Street
J. H. R. Brazleton	906 East 7th Street
Irving Dunges	R. F. D.
Mrs. E. W. Caruthers	221 West Washington Street
Miss Garry Walton	831 East 9th Street
Mr. H. V. Gear	514 East 2nd Street
H. A. Berry	924 East 10th Street
Mrs. H. A. Berry	924 East 10th Street
Mrs. A. P. Bethel	317 East 2nd Street
T. H. Traylor	112 West Noble Street
William Harrison	821 East 7th Street
Mrs. T. H. Traylor	112 West Noble Street
John Seymood	19 East 9th Street
Mrs. Eliza Seymood	315 South Broadway
K. B. Whitby	620 East 2nd Street
	907 East 3rd Street
M. Smith	815 East 2nd Street

Monrovia, Liberia,
January, 22, 1920.

Dear Sister:-

Both of your letters came in December. Mail comes pecu-
liarily out here. Your letter dated November 24th and posted
at Columbus November 25th arrived here December 19th, while
the one you wrote on November 22nd did not reach me until December 24. So you see there is something in that argument that
the first shall be last and the last shall be first.

I am very well and have been very well since I have been
on the West African coast with the exception of an injured
right leg. In landing from the steamer at the logging camp on
September 6th I cut it I thought but slightly but not having
any thing with which to treat it, it became infected and has
given me no end of trouble. I have kept the infection down
with warm water by keeping it clean but having no germicide
I have simply had to keep the infection down with plain warm
water as best I could until I sent to MayBelle for some medicine.

Thus far my dear wife has not responded. Cannot imagine
what the matter is. Surely she wouldn't delay when her husband sent for medicine knowing that he must need it, other-

15

wise he wouldn't have sent for it. The medicine proposition
is the worst proposition out here. Quinine is used for almost
all purposes. When one gets sick and dies out here it is not
because of the climate or other natural causes but because of
not having any remedial agents at hand. Quinine, Castor oil,
Salts and Terpentine are the drugs used here and when a person has something that cannot be reached with those drugs, the
doctor comes in, takes the temperature and pulse, looks at the
tongue, makes out the diagnosis, writes a prescription and
sends it to New York or Liverpool to be filled, according to
whichever place the next steamer is going. Probable a wait of
10 or 15 days will be necessary before the next steamer arrives and if the patient survives that period he probably will
be dead long before the steamer arrives at its destination.

For the life of me I cannot understand the delay. She must
have blundered in some way in sending it. Probably she sent it

I have just been plugging along here with an infected leg
depending on MayBelle and depending on MayBelle until sometimes
I become fearful lest I have depended upon her too long. Upon
the same boat which I sent the letter to her asking for the
medicine I also sent one to Governor Cox, at Columbus, Ex Gov.
Harmon at Cincinnati, Chairman Durbin at Kenton and Billy
Brumbaugh at Greenville and have received a reply from each of
of them. All of there answers came in December. Durbin's came
on the 19th and the others on the 24th. Had she sent the medicine by first class mail as soon as she received the letter
it would have been here December 19th, if by Liverpool and December 24th, if by France.

For the life of me I cannot understand the delay. She must
have blundered in some way in sending it. Probably she sent it

down to Wilberforce to be brought over by the Colonel. If so it
will probably be here by June as I understand that officer is
coming by way of France for the purpose of inspecting the Military operations of that country during the great war. Or probably she sent it by Parcel Post, in which event it will arrive
here about the middle of April as we only have a Parcel Post
mail from New York every three months, the last arriving here
January 9th.

Liberia is without a doubt the healthiest place on earth.
Two and one half million people and not a drug store or a Hospital and only eleven doctors. I have let out such a terrific
howl about there being no way to assist or protect American
citizens out here who happen to become indisposed that they
heard me in Washington and the U. S. Government is going to
equip a twenty bed Hospital and send a Physician from the Bureau of Public Health as an attendent. Guess however it will
be too late to be of service to me.

The last letter I received from MayBelle was written on
November 10th. Six mail boats have been in since I have been
expecting the medicine, four from Liverpool, one from France
and one from Spain and no results. I sent for 100 formin tablets and a small box of Tyrees Antiseptic Powder. Probably you
had better get them and send at once. Have them prepared so
that the package will carry through the mail. It has now been

17

well on to four months since I sent for the medicine. All of
this time I have had to treat it without a germicide or an
antiseptic. For the last week I have done a little better as
I have had a little tincture of Iodin. It burns like forty
but I think it is doing me a little good. An American Army
officer came down from the Interior and brought a small bottle
which I induced him to divide with me. When I am out of it I
will simply have to go back to the warm water until the Antiseptic powder comes.

Whisky is the only internal antiseptic I have so I have
become to be quite a toper. A quart lasts me about five days
more or less, depending upon how many callers I have who like
it. I am wholly unused to it and have no taste for it whatever
but I have no choice, I simply have to continue taking it until the formin comes or I go some where for treatment.

Captain Brockway, the Liberian Auditor and a citizen of
the state of New York is going home on the first boat in February, he says to die. He was a perfectly healthy man when he
came here but he had an attack of sluggish liver which could
have been righted with a few calomel and soda tablets or a few
ABS tablets in three or four days but the poor man had abso-
lutely nothing to help himself. I went to see him but was ab-
solutely powerless. He called the German doctor and he of course
proceeded to shovel in the quinine which is a very poor drug
for that trouble. Going from bad to worse, his heart finally
broke down. I have sent to Maybelle to bring a list of drugs
along which will be sufficient to protect my family.

Yours ever,

Joseph R Johnson

Assignment of Patent.

Whereas, I , Jesse H. Johnson

of New Paris , in the County of Preble

and State of Ohio did obtain Letters-Patent from the United States for certain Improvements in CORN HARVESTERS

which Letters-Patent are numbered 872821 and bear date the third

day of December 1907 ; and

Whereas, I, the Jesse H. Johnson am now the sole owner of said patent, and all the rights under the same; and

Whereas, Catherine M. Johnson

by the said Catherine M. Johnson

for her own use and behoof, and for the use and behoof of her legal representatives, as fully and entirely as the same would have been held and enjoyed by me had this assignment and sale not been made.

In testimony whereof, I have hereunto set my hand and affix my seal , this thirty first day of December A. D. 1907.

Signed at Springfield Illinois on the date above written.

Jesse H Johnson [SEAL]

[SEAL]

In presence of two witnesses:

N Dakins

W R Hale

NO LEGALIZATION NECESSARY,

Send This Ambulance Aboard
The American Relief Ship for Spain
Sailing in September
When You Help the Women and Children in Spain
You Help Defeat Mussolini and Avenge Ethiopia!

SPONSORS:

PAUL ROBESON	WILLIAM PICKENS	T. ARNOLD HILL
CHANNING TOBIAS	KATHERINE JOHNSON	MILTON P. WEBSTER
A. PHILIP RANDOLPH	LANGSTON HUGHES	EARL B. DICKERSON
MAX YERGAN	RICHARD WRIGHT	IRENE McCOY GAINES

MRS. ERNEST R. ALEXANDER   MRS. ETNAH ROCHON BOUTTE
and others

Early this year Paul Robeson sent $250 from London to the Negro People of America. He asked that it be used to start a fund to purchase an ambulance and make it a gift from the Negro people of America to the heroic people of Republican Spain. He pointed out that the fight against fascism is the Negro's fight. Mussolini moved from Ethiopia to Spain. And hundreds of Negroes now fighting in the International Brigades went to Spain "to meet Mussolini there." The fight for democracy in Spain, is the fight against lynching and Jim Crow discrimination right here.

Negro Committee to Aid Spain
with the Medical Bureau and North American Committee
to Aid Spanish Democracy
381 Fourth Avenue, New York City.

I contribute $............ for the Negro Ambulance to Spain
to sail on the Relief Ship.

Name ....

Street ....

City and State ....

I should like the ambulance to tour my city ....

The following organizations would be interested ....

The fund for an ambulance for Spain has been increased by contributions from Committees in New York (The Harlem Committee to Aid Spanish Democracy) and Chicago (The Salaria Kee Negro Ambulance Fund). To ship this ambulance to Spain additional funds are needed for equipment and medical supplies. When you contribute you may be saving the life of an American Negro boy in Spain. Make your contribution on this blank today.

For A Fully-Equipped
Negro Ambulance in Spain

A TWO-FOOT SHELF OF NEGRO LITERATURE

Composed of twelve books, selected with care and discrimination, with the idea of offsetting the silence of our educational system regarding twelve million American citizens. Add these volumes to your library. Reading them will increase your respect for the Negro race.

1. **THE NEGRO IN OUR HISTORY**—Carter Woodson ... $ 2.00
   An illustrated text-book covering the history of the Negro in America.

2. **THE BOOK OF AMERICAN NEGRO POETRY** ... 1.75
   —James Weldon Johnson. A choice selection of poems from Negro authors.

3. **THE NEGRO FACES AMERICA**—Herbert J. Seligman ... 1.75
   A scientific treatise on the color question.

4. **TWO COLORED WOMEN WITH THE AMERICAN EXPEDITIONARY FORCES**—Addie W. Hunton and Kathryn M. Johnson. A book written by two of the three colored women who were in France during the period of active warfare. The only book about the colored soldiers that has so far been written by anyone who was in France during that period. A valuable addition to the history of the Negro. ... 2.50

5. **THE NEGRO**—W. E. B. DuBois. A short history of the splendid part played by the Negro in the early civilization of the world.

6. **THE NEGRO IN LITERATURE AND ART** Brawley ... 1.50
   A history of the artistic achievements of the Negro in the United States.

7. **THE LIFE OF FREDERICK DOUGLASS**—Booker T. Washington. ... 2.00

8. **LIFE AND WORKS OF PAUL LAURENCE DUNBAR** ... 2.50
   Illustrated.

9-10. **AFRICA AND THE DISCOVERY OF AMERICA**—Leo Wiener, Professor of Slavic Language and Literature at Harvard University. A scholarly treatise designed to prove that the Africans were here decades before Columbus discovered America. **Two volumes, $5.00 each.** ... 10.00
   (A third and concluding volume is now on the press; it is larger and may be more expensive)

FOR CHILDREN

11. **THE UPWARD PATH**—Ovington and Pritchard. A reader composed altogether of selections by colored authors. ... 1.35

12. **FLOYD'S FLOWERS**—Silas X. Floyd. A story book especially valuable for its illustrations representing well groomed colored men, women and children. ... 1.50

Total $27.75

Terms: Five per cent. off for any group selected from the number, whose total cost is not less than $10.00 nor more than $20.00. Seven per cent. off for any group selected whose total cost is not less than $20.00 nor more than $30.00. Ten per cent. off for entire set. Books may be purchased one by one if desired. Remit money by Post Office or Express money order.

Express or postage extra.

KATHRYN M. JOHNSON,
576 Green Avenue, Brooklyn, N. Y.

October 31, 1921.

My dear Miss Johnson:

The President has read with appreciation your letter of October 28th and he asks me to thank you for your courtesy in sending him the copy of your book.

Sincerely yours,

Geo B. Christian Jr

Secretary to the President.

Miss Kathryn M. Johnson,
372 Grand Avenue,
Brooklyn, N.Y.

Kathryn M. Johnson
4509 Prairie Avenue
Chicago 15, Illinois
Phone Drexel 6348

My name is Kathryn M. Johnson; it is listed in
my Father's family Bible as Catherine Magnolia Johnson. The
name Catherine was changed to Kathryn on the college rolls
at Wilberforce University. That brought about confusion and
I adopted the change.

My father's name was Walter Johnson; he was born
near Lexington, Kentucky, and came to Ohio when he was twelve
years old. His father's name was Joseph Johnson, and he was
born in Virginia of a white mother and a slave father; he was
therefore a free man, as the children of white mothers were
free, and the children of colored mothers were slaves.

My father settled in Darke County, Ohio, near
Greenville, where slaveholders had settled their colored families on land near a school called the Union Literary Institute, or the Darke County Colored Seminary. It was established
by Quakers, and was one of the first schools of higher learning
established for colored people in the United States.

My mother was born in Rush County, Indiana, near
Flatrock. Her name was Lucinda Jane McCown. Her father's name
was Tarlton McCown, and her mother's name was Julia Green McCown.
They, too, moved to the colored settlement in Darke County, Ohio.
There my mother met my father, and they were married.

To this union was born Julia Anna Johnson; Nan-
cy Jane Johnson; Frederick Douglass Johnson; Thaddeus Langston
Johnson; William Henry Johnson; Joseph Lee Johnson; Jesse Hayes Johnson;
and Kathryn M. Johnson.

Of this family only three of us are living at this date,
May 23, 1947. Frederick D. Johnson, now eighty two years old,
lives at 301 Chickahominy, Dayton, Ohio. The other, William
Henry Johnson, lives at 8430 Vincennes Ave., Chicago, Ill.

My sister Nancy married Oliver Singleton, of Spring
field, Ill., and became the mother of eight children. Of these
there remain living, Walter Singleton, 422 Greely Ave., Kansas City, Kan.; Arthur Singleton, 300 East 61st St., Chicago,
Ill., and Dr. Roscoe E. Singleton, DDS. of the same address.
Mrs. Leota Harris, 6010 Elizabeth, Chicago, Ill.; and Mrs. Ethel
Goodin, 4287 West Labadie, St. Louis, Mo.

My brother Dr. Joseph. L. Johnson, now deceased, has
two living children; Travola Johnson, Adams, Thirteenth St. N.E.,
Washington, D.C. and Dr. Walter Johnson, Homer Phillips Hospital,
St. Louis, Mo.

I have never been married and have no children.

On September 19 the relatives of the McCown family met at the home of Mr and Mrs Haywood Collins in their first reunion. The family was well represented by relatives of the vicinity also Henry Lane and wife Oliver Lane and wife of Cass County Mich., Mrs Hannah Bush of Lima O., Harvey McCown and wife, Samuel Carpenter and wife of Richmond, Ind.

A very enjoyable time was had; an elaborate dinner was served from the well filled baskets to eighty five persons. Several visitors were present in the afternoon.

A temporary organization was formed and short talks were made by Henry Lane and Amos Carpenter; of the visitors present, interesting addresses were made by Shoemake, Attorney Richardson and Dr Anderson of Richmond Ind.

It was decided that the reunions be continued, and officers for the following year were elected, as follows: Jesse McCown, president, Jeremiah Burden, vice president; R.J. Collins, secretary; Elmer McCown, asst secretary.

A committee of five was chosen by the president to make the arrangements for the ensuing year, namely J.C. Clemons, J. F. Epps, David Ware, J.J. McCown, J.Q. Grant.

An interesting history of the McCown ancestry was read by Jesse McCown, as follows: We have met here today as representatives of our great grandfather, Daniel McKeon, a native of Scotland, whose birth occurred in the seventeenth century, at which time it took a vessel six months to cross the ocean. There were no steamships in our great grandfathers day. The impression of my mind is, that he was a sailor, for hr took for a wife a Hindu woman and it is not probable that there were Hindus in Scotland. Under the Mosaic law, no one could be a priest unless he could prove his lineage to Aaron. We are able to prove that we are the descendants of Daniel McKeon. He emigrated to this country about the middle of the seventeenth century, while it was still colonies. He had one son, Archibald, our grandfather, whom I remember quite well. I have heard him say that he was about twelve years old at the time of the Revolutionary War and large enough to hold a General's horse. He was probably born about 1761. He married a mulatto woman, and to them were born twelve children: Daniel, James, Sarah, John, Archibald, Charley, Elizabeth, Constantine, Mary, Tarlton, Pleasant, and Lucinda, their births occurring between the years 1796 and 1819. The most of them were born in Cushing Co., Va., between Lynchburg and Richmond - ninety miles to Lynchburg, one hundred miles to Richmond. Grandfather raised tobacco and these cities were his market places. When ready for market, he cut from the forest a chestnut or oak, split it into staves, made a hogshead large enough to hold his crop, put a frame around it, as we do our field rollers, put four horses to it and delivered it to one or the other of the towns. Getting tired of this he concluded he would go West; so loading his effects into a wagon, with six good horses, and his son Archibald (Harvey's father) as a driver, he started for Indiana, settled in Fayette county, near Connorsville, on eighty acres, entered from the government for one hundred dollars. He improved this for about three years then sold, and went about 12 miles into Rush county. Out of the 30 acres he realized enough to buy a section of land at about $1.25 per acre. So you see he had lots of push and energy.

I will give you a short history of James McCown, at whose old homestead, we are assembled today. When an orphan of twelve years, I was taken into his home as one of his already large family of children. He was born June 12, 1798, and died at this homestead 28 years ago. He was married to Rebecca Vires of Gallia county in 1824. He was a good provider. It was just like a boarding house every day. He would butcher from 10 to 12 hogs and a beef or two every year. He had lots of company and enjoyed it as well as any man I ever saw. He owned 80 acres in Rush county, Ind. and about the time of the panic of 1839-40 bought another 80 acres, mortgaged both for the remainder of the money, and had it paid out except $100 He was sued for this and the demand was that it paid in gold; one dollar in gold being worth $2.50 in paper money. He never stopped for th moment to think he could not pay for it. He sold corn at 12½ cents per bushel, wheat at 25 cents, hogs at $1.00 per hundred, his horses and cattle, except one old mare, and paid off the mortgage. This left him with nothing to support his family only by days work, which he did, while his son Alexander, age 10, tended 6 acres of corn with the old mare. For his work he received 2 bushels of corn or 1 bushel of wheat per day. In 1852 he sold the 160 acres in Rush county for $8,800; bought 603 acres in Darke county and 40 acres in Randolph, paying for both $7,580. He moved to this place with six work horses, besides the old mare, three 3 year old colts, two 2 year olds, 25 head of cattle, 75 head of hogs, his family of ten children, viz: Alexander, Mary, William, Archibald, Caroline, Martha, Hannah, Nancy, Clarissa and James; Lewis being born in Darke county. His great business capacity should be an inspiration to us as well as future generations.

ONE WHO WAS THERE.

Oct. 2, 1922.

My dear Miss Johnson: There is very little if anything more for me to say. I am sure it is not the first time that "friendship's" name has been used to threat' but one is always able to distinguish between the advice of a friend and an attack by one in a rancorous mood. I was not angry when I wrote but greatly insulted. I fear it will be as your brother said when I was trying to defend you, some day some one will have you in the meshes of the law for saying things you cannot prove. You have a very drastic and bitter way — that to say the least is not christian — but it is all right so far as I am concerned.

We will leave it, and all else — I would not spend two minutes with you in any further personal discussion of the book. I wanted to arrange it while I had time. I begin work tomorrow and if Cleveland wishes me, I leave here Friday.

I tried to show you both courtesy and consideration, first by writing and then by an interview, both of which you met in a surprisingly hostile way.

Of course I cannot sell without knowing what I am selling, but I can assign all of my interests and let you have an accounting, as they will ask. This seems

my only course out and I only take it
because you would not come to any
point with me and I think it best
to have no further interest in this edition

Friendship is a sacred rite with me —
I have friends too that I have had always
and always will have, I try never to
hurt either those who are and who are
not my friends. I leave them to themselves whom I find untrue or unkind

Very sincerely
Addie W Hunton

My dear Adele,

Not because I think my report is due you - but because
I want you to know how false were your accusations, contained in
your recent tirade of temper, am I sending you these items from the
Brooklyn Eagle Printing Department.

I say no report is due you because it was my own (?)
initiative that the original plan was changed. You were to be satisfied with being paid as I was able to pay you, but wanted to sell
out your interest in the book to publishers who you claimed (?) had
offered you a flattering price. I finally consented for you (?)
to do so, with the change that you sell your share of the rights,
instead of "your interest in the book" to avoid (?) (?) (?) of (?)
which would have given me a strange partner (?) (?) (?) (?) (?)
hard to (?) (?) to any member of (?) (?) (?) (?)
introduction.

You will see by this report that I (?) the (?)
Brooklyn Eagle all that is due them, plus the (?) (?) (?) (?)
and the binding that is yet to be done. Subtracting (?) (?) (?)
amount of $900, which I put into it, and the amount for (?) (?) (?)
copy (an amount which you will discover does not pay (?) (?) (?)
(?) expenses) you will see that you are the only one who (?)
has gotten any clear money out of the book.

Now of course you might say that you didn't know (?) (?)
Perhaps you didn't. But you knew the amount of (?) (?) (?)
was, and certainly you could not expect me to sell (?) (?) (?)
thousand books a year, unless I were a genius (?) (?) (?) it (?)
is one very easy for you to ascertain had (?) (?) (?) (?)
you, even if we had adhered to the original plan (?) (?) (?)

But you have never been interested in (?) (?) (?)
I had paid the debt, as had been able to (?) (?) (?) (?)
the money that I put into it. The only (?) (?) (?) (?)
terested in was getting money for (?) (?) (?) (?)
(?) (?) (?) (?) into a handsome (?) (?) (?) (?)
of (?) (?) (?) (?) the most inconsiderate (?) (?) (?)
and contempt (?) (?) (?) (?) (?)

It is not necessary for me to (?) (?) (?) (?)
things you said have no foundation in truth (?) (?) (?)
now, and it might be very embarrassing (?) (?) (?) (?) (?)
were to prove that they were true.

As to my being a hypocrite - all of your (?) (?)
know about this very financial accusation. The only difference
between them and me is that I have talked to you about it, and we
(?) talked to each other. They are not hypocrites either - they
simply prefer to throw the mantle of charity about your faults
and retain the friendship of what they have hitherto considered
a highly cultured and talented woman.

They have not been forced up against the wall where
they have had to fight for their lives as you have done and if (?)
they had- they would have surprised you by telling you what they
knew also.

When you wrote me letters explaining (?) (?) you were
planning to give me a strange partner - in each of (?) (?) (?) (?) (?)

tal and physical distraction was increased when you became ill far as she they were. Yet you seem to think that I should have taken all of this treatment and said nothing about it.

When I loaned you $100 to rent a house for two months, the sum to be returned in a day or two, and which you reluctantly returned many months after, I spent many sleepless nights. I needed the money, and you knew it. You promised faithfully to return it to help pay the indebtedness I had contracted. After you got your hands on it, you not only did not rent a house, but kept the money. Your slogan seemed to have been, "Pay for two weeks if you can - if you cant - lose the money you have already put into them, and see how much I care." Yet I have never called you a liar, nor a thief, or the other unprintable word some with whom your wife keeps company recently slandered our household.

When I said that I wanted to live in the house with you, I did not mean that I would have done any work.

As to my making my living on your own, that is a liability rather than an asset, and only used it because I didn't want you to think I was not giving you due credit. Henceforth I shall use it as little as possible.

Very truly yours, Kat

State of Illinois, } ss.
County of Cook }

COUNTY COURT OF COOK COUNTY, ILLINOIS

TO THE JUDGES OF ELECTION:

The bearer of this Credential *Kathryn M. Johnson*
(To be signed by candidate personally)
is a candidate for the office of *Representative in Congress,*
to be voted for at the Primary Election to be held on April 9, 1940.

Will you please extend to the bearer of this Credential the courtesy of visiting your Polling Place during the voting time and the counting of the ballots?

The bearer of this Credential is not in the employ of the Board of Election Commissioners nor the County Court. This Credential is issued as a courtesy to candidates who are personally interested in the outcome of the election in order that they may have an opportunity to observe the conduct of the election, including the count of the ballots.

WITNESS the hand and seal of the Judge of the County Court of Cook County, Illinois, this 8th day of April, A.D., 1940.

Edmund K. Jarecki,

Judge of the County Court of Cook County, Illinois.

(SEAL)

LAST WILL AND TESTAMENT.

I was one of three colored women to serve in France during
World War I. I was in the Y.M.C.A. Service. I have scrap books
and pictures which could be distributed by the Executor, in
accordance with which children or grandchildren would appreciate
them most. Also my cape, cap, and uniform.

There are a number of pictures of myself, taken in France; some
are alone and some in groups. This was because French photographers
followd us up.

Some of the books should go to the George Cleveland Hall Library;
especially Leo Wiener's three volumes on Afri ca and The Dis
covery of America.

Kathryn M. Johnson

IN THE NAME OF GOD, AMEN:

I, KATHRYN M. JOHNSON, of the City of Chicago, County of
Cook and State of Illinois, being now of sound and disposing
mind and memory, do hereby make, publish and declare this instrument to be my Last Will and Testament, hereby revoking all
Wills and Testamentary papers at any time heretofore made by
me.

FIRST:

I order and direct that my Executor hereinafter named pay
all of my just debts and funeral expenses, including a headstone
and perpetual care of grave, as soon after my decease as con-
veniently may be.

SECOND:

I hereby authorize and empower my Executor hereinafter
named to sell at public or private sale, upon such terms and
conditions as may be deemed by him to be for the best interest
of my estate, any and all of the assets thereof, including any
and all real estate wheresoever situated in which I may have
any interest at my decease.

THIRD:

In the event that my decease occurs before that of my
brother, WILLIAM JOHNSON, I direct my Executor hereinafter named

THIS IS PAGE ONE (1) OF MY LAST WILL
AND TESTAMENT MADE THIS   DAY
OF SEPTEMBER, A. D. 1953.

to hold, as Trustee, a sum not to exceed the sum of $
with which to pay the funeral expenses of the said WILLIAM JOHN-
SON.

FOURTH:

I give, devise and bequeath all the rest, residue and remainder of my estate, real, personal and mixed, of every kind
and nature and wheresoever situated, or of which I shall die
seized or possessed, or over which I may have testamentary control, or to which I may be in any way entitled at the time of
my decease, including the proceeds of any sale of property
pursuant to Paragraph SECOND above, as follows:

One-Third (1/3) to my brother, WILLIAM JOHNSON, of Chicago,
Illinois;

One-Third (1/3) to the heirs-at-law of my deceased brother,
JOSEPH JOHNSON, of Columbus, Ohio, namely: DR. WALTER JOHNSON,
of St. Louis, Missouri; and TRAVOLA ADAMS, of Washington, D. C.,
share and share alike, or to the survivor thereof;

One-Third (1/3) to the heirs-at-law of my deceased sister,
NANCY SINGLETON, of Springfield, Illinois, namely: ARTHUR B.
SINGLETON, of Chicago, Illinois; WALTER C. SINGLETON, of Kansas
City, Kansas; ROSCOE E. SINGLETON, of Chicago, Illinois; LEOTA
HARRIS, of Springfield, Illinois; and ETHEL M. GOODIN, of St.
Louis, Missouri, share and share alike, or to the survivor there-
of.

FIFTH:

I hereby nominate, constitute and appoint *Dr. Roosevelt Single*
of Chicago, Illinois, as Executor of this, my Last Will and Testa-

THIS IS PAGE TWO (2) OF MY LAST WILL
AND TESTAMENT MADE THIS   DAY
OF SEPTEMBER, A.D. 1953.

ment, with full power to settle and compromise all claims in favor of or against my Estate; and with full power to sell at public or private sale, within one year after my decease, upon such terms and conditions as he may deem best for the interest of my Estate, any and all property of my estate as provided in Paragraph SECOND above, and to make distribution as herein provided.

IN WITNESS WHEREOF, I have hereunto subscribed my name and affixed my seal this   day of September, A. D. 1953.

_____

The foregoing instrument, consisting of three (3) pages, this page included, each authenticated by the signature of the Testatrix at the bottom thereof, was subscribed by the Testatrix, KATHRYN M. JOHNSON, on the   day of September, A. D. 1953, in our presence and also at the same time declared by her to be her Last Will and Testament, and we, at the same time, in her presence, at her request, and in the presence of each other, have hereunto subscribed our names as witnesses, and do hereby further declare that at the time of the execution of said Last Will and Testament the said KATHRYN M. JOHNSON was of sound and disposing mind, memory and understanding.

_____ RESIDING AT _____
                                        CHICAGO, ILLINOIS

_____ RESIDING AT _____
                                        CHICAGO, ILLINOIS

_____ RESIDING AT _____
                                        CHICAGO, ILLINOIS

THIS IS PAGE THREE (3) OF MY LAST WILL
AND TESTAMENT MADE THIS   DAY
OF SEPTEMBER, A.D. 1953.

_____

Made in the USA
Monee, IL
29 February 2020